THE LIFE AND TIMES OF
PORGY AND BESS

THE LIFE AND TIMES OF

PORGY AND BESS

THE STORY OF
AN AMERICAN CLASSIC

HOLLIS ALPERT

ALFRED A. KNOPF   NEW YORK   1990

THIS IS A BORZOI BOOK
PUBLISHED BY ALFRED A. KNOPF, INC.

Library of Congress Cataloging-in-Publication Data
Alpert, Hollis, [date]
The life and times of Porgy and Bess: the story of an American
classic / by Hollis Alpert. — 1st ed.
p. cm.
Includes bibliographical references (p.   ).
ISBN 0-394-58339-6
1. Gershwin, George, 1898–1937. Porgy and Bess.   I. Title.
ML410.G288A68   1990
782.1—dc20   89-43367   CIP MN
Manufactured in the United States of America
First Edition

*Frontispiece: "Bess, You Is My Woman Now": Todd Duncan and Anne Brown.
(Theatre Collection, Museum of the City of New York.*

No one knew Porgy's age . . . Once a child saw Porgy, and said, suddenly, "What is he waiting for?" That expressed him better than anything else. He was waiting, waiting with the concentrated intensity of a burning glass.

—From *Porgy*, a novel by DuBose Heyward

AUTHOR'S NOTE

For those unfamiliar with *Porgy and Bess,* or for those whose memories of the details of the story of the opera need refreshing, and to avoid repetition of those details in the narrative that follows, an appendix provides a synopsis. This outline, it should be said, is of the opera as originally created by DuBose Heyward and George and Ira Gershwin. Variations from it have occurred over the years during its myriad performances, as veteran lovers of the opera well know.

The convention adopted when referring to Americans of African heritage is to employ the term generally used in the context of the time of the described events. The changes are perhaps significant in themselves.

THE LIFE AND TIMES OF
PORGY AND BESS

*George Gershwin. (Wachsman Collection, Lawrence and Lee Theatre
Research Institute, Ohio State University.)*

PROLOGUE

I T S E E M E D just about everyone who was anyone was at the Alvin Theatre on October 10, 1935, for the New York premiere of George Gershwin's "folk opera," *Porgy and Bess*. Few first nights could have boasted so many important names from theatre, music, films, finance, and that more miscellaneous group known as society. The Theatre Guild, producers of this decidedly unusual musical work, had been besieged with requests for tickets for weeks on end. Newspaper and magazine editors, noting the importance of the occasion, dispatched both their theatre and their music critics. So such important aisle sitters as Alexander Woollcott, Brooks Atkinson, and John Mason Brown were joined by Virgil Thomson, Olin Downes, and Lawrence Gilman.

There were so many celebrities present, filling the orchestra seats, that they were forced to watch one another. Leslie Howard, Joan Crawford, Norma Shearer, and Katharine Hepburn—to mention a few—from films; Lily Pons and Kirsten Flagstad from opera; playwrights included Robert E. Sherwood, Elmer Rice, and Ben Hecht; there were novelists (Edna Ferber, Fannie Hurst, and J. B. Priestley) and violinists (Fritz Kreisler and Jascha Heifetz), bandleaders (Paul Whiteman and Fred Waring) and people from publishing (Condé Nast and Harold Ross).

The true star of the evening, though, was George Gershwin, who, in his mid-thirties, was already at the zenith of accomplishment and fame. He was a rarity, a composer who had managed to bridge the difficult gap between art and money, between Tin Pan Alley and the concert hall. He found a middle ground, too, as the composer for several Broadway hit musicals. He lived in a duplex penthouse and associated with financiers, social leaders, and leading lights of the theatre. Not all that distant in memory was the day he created a sensation during a famous Paul Whiteman jazz concert with the first performance of his *Rhapsody in Blue*. From the modes of jazz and blues he had fashioned a concert work both American and universal in its acceptance. With it notice was served that the New World was finding its indigenous musical voice.

While enchanting Broadway with his musicals, he continued to refine his classical skills with a series of concert works, among them the jazzily cheerful *An American in Paris,* complete with authentic French taxi klaxons.

Tonight was something more imposing: a full operatic work, performed by a sizable black cast, with an orchestra twice the size of those ordinarily found in the pit. Many in the audience were already conditioned to expect something remarkable. News of the opera had been circulating for several months. The ebullient composer, not given to excessive modesty, had described his work-in-progress as something akin in style to *Carmen* and *Boris Godunov.* The tryout in Boston, two weeks before, had drawn lyrical raves. In New York, a favored few had already heard portions of the score; Gershwin would play selections for visitors to his apartment, sometimes singing along with his brother Ira.

The two brothers sat in a back row of the orchestra, between them Kay Swift, a composer of musicals herself. She was the most prominent woman in George's life, though not the sole recipient of his affections, and had been so for ten years. (For most of that time she had maintained her marriage to James Warburg, son of financier Felix.) Nearby were DuBose Heyward, author of the libretto and lyricist with Ira, and Heyward's wife, Dorothy, who was coauthor with her husband of the play on which the opera was based.

What was seen and heard that night after the strains of "Summertime," sung sweetly and winningly by Abby Mitchell, filled the theatre is now known throughout the world. The audience was stirred, moved (many brought to tears), by a musical event unlike any in previous Broadway history. Never had so many black singers of training and talent performed together on a Broadway stage. New stars were made: Todd Duncan, who sang Porgy in a stalwart baritone; Anne Brown, a classically trained and highly educated young singer, in the role of the wanton Bess; Ruby Elzy as the bereft Serena, whose husband is killed early on.

When the curtain fell after the last of the three acts, the tumultuous applause and cheering went on for half an hour. Gershwin was brought to the stage. So were Rouben Mamoulian, the director, and Alexander Smallens, the musical director, and, more reluctantly, the shy Heyward. The audience came to its feet and cheered and cheered.

OUTSIDE THE theatre, limousines and cars pulled up and some four hundred invitees headed uptown for a party at Condé Nast's huge penthouse apartment on Madison Avenue.

Kay Swift had done the organizing. She persuaded several friends and admirers of Gershwin's to put up the money for what would be the season's biggest bash. Contributors included such tycoons as William Paley, Jules Glaenzer, Marshall Field, and Averell Harriman. Condé Nast lent his house staff. Kay had spent days making out guest lists and sending telegrams. No one sent regrets. Enric Madriguera's Latin band was engaged for the party, and on the spur of the moment Paul Whiteman brought along twelve members of his orchestra. Eventually, after all sixty members of the cast had arrived, Gershwin took over at the piano—he needed little coaxing—and reprised much of the opera. On and on the party went, through the night. It was a wonderful party, and it petered out at seven in the morning.

Time now for the reviews.

THE RESPONSE by the New York–based critics to what would eventually be regarded as this country's greatest contribution to opera, and would later conquer many of Europe's most prestigious opera stages, was much more favorable than not, although the notion has persisted that it got a poor press. Only a very few took the work seriously to task. Mostly there seemed an air of puzzlement as to just what it was. Opera was supposed to be presented at an opera house. *Porgy and Bess* had been performed in a Broadway theatre, and the tendency was to judge it by the standards of Broadway.

Most of the drama critics were admiring. They hailed it as colorful, poignant, well sung and well acted . . . well, except for some pretty dull stretches of recitative. It was from the music critics that a more patronizing tone emerged. A few were sour indeed. Virgil Thomson called it "crooked folklore and half-way opera." Undoubtedly, the mix of opinions caused confusion among theatregoers.

The production, with its large cast and chorus and unusually large orchestra, was costly to run. The break-even point was barely reachable even with full houses night after night. The decision was made to close down after 124 performances—a longer continuous run than for any previous opera on any stage—but too expensive a show to keep going on Broadway. Even with a short tour that followed, the total capitalization, and more, was lost. Gershwin, however, was not in the least disheartened, for he had a supreme faith in his music: *Porgy and Bess* would live again, he felt certain after the closing. He was right. If ever a theatrical work conquered an entire world, this has to be the leading candidate. Fifty years after its opening, *Porgy and Bess* went into the repertory of the Metropolitan Opera.

Yet, in spite of its universal popular acceptance, it has generated a remarkable amount of controversy. For years, arguments continued over the merits of its music and whether or not it was truly *opera,* and, if not, what it should be called. Was it meant for the theatre or for the opera house? And what about the work's treatment of its black characters? Charges were flung that it contained demeaning stereotypes of American black people. Some black singers, approached for roles, refused to appear in it.

Others have pointed to the fact that because of *Porgy and Bess* hundreds of black performers, over the years, found work on Broadway stages and in opera houses and thereby advanced their careers. Nowadays the demand for classically trained black singers sometimes exceeds their availability, and the Metropolitan Opera employs dozens in its permanent company. *Porgy and Bess* has had a great deal to do with this welcome change. The work and its gifted performers have proven to be of vast cultural importance during many travels abroad.

It is taken for granted now that *Porgy and Bess* represents an epochal event in American music, but in its many manifestations it can also be seen as a kind of mirror of social change in America. The opera's history has its curious aspects, and it has been regarded differently in the decades in which it has been played. It has also been played differently.

The opera did not come into being in one single burst of creativity. Rather, it had its beginnings in relative obscurity as a first novel by a Southern poet, and nine years passed before it came to the stage of the Alvin Theatre. *Porgy,* as the novel (and then a play) was titled, had substance as a literary work and gained critical plaudits for that. It got additional attention because it was seen as a new note in the fictional treatment of Southern Negroes, which is to say, written with sympathy and understanding of their qualities and condition. Black critics, aware that the characters were based on the Gullah-speaking blacks of the Charleston, South Carolina, region, had praise for Heyward's accuracy in depicting their downtrodden lives. Yet, in later decades the opera (embodying the same characters) was attacked by its detractors for its patronizing and demeaning portrayal of blacks. Then, some of those who derided it turned around and played in it and sang its songs.

To understand all this needs some perspective. At the time of its conception the kind of separation that existed between blacks and whites was assumed to be the norm on both sides of the color line. Just in case the line was overstepped by black people, the Ku Klux Klan and other racist groups were around in force; their ranks swelled alarmingly enough to become a national issue and shame, and to bring on widespread protests. In all, sixty-one lynchings occurred during the twenties. Some Negro leaders talked of the necessity of being "separate but equal." Others, however, sought the removal of all barriers. But while black people were being hounded, kept segregated in humiliating ways, America and Europe were embracing their blues and jazz.

As a European composer put it in a song: "Here's the new world, come across the sea in splendor, to take over old Europe with a dance."

The Klan, the lynchings, the poverty, the constant discrimination propelled the Negro from the South to a hoped-for better life in the North. The shift was further abetted by the need for labor in the industrial North when the country entered the First World War. Prejudice and discrimination were not as openly apparent in most Northern states; at least black children could attend the same schools as whites. But when it came to jobs, housing, government employment, and the armed services, blacks faced almost as much discrimination as they did in the South. More is the wonder, then, of the artistic and cultural flowering that was given the name of "the Negro Renaissance" during the middle and late twenties. Harlem was its first home; Harlem was where Gershwin, as a boy, first heard the jazz that entranced him so, gave the sparkle and the blue note to his music, and led him on the path to *Porgy and Bess*.

HEADING FOR
THE PROMISED LAND

DuBose Heyward. (Wachsman Collection, Lawrence and Lee Theatre Research Institute, Ohio State University.)

1

THE ODYSSEY OF Porgy and his Bess began in Charleston, South Carolina, not long after a dance born there drifted north and was incorporated into a Negro musical, *Runnin' Wild,* to become by 1924 a national rage. In that year DuBose Heyward, a native of Charleston, an insurance salesman and sometime poet, decided to try his luck as a full-time writer. He decided on a novel, his inspiration a crippled beggar, Sammy Smalls, a familiar figure on the street corners of Charleston's business district. What made him distinctive was his means of locomotion, a hand-made cart pulled by a notably odoriferous goat.

Heyward, on the surface, would not have seemed the ideal person to tell a story of a lowly Negro and his milieu. He was white and, though hardly prosperous, a born-and-bred member of Charleston's proud if somewhat faded aristocracy. "There was about the city," a visitor of the time noted, "an aura of slow and beautiful death, a mellow decay in houses and streets." Behind wrought-iron fences were little inner-court gardens crowded with shrubs and vines. Once-proud mansions were in disrepair, vines clutching their walls like green tentacles. This condition wouldn't last long, however. The boom times were at hand and the South came to share in the rising prosperity. Already there was talk of restoration, and enterprising architects and real estate entrepreneurs were snapping up available bargains. Today the "low country," or downtown section, of refurbished Charleston has the

Cabbage Row, street view, after abandonment. The archway, center, leads to the courtyard that became Catfish Row. "A decaying pair of buildings behind which was an inner court." (South Carolina Historical Society.)

clean look of a Disney theme park. City statutes determine what can be done in the way of change or addition to the historic houses, each of which is now worth a considerable fortune. Tourists put the city on their vacation agendas, and one of the most popular attractions is the house where Porgy and Bess supposedly lived.

Nor is Charleston any longer the kind of port it once was. The cotton-bearing steamships have ceased to ply the seas, the wharves are gone, and the tony houses lining the banks of the Cooper and Ashley rivers—their conjunction defining the city—face an unblemished vista of sea and the offshore islands, one of these being Kitiwah (now usually spelled Kiawah), where the inhabitants of the opera's Catfish Row went for their picnic.

WHILE HEYWARD was developing his notion for a novel, the most popular bandleader of the day, Paul Whiteman, gave a concert at Aeolian Hall in New York which he labeled "An Experiment in Modern Music." Whiteman, a classically trained musician, was a fervent proponent of the musical value inherent in jazz. The music of the so-called common people, sometimes inveighed against as a temptation to sin and untold excess, was not, he felt, being taken seriously enough by the highbrows. There was no such problem abroad. Prestigious composers—Satie, Ravel, Milhaud, among them—were already incorporating jazz elements into their work.

Whiteman's brainstorm was to give a concert devoted to jazz works, to provide a setting in which they could be heard and judged seriously. He would demonstrate that jazz was America's true and native form of music. To this end his program included "semi-symphonic arrangements of popular melodies" and "adaptations of standard selections to dance rhythm." And he also wanted an original jazz composition. For this, he asked the busy and up-and-coming George Gershwin for a contribution to the program. Other contributors to the afternoon concert (ticket prices ranging from 55¢ to $2.20) included Irving Berlin, Ferde Grofé, and Victor Herbert. It was Gershwin, though, who Whiteman hoped would provide the pièce de ré-sistance, with his work for solo piano and orchestra, Gershwin appearing as the soloist. By this time, Gershwin, barely twenty-five, was already regarded as a songwriter and composer of exceptional talent. He had moved from Tin Pan Alley to Broadway revues and musical comedies. Gilbert Seldes, who championed such supposedly inartistic forms as vaudeville, comic strips, and jazz in his *The Seven Lively Arts,* used Gershwin to help make his points. "Delicacy, even dreaminess," he wrote, "is a quality he alone brings into jazz music. And his sense of variation in rhythm, of an oddly placed accent, of emphasis and color, is impeccable."

Gershwin, though, was showing signs of moving closer to the concert hall—an early string quartet, courses in composition and counterpoint at Columbia University, a one-act jazz opera, *Blue Monday* (inserted into George White's *Scandals of 1922*), which, while failing to impress many critics, had impressed Whiteman.

Gershwin accepted the assignment reluctantly: He was busy. His new musical was about to have its tryout. He was galvanized, however, when it was reported in the papers that he was already working on a symphonic composition for Whiteman's concert. In less than a month he finished a work that he at first titled *Rhapsody for Jazz Band and Piano.*

Whiteman was determined to impress the intelligentsia, musical and otherwise. He rounded up patrons for the concert: Kreisler, Rachmaninoff, Walter Damrosch, Leopold Stokowski, Alma Gluck, Mary Garden—great names all. Among writers, Seldes, Heywood Broun, Carl Van Vechten, Fannie Hurst, and O. O. McIntyre. An address was given before the start of the concert by Hugh C. Ernst, the writer—along with Seldes—of the pro-gram notes. He made clear that this experiment was to be purely educational, its aim being to point out the tremendous strides that had been made in popular music since jazz had captured the scene some ten years before. This was music that was in the spirit of the times. He hoped that an American school of music would evolve which would provide a stepping-stone for the masses to the understanding and enjoyment of symphony and opera.

Whiteman's usual Palais Royal orchestra of fourteen musicians was augmented with nine more. A program with notes by Seldes was printed at considerable expense, and, although the house was quickly sold out, Whiteman spent far more than came in, partly because he distributed so many free seats.

"It was a strange audience," he wrote later on, "vaudevillians, concert managers come to have a look at the novelty, Tin Pan Alleyites, composers, symphony and opera stars, flappers, cake-eaters, all mixed up higgledy-piggledy."

The program was long—twenty-five selections—and after a while signs of restlessness were apparent. Nothing being heard was all that startling or new. Twenty-three numbers were played before Gershwin strolled onstage and took his place at the piano.

And then Ross Gorman placed his lips to his clarinet and for the first time was heard what a critic described as "a flutter-tongued, drunken whoop of an introduction which had the audience rocking." This upward slide, or glissando, this bluesy wail, was not in the written score, although it has been played that way ever since. Gorman played it as a joke during one of the rehearsals, and Gershwin was so taken with it that he asked Gorman to play it similarly at the concert, and even to increase the "wail" as much as possible. A note was struck, literally, that for generations has stood as an expression of the mood and spirit of the twenties.

Rhapsody in Blue was an immediate sensation, and from that moment on, no one ever had to ask who Gershwin was. Any listing of the important events of 1924 would have to include Whiteman's concert and the premiere of *Rhapsody in Blue*. But Gershwin's was not the only innovative spirit in American music that year, the same year in which was first heard George Antheil's *Ballet mécanique,* John Alden Carpenter's *Skyscrapers,* and Aaron Copland's *Symphony for Organ and Orchestra.* Edgard Varèse, Henry Cowell, and Charles Ives completed works of importance, too.

In fact, all the arts were in a state of remarkable fecundity. While America was increasing its industrial and economic muscle, while it worried more about "Reds" than bootleggers and gangsters, its artists were venturing into new and exciting cultural territory. Some disgruntled writers, to be sure, were heading for Paris, where there was no need to drink bootleg gin, and living was cheap and easy, and love was freer. At home, though, Georgia O'Keeffe was painting her brilliant flowers, George Bellows captured Dempsey and Firpo on canvas, and Alexander Calder was constructing his abstract sculpture. In dance, Michel Fokine was organizing his American Ballet.

On Broadway, John Barrymore—until he abandoned New York to become Hollywood's highest-priced star—was presenting his renowned Freudian interpretation of *Hamlet.* The Moscow Art Theatre was paying a visit to New York, Walter Huston was being seen in Eugene O'Neill's *Desire Under the Elms,* and Paul Robeson was incurring the wrath of the Klan for his role as a black man married to a white woman in the same author's *All God's Chillun Got Wings.* And while George Gershwin collected laurels for *Rhapsody in Blue,* he and Ira were collecting royalties on their musical, *Lady, Be Good,* starring Fred and Adele Astaire. Broadway had real star power that year: Ethel Barrymore, Fanny Brice, Jane Cowl, the Marx Brothers, Will Rogers, W. C. Fields, Beatrice Lillie, Marilyn Miller, George Arliss, Leslie Howard, and Lunt and Fontanne.

The F. Scott Fitzgerald look—blue blazer, high-waisted, baggy pleated trousers, rounded-toed shoes—was fashionable for men, while women kept their skirts at the knees and wore cloche hats that came to the eyes. They were reading Edna Ferber's *So Big* and Louis Bromfield's *The Green Bay Tree,* and those of discerning taste had picked up *In Our Time,* a collection of short stories by a new writer named Ernest Hemingway. Thomas Mann and André Gide had books in the stores, Edgar Lee Masters published his *New Spoon River Anthology,* and Robinson Jeffers his *Tamar.*

I T   W A S   A   T I M E for "movement" in the arts and in literature, for revolt from convention, for experimentation. In Charleston, DuBose Heyward was one of those who thought it time for the South to come out of its literary doldrums. He and his good friend Hervey Allen, then a poet, too, took a leading part in forming The Poetry Society of South Carolina, aimed at producing a poetic awakening in the South. He and others were not happy to be known as inhabitants of the "Bible Belt," an uncomplimentary tag bestowed by H. L. Mencken. Through the society, they hoped to foster a new regionalism, to avoid the sentimentality and stale sweetness of the "old" tradition.

Heyward became the secretary of the society and by 1924 was its president. He arranged for lectures by Robert Frost, Amy Lowell, Carl Sandburg, and other prominent poets. He, too, lectured, traveling about and bringing the message about the work being done in the South. His own poetry gained him recognition, but his efforts on behalf of the society gained him more as a literary personage.

He decided, early in 1924, to abandon his insurance business and give his full time to writing. Newly married, he realized that poetry was not the medium on which to base a living; he would have to turn to fiction. He did not consciously have a fully formed idea in mind when he came across a newspaper item about the Negro cripple Sammy Smalls, but when he did, it can be said that Porgy was born—embryonically, to be sure, but soon enough to take form in the pages of a book.

Heyward had his own feeling for jazz. In some of his poems he had attempted to suggest rhythms similar to those of jazz and its form known as blues. In one, a narrative poem called "Jasbo Brown," he recalled the legendary pianist who was supposed to have played along the Mississippi and from whose name came the name for his and the nation's music. Many years later, while writing the libretto for the opera, Heyward came up with an opening scene that was not included when it premiered. In it, a character called Jasbo Brown plays in a Negro dance hall. The poem reflected what Heyward felt to be happening to the Negroes he knew and had grown up with—their being caught in the general shift from their original agrarian environment to urban settings for which they were unprepared. Heyward was not a social reformer. He knew there was a problem, but knew of no ready solutions.

In retrospect, the poems now appear like early sketches for the novel that became *Porgy*. Heyward had always taken a deep interest in the Negroes of Charleston; their ways seemed to him so different, alien, primitive even, from the polite ways of the Charleston milieu he inhabited. Like a folklorist he studied them and was attracted to and envious of their lack of inhibition. Members of his family before him had studied the speech and customs of the Gullahs of the region; his mother became a lecturer of local note on their speech and traditions. In his youth he had worked as a cotton checker with the Gullah stevedores on the waterfront; they often came to him with their problems. Hardly a block away from where he lived on Church Street in downtown Charleston was a decaying pair of buildings inhabited by Negroes behind which was an inner court. It was a noisy, overcrowded, troublesome place, which drew the police frequently to settle altercations. Ground-floor shopkeepers put their vegetable stands on the street, and for that reason the place was familiarly known as Cabbage Row.

Heyward passed it every morning on his way to work on Broad Street, a few blocks away, where his insurance business was located. On one of these March mornings, with his wife away in New York, he stopped off at his sister's house on the same street to have breakfast with her. While eating, he browsed through the day's edition of the Charleston *News and Courier*. An item in the police blotter caught his eye.

It read:

Samuel Smalls, who is a cripple and is familiar to King Street, with his goat and cart, was held for the June term of Court of Sessions on an aggravated assault charge. It is alleged that on Saturday night he attempted to shoot Maggie Barnes at number four Romney Street. His shots went wide of the mark. Smalls was up on a similar charge some months ago and was given a suspended sentence. Smalls had attempted to escape in his wagon and was run down and captured by the police patrol.

"Just think of that old wreck having enough manhood to do a thing like that," Heyward said to his sister, and he clipped out the item and put it in his wallet.

The "real" Catfish Row. The inner court after abandonment.
(South Carolina Historical Society.)

2

I T I S D O U B T F U L that Sammy Smalls ever lived in Cabbage Row at 89–91 Church Street, although the landscape architect who came along in the early thirties and rescued the site from its terminal decadence claimed that on the abandoned premises he found remnants of a little goat wagon and fragments of a goat harness. He never produced these remains, however, and he may have been seeking to trade on the fame of the fictional Porgy, who by that time had made his way to both the printed page and the Broadway stage.

Laurel Briggs, after acquiring the property, created picturesque apartments in the main three-story building and the extensions around a charming court in the rear. His aim was to attract tenants of artistic bent, and today the street front of the building boasts two small specialty shops, one of which is named, yes, Porgy, and the other, Bess.

But of the existence of the prototype for Porgy there is no doubt. Several Charlestonians remembered him, although with less than fondness.

"He was neither very virtuous nor very villainous," one recalled. If anything stood out about him it was the acrid smell of his goat. On one of his arrests they picked him up as a complete unit—goat, cart, and Sammy—and set him before the judge, who didn't quite know what to do with him. He was a nuisance in the jail, so he was usually released. Local interest in him grew years after *Porgy* appeared, but by then he was gone from view, and efforts were made to discover his history. A surviving wife was located, and a grave on Folly Island that might have been his; a few stepped forward to say that they were his relatives. There were a lot of people named Smalls.

And Cabbage Row, which soon enough became established as the model for the Catfish Row of novel, play, and opera, also aroused much interest. An old map was located that showed the double house existed as early as 1788. A local historian, Samuel Gaillard Stoney, was certain that it antedated the American Revolution. It was not a mansion gone to seed, as many assumed because of its size, but a double tenement meant from its beginnings for rental. The shape of the buildings had to do with real estate taxes in Charleston's early days. Houses were taxed according to the amount of street frontage they occupied. As a result, many of Charleston's old houses were built long and narrow, with rear courtyards rather than lawns in front.

How Negroes came to occupy the apartments of Cabbage Row is not known either. Their tenancy went back to the previous century, and before that some records spoke vaguely of its having been a "resort" — presumably a brothel — for sailors.

By the time DuBose Heyward looked upon it as a setting for a story, the place was an eyesore, bursting with as many as seventy residents, and it wasn't long before it was abandoned entirely, most of its fine woodwork having been ripped out and gone up the flues of its fireplaces.

"When I acquired it," Briggs said, "the premises weren't fit to live in." The ceilings were low, and the fairly large rooms had been cut into many tiny cubicles. One of the rooms had the word "jail" scrawled in chalk over the door. "I suppose," said Briggs, "it must have been used to confine the tenants temporarily."

''IT WAS ONE of those tragedies on the razor edge of comedy," Heyward remarked about the news item that sparked his imagination and led him to *Porgy*. From his background, he would not have been the likeliest candidate to produce a novel that would mirror the conditions of Southern slum Negroes. His forebears went back to the American Revolution. A great-great-grandfather, Thomas Heyward, was a signer of the Declaration of Independence, attested to by a brass plaque on the house he lived in. His descendant, DuBose, is now also honored by a plaque on the house he inhabited down the street from Cabbage Row.

By the time of his birth, however, August 31, 1885, the family fortunes had financially gone way downhill. So had those of a lot of neighbors whose family names also went back to Revolutionary War times. Charleston, whose Fort Sumter took the first shots of the Civil War, was badly buffeted by both the war and its aftermath. It had also suffered from fire, earthquake, and hurricanes. Heyward's grandparents on both sides had owned plantations, but by the time DuBose was born the holdings were lost and his father, Edwin Watkins Heyward, was reduced to working in a rice mill.

Ill fortune continued to dog the family when an earthquake crumbled their house. All managed to escape, but not long after, Edwin Heyward died when he was mangled in the mill machinery, leaving his wife, the former Jane Screvens DuBose, and his small son and daughter all but penniless. Jane scrimped a living for the family by taking in sewing and also running a small beach boardinghouse. She had a poetic bent and earned extra money by writing little verse advertisements for newspapers. DuBose was ten when she published a volume of verse titled *Wild Roses.* By that time DuBose was making his own attempts at verse.

The Gullahs indigenous to the region fascinated Jane. She had been brought up around black servants who spoke Gullah, and she learned their language well enough to speak it and lecture on it to the tourists who discovered the antebellum charm of Charleston in the early twenties; she included tales told her by the servants who had helped raise her. DuBose had grown up hearing those tales and others dealing with the South and her family. In a poem he wrote he paid tribute to her "gifts" to him, those "wild, fantastic legends of lost ages," far more valuable, as it turned out, than the toys she was unable to afford.

The word "Gullah," she said, was a corruption of "Angola," from where Charleston's Negroes were thought to have been brought by slave traders. Recent linguistic studies of those who still speak the patois (mainly on the sea islands of South Carolina and Georgia) have revealed its striking similarities to the languages of West Africa. But not of Angola alone. As many as a thousand Gullah words are much the same as those of Krio, the language of Sierra Leone.

Rice was an important export of the Southern colonies, and boatloads of West Africans were brought to work the fields of the Carolinas, many of them to islands near Charleston, where rice was then grown. They were resistant, as the colonists were not, to the swamp diseases of malaria and yellow fever. When rice production was all but abandoned on the islands after the Civil War, the Gullahs were left to fend as best they could in the new circumstances. They worked the wharves, became servants to the townspeople, and moved inland to the cotton plantations. Just about every family in Charleston had at least one black household servant, and, if no other, the "Mauma" who helped raise the children. It was mainly their Mauma who, in the case of DuBose and his sister, Jeannie, inculcated in them proper manners and deportment.

It was not at all strange to find whites and Negroes living on the same streets, since servants tended to live near their masters and employers. What was tantamount to segregation came only after restoration of the old homes and mansions sent their prices skyrocketing. One of the houses DuBose lived in as a boy was on a street near a wharf, where blacks also resided and where Negro fishermen and farmers from the islands brought their produce to market. Life in the neighborhood was reasonably calm during the work-week, but got wilder on Saturday nights. The cheap whiskey was brought out, and soon enough there were fights with razors and the vicious cotton hooks used by stevedores. DuBose as a child often heard the clang accom-panying the arrival of the police wagons. On Sundays he witnessed the boisterous Sunday adult baptisms in the water off the wharf.

He was a poor student, inclined toward dreaminess and absent-mindedness. School bored him, and at fourteen he simply dropped out, apparently with no objection from his mother. He delivered newspapers, then at fifteen worked full-time in a hardware store. There was no social stigma attached to this. Hard times were endemic in Charleston, and what counted most was not what you did but who your forebears were. Within a few years he came down with a disease that the doctors were unable to diagnose. He lost the use of his arms and was weakened generally. During a long period of recuperation a wealthy aunt sent him to Philadelphia to be treated in the city's Orthopedic Hospital. Belatedly, he was discovered to have had polio. Treatments helped him regain most of the use of his arms and hands, although his right arm never came back to normal and he would have serious bouts of illness throughout his lifetime.

At twenty he was able to work again, and he found himself a job on the waterfront as a cotton checker for a steamship company's warehouse. This brought him into close contact with the Negro stevedores who did the loading and unloading of the bales. He was caught, he said later, "by the color, the mystery and movement of Negro life . . . Negroes in long lines trucking cotton on the wharves; dim figures in a deserted warehouse squat-ting over a crap game; spirituals bringing me up short to listen against the wall of a dilapidated church that I had to pass on the way to work."

The steamship line failed within a year, and he had to look for other means of livelihood. He chose insurance as his new field and went into business with a friend, Harry O'Neill, who was something of a "go-getter." They did well. Heyward was able to buy a small house for the family and dabbled a bit in real estate. His courtly manners and quiet sense of humor, his gentlemanly good looks, made him one of Charleston's more eligible bachelors. Now reasonably prosperous, he took his rightful place in Charleston's hierarchal society; he joined the right clubs, attended the society balls, squired around the local belles, to whom he wrote missives in light verse. He found time to turn out a one-act comedy for a local drama group; it was performed in the South Carolina Society Hall and was followed by two hours of dancing. The evening was pronounced a fine social success. With a friend, he toured Europe prior to the outbreak of the war.

While the war raged in Europe he was recuperating in the mountains of North Carolina from a virulent attack of pleurisy. With time hanging heavy he tried to catch on canvas the mountain scenery, then turned to poetry and short stories. His true vocation, he decided, was writing, and the mountains gave him the quiet and privacy he felt he needed. He came across eighteen acres for sale near Hendersonville, a bargain because the old woman owner had the right to live there in perpetuity; after acquiring the property he built a small rustic house he called Orienta, to which he was able to escape from time to time. When America entered the war Heyward attempted to enlist but found himself "a poor bird who couldn't get by the physical and stayed home making speeches instead of getting first hand experience in the trenches." What he got instead was more experience working firsthand with Negroes; he aided in organizing Charleston's black people for war work.

When the war was over he continued his writing. One of his attempts was a melodrama designed for motion pictures; it dealt with an aristocratic Charleston family that purchases a slave girl who at the end is revealed to be pure and driven white and, surprise, the heiress to a fortune. Heyward, in offering the screenplay for sale, assured any potential purchaser that he could guarantee entrance to Charleston's famous old houses. The inducement was not sufficient.

He returned to poetry and short fiction and managed to sell a short story. He was floundering, however, and in need of guidance about whether to pursue lofty literary aims or write mainly for money.

T H E R I G H T M A N for him came along at the right time. He was John Bennett, an insurance client who wrote professionally; his children's book, *Master Skylark*, was regarded as a classic. During a visit to the office one day, he gave Heyward some advice on the kind of apples best to grow on his North Carolina property. Heyward revealed to him he was thinking of a writing career. Bennett, twenty years his senior, generous and sympathetic to other writers, soon took on the role of his counselor.

Through Bennett, Heyward met Hervey Allen, a wounded war veteran who had taken a teaching job at a Charleston military academy. From Pittsburgh originally, Allen was four years younger than Heyward and had already published two volumes of verse. The two men took to each other at once. With Bennett, they formed a little group that met Wednesday evenings to trade criticism and advice on their work. The avuncular Bennett was the cohesive force. Freshly written poems and stories were read and analyzed. (Allen would go on in later years to write the phenomenal 1933 best-seller *Anthony Adverse*.)

Heyward depended heavily on Bennett's criticism, which was sometimes severe. He was still uncertain about which way he wanted to go: the popular route, which would bring in earnings, or "something which would merit publication in a distinguished magazine." He wondered if there was a middle ground "between the melodramatic and the strong, the realistic and the romantic." Bennett, who was not above writing commercial fiction, nevertheless steered Heyward in a more literary direction, and, soon enough, Heyward's poems began to appear in magazines. One of these, "Gamesters All," was the winner of the 1921 prize given by the magazine *Contemporary Verse*.

The poem came directly from experience. On his way to work one summer morning, he heard someone shout, "Look out!" He recalled: "I saw a large Negro racing directly towards me. A second later a policeman rounded the corner, aimed coolly and carefully, and fired. The man lurched forward and died, almost at my feet." The incident affected him deeply. "I wanted to write what I had seen. It kept crowding between the pleasant, lazy routine of business and the off-hour frivolity of the hot season." He decided that he would deal seriously with "the slum Negro of the South."

In "Gamesters All" a group of Negroes are shooting craps. A policeman spots them and is about to take them in for gambling when one of them, Joe, runs off. The policeman gives chase and fires, as though it's a sporting event, and Joe drops dead. At the end of the poem a woman is heard moaning.

There is no overt "message" in the poem, and, if it made a statement, it was indirect, simply the poet's reaction to callousness and injustice. What was more unusual at the time was that a white Southerner would develop sympathy not for the white representative of law and order but for the humble craps shooter. The poem also demonstrated Heyward's knowledge of and feeling for Negro speech rhythms. And, as with his later poem, "Jasbo Brown," Heyward attempted to suggest rhythms suggestive of jazz and blues. These poems, and others with Negro themes, were heading him toward the novel that would bring him into contact with the young composer just then making his way toward Broadway.

FROM HEYWARD'S birth, there never was any doubt about his name, both given and family. But Gershwin's had to evolve, like those of a multitude of Jews born to immigrant parents. He went from Jacob to

George, from Gershwine to Gershwin. His father left St. Petersburg, Russia, in 1892 as Moishe Gershovitz. Here his name became Morris Gershvin. It was a doctor's mistake on George's birth certificate that turned Gershvin into Gershwine. In the family's drive toward Americanization, the Jacob became George. George's brother Ira, his elder by two years, was Israel Gershvin at birth; he then became Isadore, and eventually Ira. Their mother, too, underwent a name change, from Rosa Brushkin in her native St. Petersburg to Rose Bruskin in this country. As George became noted as a musician, somewhere along the line he changed his name to Gershwin. Soon after, the whole family followed suit.

"My mother's father," George said, "was a furrier. My paternal grand-father was some sort of inventor; his ingenuity had something to do with the Czar's guns. My father went to an opera occasionally, as most fathers do." But his musical ability was limited to whistling well and imitating a cornet. His mother he described as "nervous, ambitious, and purposeful." She was loving, intent on having her three sons and one daughter educated, but didn't interfere much with their day-to-day activities.

"George was a pretty wild boy," his sister, Frances, remembered. "He'd run around freely everywhere. People would say Mrs. Gershvin has nice children, but that son of hers—she'll have trouble with him someday." He was a tough little kid, by age seven or so the best roller skater in the neighborhood, the home of some noted gangsters.

When George was born on September 26, 1898, the family was living in Brooklyn, but they soon moved to the Lower East Side, where Morris worked in leather, fashioning ladies' shoe tops. As his jobs and enterprises changed, so did the residences; he liked to live near where he worked. By the time George was grown, Morris had moved the family more than twenty times. He went into the bakery business, ran restaurants, a Turkish bath, a cigar store, a pool parlor, and even spent an unfortunate month as a bookie at Belmont Park. He wasn't the most astute of businessmen, but he managed to keep his family afloat.

Via his roller skates, George explored the world of the city. While his more bookish brother Ira devoured dime novels, George darted through traffic, paused at the sound of a hurdy-gurdy churning out "Put Your Arms Around Me, Honey, Hold Me Tight," while an elevated train thundered overhead. He heard the mechanical music of the carrousels in Coney Island, and in Harlem he roller-skated past Baron Wilkins's nightclub and heard from inside the new rhythm of the fox trot. He had a memory from the age of six of standing outside a penny arcade on 125th Street listening to "an automatic piano leaping through Rubinstein's *Melody in F.* The peculiar jumps in the music held me rooted."

But beyond that, there wasn't much in the way of musical nourishment in George's family life—not until he was twelve, when a secondhand upright piano was brought through a window to their second-floor apartment. Mrs. Gershvin's married sister had acquired one, and so they should have one, too. Ira was designated to play it, but, according to George, "No sooner had it come through the window and been backed up against the wall, than I was at the keys. I must have crowded out Ira very soon."

Not only did George sit down at the piano; to everyone's surprise, he began playing tunes. "We were all flabbergasted," Frances said. Actually, George had habitually picked out tunes on pianos in the homes of his friends. One of these friends was Maxie Rosenzweig, a year younger than he, who was a child wonder as a violinist. Maxie grew up to become the virtuoso Max Rosen. "He opened the world of music to me," George admitted, "and almost closed it." Young Maxie took a dim view of young George's musical potential.

George started piano lessons at fifty cents per session, then moved up to a Mr. Goldfarb, who charged a dollar and a half. But it wasn't until he was referred to Charles Hambitzer, an orchestral musician and a composer of light opera, that he found his major formative influence. Hambitzer saw genius in the boy and sent him on for further instruction in harmony to the composer and pianist Edward Kilenyi.

At age fifteen George played in a bar, then was offered a full-time job as a song plugger at Remick's, a music publishing firm on 28th Street, the cacophonous street known as Tin Pan Alley. He was in his second year at the High School of Commerce, dutifully but unhappily following through on his mother's wish for him to become an accountant. Ira, a far better student, was at Townsend Harris High School, a sort of prep school for New York's City College, where he would soon reveal his way with words. George wanted the job badly, and his mother gave in to his entreaties to leave school. After all, the fifteen-dollar-a-week salary would have more than satisfied a high school graduate.

"Every day at nine," George said of his experience at Remick's, "I was there at the piano, playing popular tunes for anybody who came along. Chorus ladies used to breathe down my neck, and some customers even treated me like dirt." On many nights George was sent—as another means of plugging—to cafés, where he accompanied singers and dancers in the new tunes. The experience was invaluable, for he could easily sense what "played" and what didn't.

Tin Pan Alley was the pulsating heart of the nation's music business. Songwriters brought their songs, and singers, actors, and show producers came to the "professional parlors" of the publishers looking for material. Far above the run-of-the-mill composers of popular songs were Irving Berlin and Jerome Kern. It was while he was at the wedding of an aunt that George first heard Kern's "They'll Never Believe Me," as played by the orchestra hired for the occasion.

"Kern," he said, "was the first composer who made me conscious that most popular music was of inferior quality, and that musical-comedy music was made of better material." He tried imitating Kern and even paid a visit to the great Berlin, who listened to his first compositions and gave him encouragement. He wrote a tune and was paid five dollars for its sheet music publication, then added to his earnings by making piano rolls for a company in East Orange, New Jersey.

He tired of his song-plugging chores; as he put it, "the popular song racket began to get on my nerves. Its tunes began to offend me. Or perhaps my ears were becoming attuned to better harmonies." For a time he was intrigued by the Yiddish musical theatre, particularly as represented by the National Theatre on Second Avenue. Operettas were put on there for the large Jewish population and George considered trying one himself with a collaborator. It didn't come off, but his mind was now on show possibilities. He brought one of his songs to Sigmund Romberg, then the chief composer for the Shubert organization, and Romberg was impressed enough to offer him the opportunity to collaborate on some tunes for his next production—*The Passing Show of 1916*. Gershwin's name turned up on a number called "The Making of a Girl."

He gave up Remick's for good when he found out that a pianist was needed for the supper show at Fox's City Theatre on 14th Street. The job was supposed to pay twenty-five dollars a week, but the first night he missed some cues and played one tune while the girls onstage danced to another. The show's comedian took the opportunity to embarrass him further, and the red-faced boy left without bothering to pick up his pay. Soon enough, he had another job, this time as rehearsal pianist for a Victor Herbert/Jerome Kern musical, *Miss 1917*. He was now in the field he wanted to inhabit and making acquaintance with some of its most notable names. Vivienne Segal, one of the stars of the show, also gave Sunday evening concerts in the same theatre. She sang two songs that George wrote for her.

Max Dreyfus became the first true discoverer of George's talents. He heard the songs, and, as he told George, "I feel you have some good stuff in you." Dreyfus knew whereof he spoke. A musician himself, and now the head of a leading music publisher, T. B. Harms, he had discovered Jerome Kern and become the publisher of his enormously successful sheet music.

Young Gershwin had the makings, he decided, of another Kern. "I'm willing to gamble," he told George. "I'll give you thirty-five dollars a week without any set duties. Just stop in every morning and say hello." It went without saying, of course, that songs written by Gershwin would be published by Harms.

Gershwin, like Heyward, missed serving in the war. He had prepared himself for the draft by studying the saxophone, hoping that the instrument might win him assignment to a military band. But the war ended before his draft number came up, and Ira, too, escaped service.

Opportunity continued to strike for him. Through Dreyfus he was commissioned by a producer to write additional songs for a revue called *Half Past Eight*, and while the show died on its way to New York, its billboard had the honor of proclaiming for the first time in history, MUSIC BY GEORGE GERSHWIN. From this he went on to his first musical comedy, *La, La, Lucille*, which opened on June 30, 1919, at the Henry Miller Theatre, and stayed there for six months. The young producer, Alex A. Aarons, with his partner, Vinton Freedley, maintained an association with Gershwin that flowered into some of the more glorious musicals of the twenties, among them *Lady, Be Good, Oh, Kay!,* and *Funny Face.*

Irving Caesar, a young lyricist friend of George's, had an idea for a song hit. That same year "Hindustan," a one-step, was sweeping the country. "I said to George," Caesar recalled, " 'Why don't we write a one-step?' I started out with a lyric, he picked it up, and boom, we were off to the races. He wrote *Swanee* in ten minutes." The song was given a production number at the Capitol Theatre, but languished there until Al Jolson heard it and sang it in his spectacle at the Winter Garden. As a writer put it, history was made in "Racket Row." The song became a wildfire hit; a million copies sold in sheet music form and more than two million as a phonograph record. From coast to coast, and in London and Paris, the name of George Gershwin became famous, and, barely past his twenty-first birthday, he was on his way to riches.

It couldn't have been a better time for him. As movies were silent and radio still in its infancy, Broadway flourished. In fashion were the elaborate, glamorous revues such as the *Ziegfeld Follies* and *George White's Scandals,* yearly undertakings replete with extravagant sets and gorgeously costumed showgirls parading in production numbers built around strings of songs. Gershwin's association with White and the *Scandals,* which began with the 1920 version, was fruitful for both him and White. Out of it emerged some forty-five Gershwin songs, including the classic "Stairway to Paradise." The *Scandals of 1922,* odd as it may seem, provided Gershwin with the opportunity for his first foray into opera.

Jazz, and particularly "the new jazz" performed by Negro artists, intrigued Gershwin, as it did his lyricist partner for the *Scandals,* Buddy De Sylva. In the early twenties he and George talked about collaborating on an opera for black audiences, a jazz opera, in other words. They mentioned the idea to George White, who seized on it immediately and suggested they do it as a one-act insert in the upcoming *Scandals of 1922,* with white performers in blackface. The problems with make-up discouraged him, however, and he changed his mind, only to change it again, three weeks before the opening in New Haven, Connecticut.

In five days and five nights, De Sylva and Gershwin managed to turn out something unique—a one-act vaudeville opera they titled *Blue Monday.* For orchestrations, Gershwin turned to a black musician friend, Will Vodery. Among those impressed with the opera during rehearsals was Paul Whiteman, the enthusiast of the new jazz idiom and an admirer of the way Gershwin evoked a Harlem mood through his use of jazz themes. While hailed at its tryout in New Haven—the occasion was so momentous for George that he dated his nervous stomach from that moment—the piece was barely noticed in New York. One reviewer, though, delivered it a smart slap. "The most dismal, stupid, and incredible blackface sketch that has ever been perpetrated. In it a dusky soprano finally killed her gambling man. She should have shot all her associates the moment they appeared and then turned the pistol on herself."

The story of *Blue Monday* was simple, but not quite as simple as that. Its setting was a basement café in Harlem, near 135th Street and Lenox Avenue. The gambling man, Joe, intends to visit his mother, but doesn't want to reveal this sentimental streak to Vi, his girlfriend, and pretends he is being called out of town for a few days. Vi is convinced he's off to see another woman, and shoots him in Frankie-and-Johnny style, realizing her mistake too late.

The crudity of this little opera was compounded by the white actors playing and singing in blackface. Only two of the songs—"Blue Monday Blues" and "Has Anyone Seen Joe?"—stood out. George White decided that the opera's bathetic plot ran counter to what audiences expected from a lighthearted revue and excised it from the production after opening night.

Yet there was one reviewer, using the initials W.S., who had a vision of what might come from the unsuccessful effort. "Here at last," he wrote, "is a genuinely human plot of American life, set to music in the American vein, using jazz at only the right moments, the Blues, and above all, a new and free ragtime time recitative. In it we see the first gleam of a new American musical art."

DuBose and Dorothy Heyward—newly married, 1924.
(South Carolina Historical Society.)

3

DURING THE EARLY twenties DuBose Heyward devoted more and more of his time to literary matters and less and less to his insurance business. It was an exciting time to be making one's way as a writer. Ezra Pound was publishing his cantos, Fitzgerald telling his tales of the Jazz Age. T. S. Eliot saw it all as a "Waste Land," but Edna St. Vincent Millay came out with her lovely "Renascence." Up in New England there was Amy Lowell and in the Midwest Carl Sandburg. Heyward and Hervey Allen decided that the South, too, should join the general creativity.

To this end, they formed The Poetry Society of South Carolina, and Heyward became its secretary. Membership was limited to two hundred, and in hardly any time at all the quota was filled. As secretary, Heyward organized the society's meetings and arranged for lectures and poetry readings. He brought to Charleston such poetic notables as Sandburg, Lowell, Robert Frost, and Stephen Vincent Benét.

Meanwhile, Hervey Allen was published in the distinguished Yale Series of Younger Poets and gained a summer's invitation to the Edward Mac-Dowell Colony at Peterborough, New Hampshire, a retreat established by the composer's widow, Marian, for writers, artists, and composers. Heyward paid Allen a visit there and immediately saw it as the kind of place suited to his own way of working. MacDowell had built a cabin in the woods outside Peterborough and found it an ideal place to create his music. After his death, Marian MacDowell barnstormed the country giving talks and piano recitals and collected enough monetary support to establish a "colony" of twenty-five studios dispersed among some four hundred prime wooded acres overlooked by Mount Monadnock. Invitations to work for a summer in the studios were highly prized.

Mrs. MacDowell was charmed by Heyward when he paid her a visit. When he and Hervey Allen jointly published a volume of verse called *Carolina Chansons* she issued Heyward an invitation to the colony for the summer of 1922. He had his own cabin in the mountains to retreat to, of course, but the company up at Peterborough was incomparably better. There that same summer were Edwin Arlington Robinson, William Rose Benét, and Elinor Wylie, along with several others of literary and artistic consequence. However, it was the relatively unknown Dorothy Hartzell Kuhns, a small, pretty playwright, who most attracted him.

Not yet produced professionally, Kuhns had just turned thirty-two when she met Heyward, who was then thirty-seven. Born in Wooster, Ohio, to a businessman father and a mother who was an amateur musician, she developed dramatic ambitions early on. After a sensible and ladylike upbringing in Canton, Ohio, she decamped to New York and studied drama at Columbia University. The way to get into the theatre, she was told, was to get any kind of entry job in it and absorb the atmosphere. The best she could do was a stint as a chorus girl in a show that went on the road. She had to leave when she developed a crippling arthritic condition.

George Pierce Baker was the magic name for budding playwrights of the time. He ran a workshop at Harvard University that had produced many who had made their way to fame and fortune on Broadway. Dorothy Kuhns submitted one of her plays to him and was awarded a fellowship established in the name of Edward MacDowell. And from that also came the invitation to do a summer's work at the colony.

Peace, quiet, the tranquil setting of the colony, were supposed to provide the ideal surroundings for creative work. Each of the studios was of a different design. Those for artists and sculptors had high ceilings. The studios for musicians had pianos and were deep enough in the woods so that the sound would not intrude on the ears of writers. There were few rules or regulations. A practice, rather than a strict rule, was that no artist visited another's studio without an invitation. Seclusion was thought so necessary that lunches were delivered in wicker baskets and left quietly on the studio steps or porches. DuBose and Dorothy shared theirs, meeting halfway between their studios to sit under trees and discuss literature and life.

Colonists met as a group for breakfast and dinner in the dining room of the main hall, known as Colony Hall. Its main salon boasted a Steinway grand piano and a billiard table. Composers demonstrated their new works, and writers sometimes gave readings of work in progress. Relative new-comers to the arts mingled with established figures. It was a stimulating atmosphere for DuBose Heyward and Dorothy Kuhns. He courted her in his quiet, unassuming way, and Dorothy soon realized that he was in love with her and that she might well be reciprocating. But passion was kept muted. They were both hard at work, he on poems and stories, she on a play.

The other colonists soon were aware of their attachment. Both were physically fragile. "They looked," a writer said, "like Hansel and Gretel lost in a wood, perhaps of their own making." DuBose might well have proposed to Dorothy, if he had not been so hard-pressed financially. His writing and his work for the poetry society had meant less attention to and consequently less income from his business. His mother was undergoing a series of operations for which he was paying the bills. So he returned to Charleston at the summer's end, and she went back to Harvard for another year at Baker's workshop.

Both were invited back to the colony for the summer of 1923. Dorothy, though, had taken a job as dramatic counselor at a summer camp, and she didn't arrive in Peterborough until early September. Eager to see her again, Heyward now had marriage on his mind. He felt he should discuss it reasonably with her. There was the matter of his income, which was low. His absences from the insurance firm had become so frequent that he had had to give up much of his share of the partnership. His mother had undergone seven costly operations. There was his own health to consider: it was so poor that he had been unable to get life insurance.

Finally, he said, "The hell with all that. Will you marry me?"

Dorothy accepted happily. They walked together through the colony grounds to Marian MacDowell's house on the hill to announce their engagement.

To add to their celebratory mood, a telegram was waiting for Dorothy at Mrs. MacDowell's residence. It came from Harvard, and notified her that she had won that year's Harvard Prize for Drama, based on *Nancy Ann*, the play she had written in Baker's workshop. The prize carried with it the guarantee of a Broadway production for the play. It was almost too much for one day. She hurried off almost at once to New York to confer with the producer, and DuBose followed her there a week later.

JOHN BENNETT, in Charleston, received a letter from DuBose Heyward in New York. His mentor would be interested to know, DuBose wrote, "that after a brief consultation, Dorothy Kuhns and I decided that it was really no use trying to live apart any longer. We have tried it and it does not work." They had thereupon decided to march themselves promptly to the Little Church Around the Corner and into matrimony. The ceremony took place on March 22, 1923. It was a heady time for Dorothy. Here she was, newly married, and about to make her mark on Broadway, where right at this moment Elmer Rice's *The Adding Machine* was running and Lionel Barrymore was playing in *Laugh, Clown, Laugh*. She may well have been humming "I'll Build a Stairway to Paradise," still a hit from George White's *Scandals* of the previous year. As for its composer, Gershwin was on his first trip abroad, in London, writing the entire score of *The Rainbow Revue* for the sum of $1,500, plus round-trip passage.

DuBose had to get back to Charleston and his responsibilities there, while Dorothy stayed on in New York, busy with preproduction plans for *Nancy Ann*. For the next several months he saw a good deal less of his wife than he would have liked, due to her absences for casting meetings and rehearsals. Meanwhile, he had some good news. Macmillan accepted his new volume of verse, *Horizons and Skylines*. When it came out early in 1924, the reviews were heartwarming. Some even went so far as to declare him the best new poet writing in the South.

Dorothy was all for her husband devoting all his time to his writing. He had the small pink house on historic Church Street (so called because it led to the venerable Saint Michael's Church) which had some value because of the rising market for Charleston's old houses. And he had the cottage near Hendersonville in North Carolina, where they could live while they both wrote. John Bennett, though, counseled him that for all his growing reputation, writing poetry was hardly a dependable way to make a living; best to try fiction.

DuBose was already thinking along those lines, and, if he had not yet focused on it, he knew that his subject would deal with Negro life in Charleston, the life of the Gullah Negroes he had worked with and known for so many years. He had already put the pink house up for sale and announced to his partner that he would be leaving the insurance business when he strolled down Church Street on that morning in early March 1924, glanced at dilapidated Cabbage Row, and joined his sister for breakfast on the same street. He picked up the Charleston *News and Courier,* read through it, and came upon the item about Sammy Smalls.

In New York, Dorothy's play *Nancy Ann* was greeted with lackluster reviews, and it folded after only a few performances. It told the story of a stagestruck, well-bred girl—played by Francine Larrimore—who fulfills her ambitions despite the bitter opposition of her family. "I flopped with it,"

Dorothy said ruefully. The nervous strain of the whole process of getting the play on, including the apparent miscasting of Larrimore, sent her into a depression. Her doctor advised a rest cure. DuBose had his own prescription: She should give up writing plays for a while and read mystery stories for relaxation. She might even try writing one.

Both retreated to the cottage, Orienta, near Hendersonville. Dorothy loved the magnificent view of the Smokies, but creature comforts were minimal. The kitchen had a spigot, no sink. A bucket had to be used instead. There was no bathroom either. For bathing, a large tub had to be filled with buckets of water. But she read mystery stories as DuBose had suggested and got her spirits back, and he, meanwhile, was scribbling something on yellow sheets of paper.

"An idea for a novel," was all he said about it.

In June they returned to the MacDowell Colony. They shared a bedroom in the lodge reserved for married couples, and one evening there DuBose asked Dorothy if she would like to hear something of what he had been writing in his studio. "Porgo," he began, reading from his scrawly handwriting on the sheets of yellow paper, "lived in the golden age . . . in an ancient, beautiful city which time has forgotten . . . among other things it was the golden age of beggary."

Porgo, it turned out, was a beggar of indeterminate age, a cripple who got about by way of a packing case turned into a cart that was drawn by an ancient goat. He lived in "a great brick structure" called Catfish Row— though it was not a row at all—"that lifted three stories about the three sides of a court." In those few months since he had clipped out the newspaper item, Sammy Smalls had metamorphosed into Porgo and his place of abode became a thinly disguised replica of Cabbage Row. As he read on, Dorothy was astonished to learn that almost all of the characters were black people, closed in by their race, their dialect, their condition, and that the few whites in the story belonged, from the Negro viewpoint, to another, alien and powerful world.

As for its story, for her it had the stuff of drama, and even before he had finished writing a first draft she suggested trying to adapt it into a play. He scoffed at that idea. Broadway didn't go in for serious treatment of Negro people. A comic song-and-dance revue like *Shuffle Along*, yes, but there was simply no audience for plays about black life played by black actors. She would be wasting her time, he said, and besides, he wasn't too happy about her returning to playwriting. She spent the summer working away at a mystery novel.

DuBose kept John Bennett aware of what he was up to. He was having "great fun," he wrote from the colony, "hell bent on the Negro novel." He would destroy it, he said, if it didn't come out well, but, meanwhile, "I am almost sure I have closed my hands about something alive in my *Porgo*. The Spirit of God has been perched on my studio gable for a month, and where the stuff came from else, I can't imagine. I am pretty drunk over it now."

The stuff was not exactly flowing like wine, however. DuBose was a careful writer. Using a pencil with his weakened hand, he worked over each sentence and paragraph as carefully as he did his lines of poetry. He rewrote sections, moved some around, and kept eliminating all but a few of the white characters. Allowed to remain were a kindly white lawyer and a few representatives of the law.

He read some sections to other colonists. One, novelist Constance Rourke, suggested he send his manuscript, two-thirds completed by the end of the summer, to her publishers, Harcourt, Brace and Company. He did, and the manuscript came back with a note saying it was company policy not to read unfinished first novels. Heyward took this as a rejection.

Back at the North Carolina cottage, Heyward finished the novel in late November and sent the manuscript off to John Bennett in Charleston for an opinion.

Bennett was "instantly struck," he said, "by the absolutely unexampled newness of its outlook upon the Southern Negro as subject. I had never seen anything like it; there had never been anything like it." Missing from it was the kind of patronizing tone characteristic of such writers as Thomas Nelson Page and Joel Chandler Harris in their stories about black people. Heyward, Bennett felt, had taken a simple Negro beggar and transformed him into a heroic figure. He wrote a laudatory letter to Heyward, who replied, "But now what the heck do I do with it?"

It didn't take long for Bennett to supply an answer.

At the next scheduled meeting of the Poetry Society of South Carolina, an address was given by John Farrar, editor of the influential literary magazine *The Bookman,* and also a roving editor for the George H. Doran Company. Bennett took Farrar to lunch the next day and talked in glowing terms about the novel just completed by Heyward, something totally new about the Southern Negro. Farrar's editorial sense was stimulated. He had already read and liked Heyward's poetry. Bennett arranged for the manuscript to be sent to him, and its acceptance by the Doran company came quickly.

The contracts were signed in early January 1925, and publication was scheduled for the fall. There was the usual royalty schedule, but no advance payment. Heyward, however, did receive some income from Farrar for serial publication of three sections of the novel in *The Bookman,* and a fourth section, recast as a short story called "Crown's Bess," ran in another magazine of high standing, *The Forum*. In effect, Farrar arranged a pre-publication campaign for the book.

In hardly any time, Heyward became cast as an authority on Southern literature and on the Southern Negro. His activities for the poetry society had put him in touch with many noted writers.

Now, prior to the publication of the novel, Farrar commissioned him to write for his magazine an article titled "The New Note in Southern Literature." Heyward predicted a trend (he, in a sense, being the trend for the moment) toward "a psychologically true serious picture of contemporary southern Negro life" and the portrayal of Negroes "as essentially human beings." He seemed unaware of the irony implicit in that last phrase; he was, after all, in many ways a traditional, albeit humanistic Southerner himself.

His novel was originally titled *Porgo*. By April 1925 it had been changed, as evidenced by a letter he wrote to Louis Untermeyer, whom he had invited to come to Charleston to give some talks. "Oh, yes," he added offhandedly. "I have a novel, *Porgy*, with Doran for autumn publication."

Over the years, biographers of Gershwin have wondered about or tried to account for the title change from *Porgo* to *Porgy*. One theory is that the name was taken from a local variety of blackfish called a porgy favored by the black natives. Fish sellers would call out, "Porgy walk, Porgy talk, Porgy eat with a knife and fork."

Harlan Greene, archivist for the South Carolina Historical Society, made it his business to dig out the viable reason. The key lay in the lectures given in the early twenties by Jane Heyward, the mother of DuBose. In the tales of the Gullah Negroes she told to tourists she included one about Chloë, a little slave girl from West Africa who grew up to become Jane's nurse on the plantation on which she was raised. All that remained to remind Chloë of her origins was a string of beads and a little wooden doll she called Porgo and kept with her always.

Heyward knew the story from his childhood, and he also heard it again at a lecture his mother gave in 1923. But when Heyward was writing his novel, Jane changed the name of the doll in the story to Gabo. And later on, in a mutual kind of noblesse oblige, Heyward changed Porgo to Porgy.

"There is simple and elegant justice here," said Greene, "that the name of an opera about blacks has a true African beginning."

THE STORY OF Porgy has changed very little in its course through a novel, a play, and many productions as an opera. Onstage its hero, the crippled beggar Porgy, and Bess, the woman he loves, have changed in looks, age, and interpretation according to those cast to play them. The goat, which

Porgy buys with his mendicant savings, is sometimes old, sometimes young and spirited. Heyward, in creating a colorful story for his characters, included elements conducive to drama and suspense — a dice game in which one of the players is killed in a brawl, a buzzard which hovers over Catfish Row like a herald of death, a vicious hurricane that terrifies the residents.

Porgy, though a cripple with useless legs, has an upper body as strong as the stevedore he might otherwise have been, and when he fights with the brutish Crown, who has come to kill him and reclaim his Bess, he is strong enough to kill his rival. There is sex, too, in the picnic scene on Kitiwah Island, when Crown reasserts his hold over Bess and quickly seduces her. A sinister quality enters the story with Sportin' Life, the dapper purveyor of "happy dust," with which at the end he lures the hapless Bess back into her old alcohol- and drug-ridden life. In fact, without the grace and style with which Heyward wrote the story, and the reality and sympathy in his treatment of the characters, the novel might have been accused of melodrama.

In later years, the story, viewed simplistically, did meet with serious objections to and confrontations about the kind of black life it portrayed, replete with craps gaming, illegitimacy, knife fights, superstition, and poverty-stricken ignorance. But not when it first came out in book form. The artfulness of the writing, the sharp and accurate sense of detail, and the moments of true lyricism combined to skirt pitfalls of melodrama and sentimentality.

The six main sections of the book parallel the passage of the seasons from spring to autumn and allow for the capture of the changing quality of existence in Catfish Row. There is courtship, gambling, the singing of spirituals, the annual parade and picnic, the cries of vendors, death, mourning, a funeral, and the inevitable encounters with the white representatives of law and order. Most of this is seen through the eyes and mind of Porgy, the philosopher cripple.

It would be too easy to equate the author's sympathy with Porgy with his own physical weaknesses, and it doesn't necessarily make the book better or truer because much in it came from his own knowledge and experience. But there certainly was a hurricane that hit Charleston in 1911 almost exactly like the one vividly described that rages through Catfish Row (or like the Hugo of 1989).

Kate Whipple, who had known the Heyward family, remembered it well: "It was a freak storm coming out of the East and extending twenty miles along the coast and not more than five miles inland." It broke the sea wall, inundated the city and tore down roofs. A lumber schooner was washed up along the sea wall, a detail that appears in the novel. The time of the story is not directly mentioned, but its overall mood and details such as the horse-drawn police wagon indicate the period before the war in Europe (although when Heyward published the play based on the novel, in 1927, he indicated the action as "Time—the present").

Catfish Row is placed not on Church Street but near a wharf on the waterfront. Bennett revealed that Heyward had told him that he had selected Cabbage Row "for its picturesque squalor and adaptability to his story." However, Bennett said, "he transported it bodily to the waterfront and relocated it on the site of Vanderhorst's Row—the street near the wharf used by the Negro fishing fleet." Also for his story purposes, Heyward invented what had once been a large and beautiful mansion in which the people take refuge from the hurricane. This detail led many to assume that Cabbage Row had originally been a mansion.

The book came out in late September 1925. The Heywards had spent the summer at the MacDowell Colony, where DuBose started work on a new novel and Dorothy followed her husband's advice and started a mystery novel called *The Pulitzer Prize Murders*. What she was really itching to do, though, in spite of DuBose's discouragement, was dramatize *Porgy*.

When the reviews came in, one, by the brilliant Southern critic Frances Newman, seemed to echo Dorothy's feelings about the inherent dramatic value in the book. Newman wrote in the New York *Herald Tribune*: "*Porgy* falls into almost dramatic scenes which would suggest that DuBose Heyward was born for the theatre. The scenic episodes and the dialect [of the characters] are certainly its finest achievements."

There was praise for the book from all sides. It turned out to be the literary discovery, even the sensation, of the season. From *The New York Times*: "Although it is a matter for wonder that Mr. Heyward has seemed to have gotten inside his characters and their surrounding, it is cause for rejoicing that he has communicated these things he has found to the reader."

"Of a beauty so rare and perfect it may be called classic," rhapsodized *The New Republic*.

The Chicago *Daily News*: "The best novel of the season by an American author."

Heywood Broun, the biting and iconoclastic columnist ("It Seems to Me"), wrote that he was "fully prepared for another of those condescending books about fine old black mammies and the like." Instead, "a literary advance in the South must be acknowledged when the writers of that land come to realize, as Heyward does, the incredibly rich material in Negro life which so far has been neglected. He leads the way with a magnificent novel."

But would black readers like what Heyward had written? "For the people of *Porgy* are savage aliens. . . . And in recognizing an alien quality in the Negroes of his story, Mr. Heyward takes a step forward beyond the usual attitude of white writers in the South who deal with Negro life." What other writers would have regarded as inferiority, he said, Heyward saw as strangeness; and he also found "Negro life more colorful and spirited and vital than that of the white community." Broun could not resist a bit of editorializing: "If the two cultures don't readily mix, it may well be the Nordic who lags."

Locally, in Charleston, a few of the proper folk claimed to be shocked by the violence in the book and its focus on the city's poor Negroes. But there was also much pride in one of their own gaining such extraordinary national literary attention. Charleston's Negroes were not overjoyed by Heyward's selection of the sordid and downtrodden milieu as his subject, but the critic for the city's black newspaper complimented him, nevertheless, for his intuitive understanding and honesty in dealing with it. Overall, if Negroes did not join in the chorus of praise, there was no widespread objection to the book. If there was disgruntlement, it was that blacks, not whites, ought to be the ones examining their own experience.

Soon enough, *Porgy* was on the best-seller lists. Both DuBose and Dorothy were bewildered by the sudden turn of events. He was now a writer of consequence, a celebrity. In New York they were invited to literary teas and soirées. Herschel Brickell, then a young writer making his way as a critic, was with them at one. To him, the Heywards seemed dazed and as though they felt out of place. When the three left together to have dinner, they didn't know where to go and wandered into the first handy restaurant. "Outlanders, all three of us," said Brickell.

During the first few months of 1926 the Heywards were in and out of New York, fulfilling a lecture schedule that had been arranged for DuBose. More good news came, meanwhile, in the form of an offer for the screen rights from Cecil B. DeMille, who had broken off with Paramount and joined a New York group called the Producers Distributing Corporation.

DeMille's new story editor in New York was a young Columbia University graduate, Charles Beahan, whose main job was to sniff out promising material for movies. John Farrar sent him the galleys of Heyward's novel, telling him it was a good and beautifully told story, but probably not suitable for the movies. Beahan read the galleys in a sitting, conveyed his enthusiasm to his supervisor, who got hold of DeMille over long-distance telephone. "It sounds like it's got problems," DeMille said, "but it's a challenge for us. Buy it—but $7,500 is the absolute limit."

The economy-minded Beahan closed the deal for $4,500, a sum Heyward was more than happy to have. In fact, always the soul of courtesy, he dropped by to see and thank Beahan, who took him around the corner to a speakeasy, where they toasted each other over an Italian version of mint juleps. Beahan was asked to scout black actors for the leading roles. His choice for Porgy was Paul Robeson, then appearing at the Princess Theatre in *The Emperor Jones*. Robeson was signed, at $250 a week, but the movie was killed before it got started when the head of sales for P.D.C. decided it was a hopeless commercial proposition, since it would be impossible to play it in the South.

Heyward was unhappy to learn of the film's abandonment, but the money he received was enough to get started on building a new and larger house on the property in North Carolina. When they returned there, Dorothy continued working on her mystery novel, or so she told her husband. Actually, she was secretly making a play out of *Porgy*.

4

WHILE HEYWARD was enjoying his novel's success, Gershwin was closing out 1925 in a dazzling display of accomplishment. The month of December saw the first two performances, at Carnegie Hall, of his concert work commissioned by Walter Damrosch, the Concerto in F. The applause that greeted him at the finish was thunderous. Three weeks later, his new musical, *Tip-Toes,* with lyrics by his brother Ira, opened at the Liberty Theatre. Two days after that, another musical, *Song of the Flame,* for which he had composed the score with Otto Harbach, began its lengthy run at the 44th Street Theatre. And the reprise of his one-act opera, *Blue Monday,* was also performed at Carnegie Hall.

It now bore a new title: *135th Street.* Paul Whiteman, long enamored of the little blues opera, decided to give it a rehearing at a Carnegie Hall jazz concert. It was impossible that month to pick up a newspaper without coming across the name George Gershwin. Consequently, hundreds waited in line for more than two hours to buy tickets to what was essentially a concert performance, given in front of the orchestra with only a few props — a bar, a table, some chairs — as a setting. The audience was pleased, but again, the critics less so. Gershwin was not dismayed; he thought the critics rather forbearing in view of the barren staging — and he was still intent on someday composing a full-length opera with jazz motifs.

His social stock was on the rise, too, and the gregarious George now moved among the rich, the talented, the famous. In his theatrical circle were

Noel Coward (in New York to perform in his play, *The Vortex*), the Astaires, Gertrude Lawrence, and Beatrice Lillie. There were parties, parties, parties; they were given by Carl Van Vechten, the Alfred Knopfs, Condé Nast, Jules Glaenzer of Cartier's, and Otto Kahn, the imposing patron of the Metropolitan Opera. George stayed out late at night, loved to dance, seldom was in bed before dawn, and slept until noon.

He had rugged good looks and an athletic body, and he attracted women easily. "Here's this young and handsome guy," said Edward Jablonski, one of his biographers, "and here he is, an American composer, playing concertos in Carnegie Hall." While Ira married, George remained a bachelor. He formed several minor attachments until he met Kay Swift. Her father was a music critic, and she had been given a musical education, then went on to compose the scores of two shows for Broadway. With Gershwin she formed a long-lasting, warm, and intimate, but not exclusive, relationship which eventually led to the breakup of her marriage.

Ira was the opposite of George in that he liked staying in to read or talk with one or two friends. At parties, George enjoyed—some said, claimed—the center of attention and was easily persuaded to sit down at the piano. Or, as some have suggested, it was the other way around; he sat down at the piano to become the center of attention. An evening with George Gershwin, said his friend Oscar Levant, became a Gershwin evening. George's presence at the piano in apartments in Manhattan and in posh Long Island homes was so well known that it brought mention in a Cole Porter musical, *Jubilee*. An Elsa Maxwell–like character, who is planning a wonderful party, remarks, "It will be different in every way. Gershwin's promised not to play."

Still, he maintained close, cohesive ties with his family. As each of the brothers prospered, they moved often within Upper West Side Manhattan, carrying on their father's tradition of restlessness. There was a five-story house at 3 3 Riverside Drive with plentiful room for George, his parents, and Ira and his new wife, Leonore. But it became so filled with friends inclined to drop in at almost any hour that George soon had to take two rooms in a nearby hotel for peace while composing.

Vernon Duke, a young composer friend, remembered there was always a contingent of pretty girls at the house—"young actresses and showgirls mostly, with an admixture of café society. These enchanting damsels had a habit of sharing the piano stool with George when he would install himself there—not to leave it again for two or three hours. No one seemed to mind his almost continuous usurpation of the instrument. What we did mind was that the sirens present never volunteered to share the piano with anyone but their host."

In the early months of 1926 he was in London getting *Lady, Be Good* ready for its London premiere. Then on to Paris for a visit with friends. While there, a theme struck him which he would eventually use in *An American in Paris,* and so firmly did he have it in mind that he went shopping for the taxi horns that would be heard in it. On his return he began work on the score for a new musical, *Oh, Kay!,* to star Gertrude Lawrence. During rehearsals in the summer of 1926 he came home to the Riverside Drive house too stimulated to fall easily asleep. He picked up a book that was recently on the best-seller list and found it even harder to fall asleep. The book was *Porgy.* He didn't put it down until four in the morning, by which time he had read it straight through. So excited was he by the story and by its author's apparent musical sensitivity that he quickly wrote and mailed off a letter suggesting they collaborate on an opera based on the book.

THE LETTER arrived at the Heywards' home in North Carolina as Dorothy Heyward was close to completing a dramatic treatment of her husband's book. She had spent seven secret months at it. During that stretch three playwrights had contacted DuBose, asking for the dramatic rights to *Porgy,* but he was still convinced that the book would not make a play of any worth. Dorothy was panicked by the Gershwin proposal. Here now was a far more powerful threat to her play. "DuBose was delighted," she related. "But when Gershwin came into the picture I had to come out into the open."

She told her husband she wanted him to listen to something she had been working on and began reading the play. He was surprised and moved. More than that, he liked what she had done and had to admit that the story now seemed workable for the stage. And yet, the opportunity to collaborate with the renowned and brilliant George Gershwin was all too tempting. "He was torn," Dorothy said, "between the prospect of the play and the opera. We both thought of it as 'or.'"

The play, and perhaps the loyalty of DuBose to his wife, prevailed. He wrote Gershwin, telling him that a play based on the book was already in process and that it would have to come first. Gershwin wrote back saying in essence that to have a play would not at all affect his writing an opera. Actually, he was stage-wise enough to know that it would be better for his purpose to have a firm stage structure than create one from the more amorphous form of a novel.

The Heywards were delighted. Now there was the possibility of both a play and an opera. And now DuBose became his wife's collaborator. At first, he offered suggestions. Then he shared the job of rewriting. "During the numerous rewritings," Dorothy said, "changes of course crept in and some characters came out different from their original conceptions."

The dialogue presented a problem. There wasn't much of it in the novel, but what there was of it was in reasonably faithful but difficult-to-say Gullah speech. Dorothy's dialogue tried only to suggest its qualities.

DuBose concentrated on providing a semblance of the Gullah speech. Dorothy would write, for example:

"I sure am tired tonight."

DuBose would change it to: "Lord, I be tired tonight."

DuBose had been nettled the year before when Franklin Pierce Adams, in his "Conning Tower" column in the New York *World,* had complained about Heyward's faulty knowledge of craps in the novel. His Pepys-like entry in his "Diary" reads: "Mr. DuBose Heyward appeareth to know a vast deal about the life of the Negro. But he does not know about their game of craps, for he telleth about how a player lost the dice on the first cast, which is not possible."

With the dice game and the tragedy it leads to as the critical opening scene of the play, DuBose wrote to a lawyer friend in Charleston, Paul Macmillan, for confirmation about the rules of craps and for expressions used by the players. Macmillan wrote back, explaining that it was possible, as the character Robbins had done in the novel, to give up the dice on rolling a two, three, or twelve. He had an option, in other words, especially if out of money and unable to make a bet. For the talk, though, he wrote, "You should get a real darky [sic!] to do it." Whether Heyward researched the talk further isn't known, but he did add a clarifying line in the play. Robbins says, upon rolling box cars (two sixes), "I goin' pass 'em along an' see ef I kin break my luck."

But it was Dorothy who made the key suggestion for the ending. Bess, as they first had it, would be taken off to New York (not Savannah, as in the novel) by Sportin' Life, but instead of letting Porgy accept this sadly and philosophically, he would take off after her in his little goat cart. Pathos would remain, but Porgy would maintain his indomitable spirit and love for his woman. DuBose liked it. They finished the play in the early summer of 1926, titled it *Catfish Row,* and Dorothy laboriously typed up three copies and sent them out to the Theatre Guild and two other producing organizations. To their astonishment, hardly a week went by before the play was accepted by all three and they had the luxury of choice. They decided on the distinguished Theatre Guild.

THE THEATRE GUILD had entered into the ranks of the Broadway theatre in 1919 as a professional offshoot of the Washington Square

Players, a group made up of aspiring playwrights, directors, producers, and actors formed in 1915 to present plays of artistic merit, principally of American origin, aside from commercial considerations. They moved uptown from Greenwich Village but kept ticket prices to the minimum—fifty cents. In line with their idealism, most everyone involved worked for free.

Unfortunately, in spite of the many new one-act (and a few full-length) plays that were presented, the group almost died because of poor acting and directing. Ticket prices were raised to a dollar and salaries were instituted— twenty-five dollars weekly—and matters improved. The Washington Square Players were well on their way to success with the critics and public when America entered the war and they were forced to cease operations because so many of their best performers went into the armed forces.

After the war, Lawrence Langner, a patent attorney and part-time playwright who had been with the group, took the lead in bringing former members into a new organization with similar aims. The Theatre Guild, as it was named, would still be dedicated to artistic and experimental theatre; new American playwrights would be fostered and works would be aired by European playwrights hitherto ignored by Broadway's commercially minded theatre managers. There would be, however, significant differences from the way the Players had operated. There would be no more amateurism, for one thing, and instead the highest standards of professional production. For financing, the founders came up with the then novel idea of a subscription audience large enough to guarantee a minimum run of four weeks for each play produced.

Enough money was raised to put on their first play, Jacinto Benavente's *The Bonds of Interest*, at the Garrick Theatre, but only with the help of Otto Kahn, who arranged for the fledgling Guild to have it rent-free. Critical support was immediate, but the popular audience stayed away. Langner, and a banker, Maurice Wertheim, came up with the funds, and hardly a penny over, needed to put on a second production, St. John Ervine's *John Ferguson*.

This time they had a hit. But then the Actors Equity strike of 1919 was called, and it halted all Broadway production—all, that is, but the Theatre Guild's. The actors' organization favored the Guild because it shared its profits with its casts, something regarded as highly desirable for performers. So, while noted actors and actresses marched up and down Broadway and shouted slogans and called for solidarity against the wicked theatre managers and producers, *John Ferguson* was just about the only show in town, and the theatre was jammed.

The Guild was run by a six-member board of managers that included Langner, the actress Helen Westley, director and playwright Philip Moeller, and Theresa Helburn, a teacher, drama critic, and playwright who had come out of George Pierce Baker's playwriting workshop. She was appointed play representative for the organization, and so valuable and dedicated were her services that eventually she became its executive director. A group vote decided the choice of plays.

During its first few seasons the Guild's record was impressive, except for the noticeable lack of original American works. One critic dubbed the board "Six Characters in Search of an American Author." Their tastes seemed to lean toward European drama, but it was difficult to find native plays beyond the artistic range of commercial theatre, by no means all dross. George Bernard Shaw was a Guild specialty, beginning with his *Heartbreak House.* There were productions of Strindberg's *The Dance of Death,* A. A. Milne's *Mr. Pim Passes By,* and *Liliom,* by Ferenc Molnár. Alfred Lunt and Lynn Fontanne brought great style (and welcome box office) to such plays as *Arms and the Man* and *The Guardsman.*

The list of subscribers lengthened, and a bond campaign was successful enough for the Guild to build its own theatre to its own design. A permanent production staff was maintained, and a Guild acting company was established, large enough to move between two simultaneous productions. When the new theatre was opened, an actors' school was founded. Meanwhile, subscription lists were being built in six other cities so that plays could be sent on the road at the end of their New York runs.

When the Heywards sent in their play, it could not have come at a better moment. Not only did *Catfish Row* strike the Guild board as a good *American* play, but its drama of seething Negro life was seen as "a window" that could be "opened to give us a peep into an alien world." On the other hand, because of the massive setting needed for it, it presented a staging challenge to the Guild's production resources. The Heywards themselves presented an obstacle: they insisted on its many Negro characters being performed by Negro actors, which meant that a whole unfamiliar company would have to be recruited.

IN HARLEM, something of a theatrical surge was noticeable. There were the popular black revues and vaudeville, a "little" theatre movement, and some stock companies that performed for black audiences. Lacking, though, was a black company with the qualifications (at least so it was thought) needed for acceptance by Broadway's white theatregoers.

Yet many Negro performers were advancing in their craft and gaining recognition, and had been doing so for several years. Paul Robeson was impressive in *The Emperor Jones.* And at the time that the Heywards were writing their play, several black actors were winning praise at the Province-town Playhouse in Paul Green's *In Abraham's Bosom.* This play, about a young Negro who loses his life while attempting to elevate himself and his people through education, was given the 1927 Pulitzer Prize for drama.

A lead actor in the play was Frank Wilson, who had been a Manhattan mail carrier for ten years. He had also produced, written, and acted in one-act plays in Harlem's Lincoln and Lafayette theatres. He studied at the American Academy of Dramatic Arts, then played in *All God's Chillun Got Wings* at the Provincetown Playhouse before joining *In Abraham's Bosom.* When the play moved uptown to the Garrick he took on the starring role of Abraham McCranie and was so effective the critics proclaimed him one of the outstanding actors of his generation.

Before that, an all-black musical, *Shuffle Along,* had created a new Broadway fad. This, with a score by Noble Sissle and Eubie Blake, reached the Great White Way in 1921 after playing to standing room only in black theatres in Washington and Philadelphia. It was helped along by such captivating hit tunes as "I'm Just Wild About Harry" and "Love Will Find a Way." A sensation of her own was created by a diminutive charmer, Florence Mills. Miss Mills, a performer since childhood, played in vaudeville and Harlem nightclubs until cast in *Shuffle Along.* In the chorus was another girl who would blaze her own trail: Josephine Baker.

It was Miss Mills, though, who was the pride, the joy, of Harlem for the next several years. "Her name," a black historian remembered, "was on the lips of everyone in the community. People sat in parlors, on stoops, or stood in hallways trying to find words that might describe her." After spending a year with *Shuffle Along* she went into *Plantation Revue,* another black show that was expanded for Broadway after a tryout in a Harlem nightclub.

In 1927 she returned to New York to appear in Lew Leslie's revue *Blackbirds.* The show had been taken to Paris for six months, then to London, where the gossip was that Edward, Prince of Wales, was so capti-vated by Miss Mills that he returned to see her again and again. Her return to New York was greatly anticipated, especially her specialty number, "I'm a Little Blackbird Looking for a Bluebird." Sadly, she had postponed an operation for appendicitis, and it came too late to save her.

Florence Mills was mourned by thousands of Harlemites who lined the streets as her funeral procession passed by and an airplane flew overhead and released a flock of blackbirds.

In 1926, *Deep River,* billed as "a native opera," came to Broadway with an all-black cast. Rose McClendon and Jules Bledsoe made strong impressions, but its flimsy libretto by Laurence Stallings and its jazzy score impressed no one and it lasted only a few weeks. The trend, though, was beginning to turn from the lighthearted and comic black revues toward a more dramatic treatment of Negro themes. In the same year, *Lulu Belle,* a play by Edward Sheldon and Charles MacArthur set in Harlem, starred Lenore Ulric and Henry Hull (both white) as a black prostitute and a black barber. The cast mingled white and black actors, and although the acting was good enough to sustain the show for a while, David Belasco's production, with its evocation of Harlem street life, was the main focus for audiences.

Another play, *Harlem* (1929), took a grimmer look at the same locale; its main distinction was its relative realism, and another was that its author, Wallace Thurman, was black and knew his subject well.

The Harlem of reality was becoming, as the prominent black writer Alain Locke wrote, "a Negro race capital." Attracted there were "the African, the West Indian, the Negro American . . . the peasant, the student, the businessman, the professional man, artist, adventurer, worker, preacher . . . and exploiter."

Early in the century a real estate boom in that uptown area of Manhattan had collapsed, and as a desperation measure landlords began attracting black people, then crowded in downtown tenderloin areas, with low rents to fill empty apartments. By the mid-twenties Harlem was being called the "Negro capital of the world." In 1925, the New York *Herald Tribune,* noting the creative vitality in the area, coined the term "the Harlem Renaissance" to describe the movements in theatre, writing, and painting.

The development continued through most of the twenties, supported by black leaders and prominent whites. A literary contest for black writers had as judges Van Wyck Brooks, Eugene O'Neill, and Robert Benchley, along with James Weldon Johnson and Alain Locke. Prize winners included Langston Hughes and Zora Neale Hurston. A deliberate aim of the leading black organizations, the NAACP and the Urban League, was the promotion of cultural and artistic excellence. White foundations, such as the Rosenwald Fund, joined in with grants, fellowships, and awards.

Langston Hughes recalled it as a period "when almost any Harlem Negro of any social importance at all would be likely to say casually: 'As I was remarking the other day to Heywood . . .' meaning Broun. Or, 'As I said to George . . . ,' referring to Gershwin." The Dark Tower, a popular gathering place for both black and white socialites, was a large brownstone on 136th Street, where A'Lelia Walker, who had earned a fortune with her hair-straightening formula, entertained in her grand salon.

Whites also came to Harlem in search of "hotter" entertainment in nightclubs and cabarets than could be found downtown. Black "hosts" were on hand to fee-guide them to the most interesting places. Jazz was the nation's music now, and the great black jazz bands played at that Harlem mecca, the Savoy Ballroom.

The Negro, as Hughes said, "was in vogue." More and more books by and about blacks appeared. In art, sculptors and painters took inspiration from African primitive discoveries. Heyward may not have realized he was hitting a nerve with *Porgy,* but its success owed much to the light it shed on what was previously regarded as a strange and exotic world.

Gershwin was well aware of the trends. For a guide he had Carl Van Vechten, who took an enthusiastic interest in the Negro arts and who, in fact, would suggest to Gershwin a black opera for which he would supply the text.

The Theatre Guild managers felt they had something new and important in the Heywards' play (retitled *Porgy* to identify it with the novel) and, though pessimistic about its commercial chances, were determined to stage it. The Heywards were hopeful for a production during the Guild's 1926–1927 season, in its brand-new theatre.

They came north in September 1926 for casting and whatever rewriting would be required. The Guild assigned the direction of the play to one of its regular directors, Robert Milton, but after some halfhearted efforts to find a cast, he put the play aside to work on another. The Heywards were discouraged, and not much heartened by the Guild's professions of firm belief in their play—although they expected to lose money on it. Regardless of audience reception, they at least could count on a four-week subscription run. While waiting for things to happen, the Heywards left New York for the off-season quiet of Atlantic City, where DuBose occupied himself with a new novel. "The usual heartbreaking stuff," he wrote John Bennett, "postponements and delays . . . and now it might not see the light until next season."

In Atlantic City that fall, Heyward and Gershwin had their first face-to-face meeting, when Gershwin came down from Philadelphia, where *Oh, Kay!* was having its pre-Broadway opening. They talked only in general terms about the opera-to-be. DuBose learned that Gershwin was not in the slightest hurry to get to work on putting *Porgy* to music. For one thing, he thought it would be some years before he was technically prepared to compose an opera, although his desire to make one from *Porgy* was not lessened.

In spite of what looked to be another postponement, Heyward was vastly impressed by Gershwin, "a young man of enormous physical and emotional vitality, who possessed the faculty of seeing himself impersonally and real-istically." He was amazed that someone of Gershwin's extraordinary success could appraise his talent with such complete detachment. But only a vague verbal agreement to someday do the opera together resulted from that meeting.

Not long after, with no play production in sight, the Heywards left for England in search of more quiet for writing. They were occupying a fisher-man's cottage on the Cornwall coast when in June of 1927 a letter came from Theresa Helburn, now the Guild's executive director, that Robert Milton had been dispensed with and that a new director had been hired for their play. Not only would it go into rehearsal in early September, but it would open the Guild's new season in October. The new director's name was Rouben Mamoulian. The Heywards had never heard of him.

5

To the people at the Theatre Guild, Rouben Mamoulian was familiarly known as "the mad Armenian," mainly because of his energy and a mind bristling with innovative ideas about stagecraft, particularly his tendency toward what he called "rhythm" and poetic stylization. Lawrence Langner came across him when the Guild brought the American Opera Company of Rochester to New York City for a short summer season. "A tall, bespectacled young man," as Langner described him, "he begged me to visit him in Rochester and see some of his work."

The Guild at the time was attempting to establish an adjunct theatre school, but without much success, although its new theatre was specifically designed to have adequate space for classes and demonstration productions. The two teachers hired had already defected when Langner happened to be in Rochester on patent business. There, Mamoulian was directing operas and conducting drama classes on the side. Langner was sufficiently impressed by what he saw to offer him the directorship of the Guild's drama school.

Mamoulian was part Armenian, part Russian. He had been born in Tiflis in 1898 in what is now Soviet Georgia, where his father was a bank president and his mother the president of the Armenian Theatre. Some of his first years were spent backstage at the Tiflis theatre while his mother directed production, and others at the Lycée Montaigne in Paris, where his family lived for a time. His stage ambitions were discouraged by his father, who sent him to Moscow University to study criminal law.

It wasn't long before he joined the Studio Theatre of the Moscow Art Theatre, directed evenings by Eugene Vakhtangov, a Stanislavsky disciple. Upon his return to Tiflis he wrote drama criticism for a local newspaper and founded his own drama studio. The Revolution was not to his liking, so on the pretext of visiting his sister he went to London and stayed, joining a group of Russian expatriate actors and organizing them into the Russian Repertory Theatre. After touring England with the group he directed a play in the West End, Austin Page's *The Beating on the Door,* with considerable success.

"To direct a professional production in London at that early age," he remembered, "was unprecedented. The management put into my contract a clause saying that whenever I was asked, in public or in print as to how old I was, my answer should be 'around thirty.' In the direction of *The Beating on the Door* I was totally under the influence of the Stanislavsky Method—utter realism—chopping wood, real wood, naturalistic action and all that. This was the first and last production I directed in this manner."

After that first success he had a crucial choice to make: whether to accept an offer to join the Théâtre des Champs-Elysées in Paris or to help George Eastman (of Kodak) organize and direct his new American Opera Company. "To me," Mamoulian said, "the appeal of the 'New World' was irresistible." Before leaving, though, he spent two weeks at the British Museum, "boning up on opera."

In Rochester over the next three years he directed a wide range of operas and operettas, from *Tannhäuser* to *The Merry Widow,* from *Boris Godunov* to Gilbert and Sullivan. In Maurice Maeterlinck's *Sister Beatrice* he began putting into effect his ideas about the integration of dialogue, dramatic action, dance, song, and music. With Eastman he clashed about another of his aims, the establishment of an important dramatic theatre. Eastman was resistant to this, and Langner's offer for Mamoulian to join the Guild came at the right moment.

In New York, Langner said, Mamoulian "began to pester the Guild directors in a most irritatingly efficient manner to come and see the plays given by his pupils and, of course, directed by himself. Finally he prevailed and we went to see a school production of *The Seven Keys to Baldpate* at the Garrick Theatre." The directors explained to Mamoulian that they had only limited time and he was not to feel dismayed if they left after a few minutes. No one, however, could budge from a seat before the final curtain. And it was at this point it occurred to Langner and Theresa Helburn that here was the man who might be able to direct *Porgy.*

Rouben Mamoulian, director
of the play Porgy and the first
production of Porgy and Bess.
(Wachsman Collection, Lawrence and
Lee Theatre Research Institute,
Ohio State University.)

Robert Milton, and other directors contacted, had been reluctant to take it on. Langner said the reason for this was the play's requirement for a large, all-Negro cast. "There were many tales (mostly untrue) of the irresponsibility of Negro actors." The other members of the board at the Guild were not convinced about Mamoulian's suitability for the job, but Helburn and Langner were persuasive, and it was "in despair," said Langner, that the others acceded.

In a letter to the Heywards, Theresa Helburn assured them that she had "great confidence in Mamoulian . . . and, while he is Russian, he has lived here long enough to speak the language and understand the American temperament. He is very keen on working with the Negroes, has kept in touch with their Harlem performances and is planning to go down to Charleston this summer to get acquainted with the locale. The way he has taken hold of the script and the casting has convinced us we have not made a mistake, and between ourselves, we are all glad to be free of the burden of Mr. Milton's unreliability."

Mamoulian had ideas about the script that meant more work for the Heywards. The part of Porgy, he felt, needed to be strengthened in a way that would bring him closer to his more sensitive, mystical, and philosophical counterpart in the book. Porgy should also show an earlier interest in Bess to sharpen the conflict between him and her lover, Crown. He wanted more made of Sportin' Life and the "happy dust" with which he lures Bess to her unknown fate. And he suggested that the play's three acts be rearranged into four.

Heyward wrote back suggesting that in Charleston Mamoulian look up John Bennett, who would help him get the feel of the locale. Mamoulian arrived with Cleon Throckmorton, the set designer. With Bennett as their guide, they explored the city and the nearby sea islands. The picturesque shabbiness of Cabbage Row appealed to their theatrical instincts, and Throckmorton carefully sketched its details. During their long walks and drives with Bennett, they peppered him with questions. The play took on more reality for them when they were shown a familiar figure known as the Honey Man, whose cries resounded through the street. Nor had Heyward exaggerated the colorful Sunday clothes of the local Negroes, their festive picnic costumes, the badges, ribbons, and sashes of the parade marshals. So intent were they on creating a realistic atmosphere that they made notes on forty-nine different sounds characteristic of the city's streets and wharves.

Back in New York, Mamoulian searched for a cast. In Harlem he combed through black theatre groups, vaudeville houses, and cabarets. Agencies for black performers offered little; they mostly represented dancers and singers. Mamoulian had an eye on Frank Wilson, the star of *In Abraham's Bosom,* for the role of Porgy, and, just in time, his show closed, and he became available. So did Rose McClendon from the same play. She was cast as Serena, the wife of Robbins, who, early in the play, is killed by Crown in a crap game. Mamoulian found his Bess, Evelyn Ellis, and his Sportin' Life, Percy Vervaine, in a Harlem musical stock company, but harder to locate was Crown, the burly villain of the piece.

Mamoulian went to the length of stopping likely-looking prospects on the street. He saw one young man in the chorus of a Harlem revue and asked him to appear at an audition. The idea of acting in a Broadway play seemed so remote to the man that he didn't bother to show up. In fact, a good many of those contacted for the twenty-two speaking parts had little notion of the kind of opportunity they were being offered.

After months of searching, enough candidates were finally gathered together in the library of the Guild Theatre for readings and assignment of parts. "With few to choose from," Heyward related, "casting resolved itself into taking those who were there." But with the experienced actors he was unhappy, too. Frank Wilson was too young to fit his vision of Porgy. Nor did he think Evelyn Ellis right for Bess. "The Bess of my novel," he later complained, "had been a gaunt, tragic figure such as I had often seen on the Charleston waterfront." But "Evelyn Ellis was young, slender, and imme-

Frank Wilson, the first Porgy—in the play, 1927. (South Carolina Historical Society.)

Evelyn Ellis, discovered in a Harlem stock theatrical company, was Bess in the play, although Heyward regarded her as unlike his conception of the character. (South Carolina Historical Society.)

diately noticeable for a certain radiant charm." As a result of this casting, the roles of Porgy and Bess became more or less fixed as much more youthful than Heyward had imagined them.

But even with casting completed, Heyward's ordeal was only beginning. Many of the actors were vaudeville-trained, which meant that they usually addressed the audience when speaking lines. When asked to register high spirits they broke into the Charleston or some other dance of the moment. Mamoulian, though, was undismayed. With patience and tact he worked at breaking the actors of "bad" stage habits and guiding them toward what he wanted from them.

"They had no conception, at first," Mamoulian said, "of the significance of their work. They showed little interest in the play. They would arrive an

Rose McClendon, a leading dramatic actress of her day,
created the role of Serena in the play.
(Theatre Collection, Museum of the City of New York.)

hour late at rehearsal, would forget to learn their lines, and after I had told
them several times how to do a scene, they would do it again the wrong way."
No point in threatening dismissal if replacements were unavailable. The
fears of the directors who had stalled about doing the plays seemed justified.
Most of these performers were new to Broadway's demands, and the language of the play itself was unfamiliar to them.

At curtain's rise, Catfish Row, in the stage directions, "reechoes with
African laughter and friendly banter in 'Gullah,' the language of the
Charleston Negro. The audience understands none of it. . . ." Neither did
the people in the cast. They were Northerners; many had never been near the
South Atlantic seaboard. Nor were they "primitive" Negroes. Gullah was a
foreign language to them.

It was decided that some tempering was needed, for the audience's sake,
too. Many of the Gullah-based words were made more intelligible and
spoken more distinctly. "It was undoubtedly not the part of wisdom,"
Dorothy Heyward said, "to discourage your audience at the very rise of the
curtain—so the Gullah was blurred into the atmosphere." She added,
"Should it ever fall on the astonished ear of Porgy's prototype, he would
never know what it was all about."

Dorothy was surprised by one objection to the play by the cast members. They were distressed by the word "nigger," which occurred frequently in the dialogue. "I had used it in writing the play," she said, "when one Negro was speaking to another, just as DuBose did in the novel. We heard it [in Charleston] fifty times a day." Nevertheless, the word remained, and it did not disappear until many years later, when Ira took matters into his own hands and excised it from the libretto of the opera.

THE PLAY WAS scheduled to open the Guild's new season, and on the stage of its theatre Catfish Row was emerging—a huge set rising three stories, with an open court in the center and a wrought-iron gateway toward the rear. The audience would see twenty windows with shutters that opened and closed and growing plants in pots on the sills. While it was stylized to a degree, Mamoulian wanted the set to carry the illusion of reality and the flavor of authenticity and, in overall quality of color and mood, to reflect the Charleston of 1912. He remembered a profusion of vines from his visit to Charleston, and so vines climbed discolored walls that held fishing nets spread to dry. Seen through the gateway was a cobbled Charleston street and, in the distance, the harbor and Fort Sumter.

With the call "Everybody in his own house," rehearsals would begin. Mamoulian was popular with the actors. Hard as he made them work, he was infinitely patient, whether drilling an individual or organizing the crowd of extras in simulating the teeming life of the quarter.

"The mad Armenian" had a method—and a theory—which was that in the timing of action and speeches in a play there was a rhythm similar to that in music. He put the theory to use in the play's last scene, which begins at dawn. He had the characters appear one by one and start on their usual tasks. The sound volume on the stage would rise with the activity—pounding, shouting, tooting, laughing. He had it done to a count: first one-two time, then faster and faster. In other scenes rhythmic punctuation came from the bells of Saint Michael's Church that tolled at regular intervals. Rhythm came, too, with the swaying to the spirituals interlarded in the play.

These spirituals had not been recorded. DuBose Heyward, like his mother, had a keen interest in Negro spirituals; from memory he sang and hummed them so they could be set down in notation. He had his own theory—that the quality of rhythm was a unique characteristic of the Negro, individually and in the mass. It was a "secret law," he said, "and a sort of race personality" that was important in energizing his own imagination.

To help the actors identify more closely with the characters they played, an authority on Gullah speech, Samuel Gaillard Stoney, came up from South Carolina. He gave the cast a sense of the way it was spoken, and he also told them stories about the way of life of the Gullah people. One member of the cast had spent some of his boyhood in Charleston, and he remembered an old crab vendor. He was commissioned to create the crab vendor for the play, and the character has remained since.

The labor being put into creating atmosphere began to affect the playing by the actors, who fell more easily and naturalistically into their parts. This didn't happen overnight, however. It took a long time for the performances to crystallize, and some on the board of managers began to talk ominously about abandoning the production.

Dorothy Heyward was sitting out front watching Mamoulian drill an actor over and over in his lines, when she noticed one of the managers, Lee Simonson, prowling the aisles with an anguished expression. "Take it again," Mamoulian said. Simonson cried out in pain, "Not again! I can't stand it!"

He came to Theresa Helburn, sitting in the seat next to Dorothy, and not seeing the playwright in the darkness, asked, "How much have we sunk in this damned thing?"

Helburn whispered, "Too much to go back now," and she gestured toward the costly set.

It was Dorothy's feeling that Throckmorton's imposing structure and its lavish props saved the production.

Then there was the goat that drew Porgy in his little cart. Good as Mamoulian was with the human actors, he was less so with the goat. As the time for dress rehearsal came closer, the goat's behavior was not always predictable, and his entrances were narrowed down to two: when Porgy first comes onstage and the last scene, in which Porgy is about to ride off to New York in search of Bess. Frank Wilson made it his job to form a good working relationship with the goat, and when the time came for the dress rehearsal he assured Mamoulian that he and the goat had come to a harmonious understanding.

Dress rehearsals, by invitation only, at the Theatre Guild were regarded as almost as important as opening nights. The *Porgy* dress rehearsal was attended by a fashionable full-house audience which reacted well to the play, that is, until just before the end, when Porgy was lifted into his cart and was about to drive offstage. The goat had been docile during his first entrance; now it began to behave more like a mule. Instead of going through the gateway it headed for the wall of a house, then to the footlights, where it gazed for a moment at the audience and at last was maneuvered with the help

The stage setting for the play version was created by Cleon Throckmorton after a visit to Charleston. (Lawrence and Lee Theatre Research Institute, Ohio State University.)

of cast members to the exit. But even there it managed to snag the wheels of the cart in the ironwork. The house rocked with laughter, to the utter dismay of the Heywards at the ruin of their ending.

After that, no chances of goatish misbehavior were taken. The goat was to be led in and firmly led off.

THE OPENING of *Porgy* occurred on schedule, October 10, 1927, a year when Broadway reached an apogee of activity: 268 plays, some two hundred of them original, were presented. First-line critics, such as George Jean Nathan, Brooks Atkinson, John Mason Brown, and Alexander Woollcott, found themselves hard-pressed to cover all the openings. *Porgy*, however, was a production of the Theatre Guild, its record by this time so distinguished that it automatically brought out the big-name reviewers.

Gershwin, incidentally, was not there (though he came later on). He was busy with out-of-town preparations for a new musical, *Funny Face,* which would have its opening a month later just across 52nd Street at a new theatre, the Alvin, named for the first syllables of the names of the owners—and producers—Alex A. Aarons and Vinton Freedley, much of whose success had come from their association with the Gershwins.

Aside from the fever and fervor of Broadway, would there ever be another such year to fascinate so continually the American populace? The excitements seemed to come one after another. There was Babe Ruth, who spent the summer assaulting and breaking the home run record. Lindbergh flew the Atlantic in his single-engine plane. Gene Tunney went down for the historic "long count" and rose to wrest the heavyweight championship from

Lawyer Frazier (A. B. Comathiere) in the play version, 1927.
(Theater Collection, Museum of the City of New York.)

Jack Dempsey, thus creating a never-ending controversy. An unpretentious musical, *The Jazz Singer,* was running on Broadway, and later that year came along as a *talking* film. Few yet realized that, partly because of it, the very life of the theatre would be endangered. Meanwhile, it was in awed silence that moviegoers watched the steamy embraces of Greta Garbo and John Gilbert in *Flesh and the Devil.*

On Wall Street the boom was on, as it was in the illegal liquor business, too. Al Capone's gang made $100,000,000 that year, and its tax-beleaguered boss decided to retire to Florida, although soon enough the government provided him his living quarters. The year featured one of the decade's juiciest murder trials, that of Ruth Snyder and Henry Gray, both convicted of her husband's murder. "You did nothing to make your husband unhappy?" Ruth Snyder was asked. "Not that he knew about," she replied.

"The frothiest year of a frothy decade," one historian called it. But it had its somber side. Sacco and Vanzetti were executed, in spite of the protesting presence outside the Boston courthouse of Dorothy Parker, Edna St. Vincent Millay, and John Dos Passos. Albert Einstein, John Galsworthy, and George Bernard Shaw protested, too. But, as the now infamous Judge Webster Thayer said, "Although he [Vanzetti] may not actually have committed the crime . . . he is the enemy of our existing institutions." It was that kind of year.

In France, the svelte and iconoclastic dancer Isadora Duncan got her scarf tangled in the wheel of a moving car and died of a broken neck. She was an advocate of "free love," as were others that year, including Mrs. Bertrand Russell and Judge Lindsay, who thought companionate (without benefit of license) marriage was a wholesome idea whose time had come.

All this was not reflected on Broadway to any great degree. Ira and George Gershwin, to a book by George S. Kaufman, tried satire (of jingoistic patriotism) in *Strike Up the Band,* but the musical closed out of town and would not be brought back for several years. They would have much better luck with *Funny Face.* Kaufman, with Edna Ferber, also fared better with a spoof of the Barrymores, *The Royal Family.* Jeanne Eagels appeared with Leslie Howard in *Her Cardboard Lover,* and Bela Lugosi brought *Dracula* to the big city. Florenz Ziegfeld built a theatre, named it after himself, and, instead of filling it with *Follies,* brought in *Show Boat,* a musical of such solid quality and popularity that it all but revolutionized the form.

As can be seen from this brief overview, *Porgy* came along in a time of general ebullience, of change and portents of change, although few were paying much attention to Philo T. Farnsworth's model of a television receiver or Werner Heisenberg's pronouncements of the uncertainty principle. But

New York and New Jersey commuters greeted with pleasure the opening of the Holland Tunnel beneath the Hudson River, and a good many of them drove through it in Henry Ford's new Model A. And note the names on the book lists: Ernest Hemingway with *Men Without Women,* William Faulkner with *Mosquitoes,* Willa Cather with *Death Comes for the Arch-bishop,* Sinclair Lewis with *Elmer Gantry,* Virginia Woolf with *To the Lighthouse,* and a translation of Thomas Mann's *The Magic Mountain.*

Dorothy and DuBose Heyward sat at the back of the theatre on their opening night, jittery with fear that some unknown disaster might strike as it had the night before. But all worked well—that is, until a clap of thunder was supposed to be heard when Crown shouts to the sky, "Gawd laugh and Crown laugh back." Crown laughed, but the thunderclap came late, and the point was lost. Yet the spirituals were sung so movingly that for DuBose they had a heartbreaking quality. And what worked most effectively were the strange shadows thrown on the wall during the scene in which Catfish Row residents gather to mourn the death of Serena's husband. During a rehearsal a stagehand had left one light on in the footlights that caused the shadows.

Crown defies the elements during the hurricane scene in Porgy.
(Lawrence and Lee Theatre Research Institute, Ohio State University.)

Lawrence Langner thought it made for an unusual effect. "We'll use it," Mamoulian decided at once; it became a virtual trademark in his subsequent career.

The Heywards were already jittery enough about the reception of the play when they noticed the rotund Alexander Woollcott leave his seat before the last scene and stride heavily up the aisle to the exit. To Heyward, "he seemed forty feet tall, thirty feet broad, his mouth that of a medieval executioner." His leaving before the finish seemed to them an ominous portent of the play's chances. And their anxiety was not relieved to any extent by the first review that came in, that of J. Brooks (as he was then known) Atkinson of *The New York Times.*

It was not a bad review. It had nice things to say. But it was not the enthusiastic kind of review, particularly from *The New York Times,* usually needed to breed a hit. Its first words were like a dash of cold water in the face: "In spite of many obvious weaknesses in the texture of the performance . . ." But it continued: "the dramatization of *Porgy* turns out to be steadily interesting in the best tradition of the Guild." Atkinson had admired the novel, but "transformed into a play it is not crisp and only spasmodically vivid; it is rather a chocolate-colored lithograph strip, splashed with color, disorderly, unwieldy, heavy and spontaneous by turns, yet always true."

Although other reviews were more positive, the managers of the Theatre Guild met immediately with the Heywards and asked for a thorough rewriting and condensation of the last act. The Heywards returned to their hotel room, locked themselves in, and for three days wrote themselves into near-exhaustion. But they did not like their reconstruction, which to them seemed no improvement over the original.

After finishing it, Dorothy said, "we started for the theatre . . . It was raining. Our dejection was so deep that we were only mildly curious about the umbrellas outside the theatre. There seemed to be a long line of people stretching down the block, foolishly standing out in the rain."

When they entered the Guild office with their new manuscript, they received strange looks. Heyward handed in the new script and announced that they had done all they could in the way of changes.

"You're crazy to want to change it," Lawrence Langner said. "We're a hit."

But why hadn't they been told, DuBose wanted to know.

"We would have," Langner said, "but it's just happened."

It was true that in the first day or two there had not been a great surge of ticket-buying, probably the result of Atkinson's equivocations and the so-called power of the *Times,* but the other reviews more than made up for its lack of enthusiasm. And in his Sunday follow-up column Atkinson warmed

Serena is at first resentful of Bess after her husband's murder: Rose McClendon, Evelyn Ellis, Frank Wilson. (Theater Collection, Museum of the City of New York.)

up enough to call *Porgy* an "illuminating chronicle of American folklore. In producing it the Guild keeps the faith with its subscribers and friends who look on it for leadership, even for pioneering, in modern drama."

As for Woollcott, in spite of his missing the final scene, he declared it to be "an evening of new experience, extraordinary interest, and high, startling beauty. In a dozen years of first nights I have not seen in the American theatre an example of more resourceful and more outstanding direction." Somehow he was omnisciently aware that at the end "the crippled but mighty Porgy gets into his little goat cart and starts for New York to recapture his woman."

The "dilapidated grandeur of the Catfish Row setting" won praise from all the reviewers. Mamoulian's career was immediately made by a torrent of accolades. "To his vivid direction," said the *Herald Tribune*'s Percy Hammond, "may be ascribed much of the play's popularity." All were impressed by "the ghostly shadows on the wall" of the mourners in Serena's room. Several saw the play, with its "scrupulous veracity," as a distinct advance in Broadway's treatment of Negro characters. And Woollcott complimented the Guild for its avoidance of the temptation to darken the faces of Alfred Lunt and Lynn Fontanne for the roles of Porgy and Bess.

Praise came, too, from the black quarter. James Weldon Johnson, an important black spokesman of his generation and a leader in the NAACP, lauded the show's use of more than sixty Negro performers, something unheard of previously on Broadway. "In *Porgy*," he wrote, "the Negro removed all doubts as to his ability to do acting that requires thoughtful interpretation and intelligent skill." For him the play "loomed high above every Negro drama that had ever been produced . . . it carried conviction through its sincere simplicity."

Black attitudes about the play and its characters would change in later decades. In that year, 1927, the NAACP had only begun to speak of a need for more positive images of black Americans in theatre and literature. And the call was aimed less at whites than at blacks. W. E. B. DuBois, its leader, urged the development of a drama written and produced by Negroes and supported by Negro audiences. New organizations sprang up in Harlem, notably the Negro Art Theatre and the Harlem Experimental Theatre.

The spirituals sung so well in *Porgy*, and new to the ears of Broadway audiences, not only added to the play's success but helped popularize the form. Alan Dale in the New York *American* wrote: "To hear the spirituals sung as they were is worth twice the price of a seat at the Guild Theatre. There were the fervor, the hysteria, the emotionalism, and the curious abandon that must accompany such outbursts. All the colored 'folks' raised their voices, gesticulated, gyrated, as they joined in the volcanic choruses. It was something new to most of us—may I say to all of us."

George Gershwin and Kay Swift saw a performance when the composer returned to New York with *Funny Face* for what turned out to be a long run. "He cheered it enthusiastically," she remembered in her ninetieth year, "and still wanted to convert it into an opera."

EVEN WHILE *Porgy* flourished at the Guild Theatre, then on the road for several months, and in a return engagement at the Republic Theatre (available again after a seven-year run of *Abie's Irish Rose*), DuBose Heyward did not lose sight of an opera eventually being made of the play. With the success of *Porgy* in both novel and play forms he was now in the position, whether asked for or not, of being a recognized interpreter of Negro folkways, and it was a role he took seriously, as was reflected in a new novel, *Mamba's Daughters.*

Porgy had been a small and relatively compact tale that owed much of its effect to its almost poetic prose. An example:

> Far away St. Christopher struck the hour. The mellow bells threw the quarter hours out like a handful of small coins to ring down upon the drowsy streets. Then, very deliberately, they dropped ten round, heavy notes into the silence.

Mamba's Daughters, on the other hand, was a large, ambitious, generational story whose principal character was a black woman who might well, at one time, have lived in Catfish Row, and of her daughter and granddaughter. Mingled with their vicissitudes was a tale of the varying fortunes of a poor but aristocratic white family, with a scion not unlike Heyward himself. Oddly, Porgy appears very briefly in the novel, now relegated only to the atmosphere of Charleston.

Heyward's Charleston-bred view of the Negro had broadened from sympathy and concern for, as he put it, "an unfortunate race," to a far more admiring one of its great potential. Through the production of *Porgy* he was in contact with people of distinct and distinctive talent. He had been thrilled by the wonderful singing of the spirituals he had helped to bring north. Now he foresaw Negroes breaking down the bastions traditionally reserved for whites. He did not foresee a fully integrated world; it was on a separate but eventually equal basis that he felt Negroes would fulfill themselves as a race.

So much was this evidently on his mind that he concluded *Mamba's*

Daughters with the performance of an all-Negro opera on the stage of the Metropolitan Opera. Making her debut as the star is Lissa, the granddaughter of Mamba, the black servant to Charleston white folks. The novel was finished in 1928—when no black singer had as yet appeared on the sacrosanct stage—and published in 1929 to a large success. (It would be dramatized in 1939 with Ethel Waters.)

Heyward, in the novel, foresees what might happen to a Negro opera sung at the Metropolitan, as he undoubtedly hoped his own would be. In the audience someone comments: "What's it anyway—a play—an opera—a pageant?"

"For heaven's sake, don't label it," another replies. "Can't you see it's new—different? Can't you feel it's something of our own—American—something that Stallings and Harley got a glimpse of in *Deep River*—that the Theatre Guild caught the pictorial side of in *Porgy;* that Gershwin actually got his hands on in spots of 'Rhapsody in Blue'? It's epoch-making, I tell you!"

Then Wentworth (the character most based on the author) thinks: "God! What music! Primitive?—Sophisticated?—neither—both. Savage, tender, reckless. Something saved from a whole race's beginnings and raised to the nth degree by Twentieth Century magic—a blues gone grand opera. Not a bad idea that . . ."

Having imagined the great Negro opera, and the triumphant emergence of a great Negro singing star, Heyward does not stop there. Lissa, now a prima donna, is not content merely to take her bows and acknowledge the frenzied applause. She steps forward on the stage and, unaccompanied, sings the "Negro National Hymn," actually a poem by James Weldon Johnson. In the novel, it is set to a marching rhythm by the Negro composer J. Rosamond Johnson, James Weldon's brother.

"Lift ev'ry voice and sing," it begins, "Till earth and heaven ring, Ring with the harmonies of liberty . . ."

Heyward had sought Johnson's permission to use the poem, and it was given cordially. Later, he wrote Heyward to tell him how pleased he was with the way his words were used in the novel. Today, *Mamba's Daughters* can stand as an example of a sensitive white Southerner's view of possibilities of change in relations between blacks and whites. Idealism of a sort is there, and also some smugness. That the attitude was shared is evident from the enthusiastic reviews and the popularity of the book.

Regardless of what might happen eventually at the Metropolitan, the major interests to blacks at the time were, according to historian Loften Mitchell, "to be free, to eat regularly, live decently, and get white feet off their necks." To them, most of the fictions of white playwrights and novelists—with the possible exception of *Porgy*—were fairy tales that were more likely to induce prejudice than combat it and perpetuated the denial of status to blacks in their own land. But the pioneers of the "Renaissance," Mitchell wrote, "were engaged in a reform movement, not a revolution. They fought a defensive action, rather than an offensive one."

In New York Gershwin was also thinking about a grand opera, but it was not *Porgy.* On his mind was an opera made from *The Dybbuk,* a Yiddish play by the Polish-Jewish Shloyme Rappaport (who used the pseudonym S. Ansky). He was encouraged—to the point of being offered a roving commission by Otto Kahn—to compose an opera of his choice for the Metropolitan. Gershwin began sketching out some musical ideas, assuming the rights to the play were free and clear. But soon he discovered that the rights belonged to an Italian composer and that a performance had already been given in Italy.

Word of Gershwin's doings usually got around fast. The New York *World* announced: GERSHWIN SHELVES JAZZ TO DO OPERA. To Isaac Goldberg, a music critic already engaged in chronicling the young composer's biography, he divulged his feelings about the operatic form. "I am frankly," he told him, "not interested in the traditions of opera. I am a man without traditions as concerns music."

At the time the conversations took place he had given up the *Dybbuk* project. "When I think of a grand opera of my own, I simply cannot think in terms of Wagner or Verdi. I want, in turn, to be myself."

He was thinking of New York, his own city, as a subject. He would like to write an opera "of the melting pot of New York City," he told Goldberg, "which is the symbolic and the actual blend of the native and immigrant strains. This would allow for many kinds of music, black and white, Eastern and Western, and would call for a style that would achieve an artistic and aesthetic unity." He wanted, he said, to catch the rhythm of the interfusing people, to blend the humor of it and the tragedy. Above all, he wanted a libretto free of conventional sentimentality. But during these conversations with Goldberg, no mention was made of *Porgy* as the basis of that libretto. It was as though it had fallen into a basket of possibilities from which Gershwin would pick the one of his choice.

Meanwhile, someone else was interested in *Porgy.* Al Jolson requested permission from the Heywards to do a short adaptation for radio. Permission was given, and the show broadcast, but because of poor reception the Heywards were able to hear only spurts of words and snatches of spirituals as sung by Jolson. By then they were commuting between their new house (called Dawn Hill) at Hendersonville and a cottage on Folly Island, near Charleston.

Jolson had become a great star in the new "talkies." The Theatre Guild had not purchased film rights to *Porgy,* since the rights to the novel still belonged to Paramount, but now, with movies talking, they asked the Heywards for rights to the play. Perhaps the managers of the Guild were aware of Jolson's interest in the property. In any case, very soon after the Heywards gave them a share of the film rights they were told that Jolson had offered $30,000 for a talking picture version. Heyward, who had so strenuously fought against an actor in blackface playing Porgy, agreed to the sale. As he saw it, talkies were a novelty, an artificial and inconsequential medium, and no real harm would be done to his work by Jolson playing in blackface.

Jolson's talking picture never materialized. What kept it from the screen is not known, although the prior sale of the novel for a silent version may have complicated negotiations. The great stock-market crash of October/November 1929 had by then happened, America's bull-market prosperity had collapsed, and with the onset of the Depression the entertainment industry, as with the general economy, was in retreat.

The Heywards were affected, too. From 1927 on, they had been on a roll. Royalties from the play and books had poured in. "We were scarcely able to believe our good fortune," Dorothy remembered later, "when we were relieved of all necessity for believing in it. It just went away, and we were back to the more accustomed ground of needing the money." They, like most everyone else, had invested in the great bull market, but most of their savings went in the collapse of a large New York bank.

It was during this period of DuBose Heyward's personal depression that a letter came from George Gershwin stating his renewed interest in making an opera from *Porgy.*

6

GERSHWIN'S LETTER, written to Heyward on March 29, 1932, sounded as though, in the midst of a busy life, he had come across some neglected but still feasible possibility. But, after all, six years had gone by since the night when he had first read Heyward's novel. "In thinking of ideas," he wrote, "for new compositions, I came back to one I had several years ago—namely *Porgy* and the thought of setting it to music. It is still the most outstanding play I know about the colored people.

"I should like very much to talk with you before I leave for Europe, and the only way that I imagine that would be possible would be by telephone. So, if you would be good enough to either telephone me collect at TRafalgar 7-0727—or send me your telephone number by telegram, I will be glad to call you."

Heyward was elated. He had kept his faith that Gershwin would someday come around to doing the opera he had already envisioned in *Mamba's Daughters*. He wrote back, assuring Gershwin, "I would be tremendously interested in working on the book with you. I have some new material that might be introduced, and once I got your ideas as to the general form suitable for the musical version, I am pretty sure I could do you a satisfactory story."

A month went by before another letter came from Gershwin. In the interim the composer had canceled his trip to Europe because of his father's death. He was very glad to know that the rights were free and clear, but "there is no possibility of the operatic version's being written before January,

1933." He did say, however, that he would "read the book several times to see what ideas I can evolve as to how it should be done."

The death of the elder Gershwin came at a time when there might otherwise have been family rejoicing. Almost at the same moment, the Pulitzer Prize for drama was awarded to *Of Thee I Sing,* the musical for which George had written the score and Ira the lyrics. In the previous year *Strike Up the Band* had been brought back with much more success than in its first go-round. Satire played better in these dark times, and what amounted to a satirical trilogy was eventually completed with *Let 'Em Eat Cake.* The sparkle of George's sophisticated songwriting and Ira's witty lyrics were causing critics to hail them as "the American Gilbert and Sullivan."

The musicals took a wry stance toward the American political scene, and, after the ebullience of the late twenties with their promise of prosperity for everyone, audiences were ready for the wicked slants at pompous politicians in their smoke-filled rooms. *Of Thee I Sing* became the most successful of all the Gershwin musicals, lasting 441 performances.

George was turning over new ground with his more serious orchestral work, too. So busy was he in 1932 that it is a wonder he was still thinking of composing the opera. His Second Rhapsody (for Piano and Orchestra) had its premiere in January; then, in May, he made a brief trip to Havana and came back with thematic sketches for a *Cuban Overture,* first heard outdoors in August in an all-Gershwin evening at New York's Lewisohn Stadium. That year, too, he published *George Gershwin's Song-Book,* containing eighteen of his songs as first composed, with added variations as he played them in concert and at parties.

Al Jolson had not lost interest in *Porgy,* and soon after the exchange of letters between Gershwin and Heyward, he came to the Theatre Guild with a new proposal—this for a musical stage version, starring himself in blackface as *Porgy,* with a book by Oscar Hammerstein II and music by Jerome Kern. With this imposing array, the Guild people were all for it, and they urged immediate acceptance on the Heywards. This put Heyward in another quandary. He felt himself committed to Gershwin, and, in any case, he was hoping to do the libretto himself. At the Guild there was skepticism. When would this happen, they wanted to know, and did the Heywards realize the riches that could come their way from a work involving Jolson, Hammerstein, and Kern?

The Heywards were still in their financial doldrums, and they also had a child to support—their daughter, Jenifer, born two years before. Audrey Wood, DuBose's agent, joined with the Guild in supporting the deal with Jolson. In September 1932 Heyward felt it necessary to write Gershwin and tell him about his dilemma. He was as strong as ever in his desire to collaborate with him, he said, but he also was aware of how valuable an asset he had in his *Porgy*. "And, in these trying times, that has to be considered." He was, of course, hoping to light a fire under Gershwin and, if that didn't work, to be morally free to pursue the other offer. He was anxious to have a production in the following year at the latest and even made a suggestion that could only have come from desperation. "Would it be possible to use Jolson and arrange some sort of agreement with him, or is that too preposterous?

"Before I turn this down flat," he went on, "I think we should exercise the customary agreement with your producer, and with whom I presume you have already been discussing the matter . . . Neither of us would wish to put our time on it without this protection." It was about as strong and forthright a letter as the ever courteous Heyward was capable of. Dorothy called it "a sort of Madison Avenue letter. Our product is in great demand."

Gershwin again refused to be hurried and, in fact, as he was already engaged in writing the score for a new musical, *Pardon My English*, could not be. "I think," he wrote back, "it is very interesting that Jolson would like to play the part of Porgy, but I really don't know how he would be in it . . . It might mean more to you financially if he should do it—provided that the rest of the production were well done. The sort of thing I have in mind is a much more serious thing than Jolson can ever do. If you can see your way to making some ready money from Jolson's version, I don't know that it would hurt a later version done by an all-colored cast." In any case, he said, what he had in mind was "more of a labor of love than anything else."

He had no producer as yet in mind, he admitted, although Herman Shumlin, who had produced the successful *Grand Hotel*, had expressed interest. "I should like to write the work first and then see who would be the best one to do it."

Heyward decided it was time to bring matters to a head. So, from North Carolina he entrained for New York and met briefly with Gershwin, again with no firm commitment about a starting date, and then with Audrey Wood, who also spoke with Gershwin in hopes of firming up the project. Gershwin told her almost exactly what he had already told Heyward—that a Jolson musical would not kill *Porgy* for his own operatic purposes.

Heyward felt forced to give his assent to Audrey Wood to work out an arrangement with Jolson, but at the same time wrote Gershwin laying out the situation as he now saw it, enclosing a carbon of his own letter to his agent. He explained:

As a matter of fact, upon my return here after my talk with you I learned of circumstances that have put me in a tight spot financially, and that alone has prompted me to write Miss Wood. Of course what I would like to be able to afford would be to wait indefinitely for your operatic version, and to work with you myself without the least thought of the commercial angle.

He would not work on the Jolson musical, he assured Gershwin, but merely sell the story, and he remained all the more eager to work with him someday "before we wake up and find ourselves in our dotage."

The Jolson musical never materialized. It was not that Jolson lost interest, but that the enormous success of Hammerstein and Kern precluded their working on a book for the *Porgy* project. First came their *Music in the Air,* and then they separated, Kern to his smash hit *Roberta* and Hammerstein to London for *Ball at the Savoy.* That left *Porgy* in limbo. The withdrawal of the Jolson forces left the way open for Gershwin once again. Meanwhile, Heyward gained some needed cash when he wrote the script for the screen version of *The Emperor Jones.* The two months' work, he wryly observed, may have cost him the friendship of the playwright, but it enabled him to sustain himself for an entire year.

During the summer of 1933, Gershwin telephoned Heyward and told him he was clearing his desk of assignments and was ready to begin work on their opera. Heyward, understandably, now wanted a contractual arrangement between them, and Gershwin was willing. They talked of producers. Otto Kahn had already offered Gershwin a $5,000 inducement if he would bring *Porgy* to the Metropolitan. But he was more inclined, George told Heyward, toward a Broadway production with its potential for a long run. Heyward favored the Theatre Guild, which had produced the play and was still ready for its first large-scale musical venture, especially now that Gershwin had committed himself. On October 17, 1935, the contracts were signed between all the parties.

AS SOON AS he returned to Dawn Hill, at Hendersonville, Heyward went right to work on the libretto. He and Gershwin had agreed that the play would have to be cut by about 40 percent and that the dialogue would have to be rearranged for musical treatment. It took him only a few weeks to have the first scene ready to send to Gershwin.

"I have cut everything possible," he wrote on November 12, enclosing the manuscript, "and marked a couple of possible further cuts in pencil on ms. As a matter of fact, this is now a very brief scene considering that it carries all the exposition necessary for the play." Obviously enthused by the task of creating the foundation for a grand opera, he bubbled with ideas. "I feel more and more that all dialog should be spoken." This, he said, would enable Gershwin, as he had already suggested, to carry the orchestration straight through the performance, with the singing growing out of the action. Certain scenes, such as the fight between Crown and Robbins, could be treated as a unified composition "drawing on lighting, orchestra, and the wailing of crowd, mass sounds of horror from people, etc. instead of singing. It can be lifted to a terrific climax. That fight was treated with a great deal of noise in play. That is not my idea of best art in handling it."

He had a new opening to suggest. Not the "riot of noise and color" as in the play, but one that would merge with the overture. "The curtain rises in darkness, then the first scene will begin to come up as the music takes up theme of jazz from the dance hall piano [played by Jasbo Brown]. The songs which I have written for this part will fall naturally into the action and mood of the separate flashes of Negro life."

He mentioned, too, that on December 1 he would be moving himself and his family to their cottage on Folly Beach. Before they left, a letter came from Gershwin complimenting him on the work he had done so far. "Think you have done a swell job, especially with the new lyrics." But of Heyward's suggestion about using unsung dialogue he had his doubts. "There may be too much talk." Good news for Heyward was that he would be meeting with Gershwin face-to-face in less than a week.

"I am leaving with my friend, Emil Mosbacher," the same letter said, "the night of December 2nd, for Charleston. I expect to stay two or three days and then leave for Florida. I hope you can arrange it so as to spend some time with me. I would like to see the town and hear some spirituals and perhaps go to a colored cafe or two if there are any."

Gershwin was heading south for other reasons than the opera. He had agreed to make a tour of twenty-eight cities in as many days to celebrate the tenth anniversary of *Rhapsody in Blue* and had also agreed to come up with a new composition for piano and orchestra to be played on the tour. The piece, called *Variations on "I Got Rhythm,"* was not yet complete, and he planned to finish it in Florida and at the same time get in some golf and sun.

Mosbacher, who had made a fortune in oil and other investments, had rented a spacious home in Palm Beach for his wife and three children. On the way, in Charleston, Gershwin spent two days with the Heywards, looked around the city, and promised another visit on his return from Florida. During the stay with Mosbacher he completed the variations, played some golf, and rested in the warm weather for the strenuous tour that lay ahead. On December 19 he wrote Heyward, saying, "My plans for returning home are finally made and they include the stop-over at Charleston as I anticipated . . . I hope I can hear some real singing, as well as have a final discussion on the first two scenes of the opera."

On his return to New York on January 4, 1934, he was ready to announce to the press that he would be writing an opera "about blacks" and that though he would maintain his own style, "the Negro flavor will be predominant throughout." And he already had a candidate, he said, to play and sing the lead: no one less·than Paul Robeson.

While Gershwin toured through January and on into February, Heyward worked away on the libretto. New scenes were waiting for Gershwin on his return to New York, and some new ideas. "I have discovered a type of secular dance," Heyward wrote, "done here that is straight from the African phallic dance, and undoubtedly a complete survival." He said he had also seen a native band of "harmonicas, combs, etc. It will make an extraordinary introduction to the primitive scene of passion between Crown and Bess."

Heyward was in search of more authentic color and to this end, he said, he had cut from the play "the conventional Negro vaudeville stuff."

At the Theatre Guild, Warren Munsell, its production manager, was asking how the collaborators were getting on. He was hoping, as was Heyward, to have the opera for the Guild's next season, the fall of 1934. Before printing up announcements to go out to the subscribers he needed an assurance of when the opera would be ready. This Gershwin was unable to give.

For something else had come up. To devote himself to the arduous composition of an opera would require giving up income that sustained his luxurious life-style. He was home from his exhausting tour for only two weeks when he began a radio program called "Music by Gershwin," a fifteen-minute show heard on Monday and Friday evenings over New York station WJZ and a national network. The salary was a pleasant $2,000 weekly, but he complained about the amount of work involved, which meant preparing an entirely different musical program for each broadcast.

Heyward heard the show in South Carolina and wrote Gershwin, "Swell show, George, but what the hell is the news about PORGY!!" He, however, later gave credit to the radio program for an important but indirect contribution to the opera. "Out of [25,000,000 radios] for a half hour each week poured the glad tidings that Feenamint could be wheedled away from virtually any drug clerk in America for one dime — the tenth part of a dollar. And with the authentic medicine man flair, the manufacturer distributed his information in the irresistible wrapper of Gershwin hits, with the composer at the piano.

"There is, I imagine, a worse fate than that which derives from the use of a laxative gum. And, anyhow, we felt that the end justified the means, and that they also served who only sat and waited."

Gershwin, in spite of his radio chores, was able to start his actual writing of the opera's music. "I have begun composing for the first act," he wrote Heyward on February 20, "and I am starting with the songs and spirituals first." By this time he had received the second act of the libretto, and he told Heyward, "I really think you are doing a magnificent job and I hope I can match it musically." He made a good start; the first song he wrote to a Heyward lyric was "Summertime."

He was hoping, too, that Heyward would be able to come north and "live in my apartment—if it is convenient for you—so we can work together on some of the spirituals for Scene 2, Act I. Perhaps when the weather grows a little warmer you will find time to do this. I cannot leave New York to go South as I am tied up with the radio until June 1st; then I have a two months' vacation—which time I shall devote entirely to the opera."

Both worried that a Virgil Thomson–Gertrude Stein opera, *Four Saints in Three Acts,* with a Negro cast, might steal their thunder. It had premiered in early February 1934, in Hartford, Connecticut, and, after the enthusiastic response, was due to reach Broadway the following year. Thomson, some years before, had asked Stein to write an opera for him. She wrote it about two of her favorite saints, Saint Teresa of Avila and Saint Ignatius Loyola. The "four" came from her making Saint Teresa into two character aspects, sung by a soprano and a contralto, and having Saint Ignatius also appear in two guises.

For some five years Thomson played and sang the opera himself in various Paris and New York drawing rooms. The lyrics had charm, even humor, if one didn't try to make literal sense of them. Thomson said the opera was really about the literary life of Paris in the twenties, that Saint Teresa was Gertrude Stein and Saint Ignatius James Joyce, and the rest of the cast their hangers-on and disciples. It took a certain amount of stretching to discover the parallels.

Then, with a modest budget of $10,000, the young director John Houseman took on its production. Thomson had already decided to have his Spanish saints played by black singers. It was an inspiration that came when he heard Jimmy Daniels in his Harlem nightclub and was impressed by his clear enunciation. Black singers, he said, had the voice quality and speech clarity he wanted and the ability to move with both grace and dignity.

There was a quite extraordinary artistic ferment in this mid-Depression time, especially in New York. Its range can be gauged by the two black operas: one, a stylized, fanciful experiment, inventive in costuming and stage design, but with no discernible drama; the other a gritty story set against a shabbily realistic background of poor Southern life.

Many books would come out of the developments in the period. In music, George Antheil, Roy Harris, Arnold Schoenberg, Walter Piston, Edgard Varèse, and John Cage were setting a new tone, not to mention tone scales. In painting, Thomas Hart Benton, Paul Cadmus, William Gropper, and Charles Burchfield gave a sometimes harsh, sometimes poetic realism to American painting. In 1935 the Federal Art Project was born and gave employment to a more abstract and eventually more influential group that included Jackson Pollock, Arshile Gorky and Willem de Kooning. Faulkner, Fitzgerald, Hemingway, Henry Miller, John O'Hara, Sinclair Lewis, John Steinbeck, William Saroyan, and Nelson Algren were all writing and being widely read.

All this created talk, and some of the most lively occurred in salons hosted by Carl Van Vechten and Constance and Kirk Askew. In what came to be known as "the Askew Salon," notables in the arts gathered and gossiped every Sunday afternoon. On one of those afternoons John Houseman encountered Virgil Thomson and they talked of staging *Four Saints*.

"I saw it," Gershwin told Heyward. "The libretto was entirely in Stein's manner, which means that it had the effect of a 5-year old child prattling on. Musically it sounded early 19th century, which was a happy inspiration and made the libretto bearable—in fact quite entertaining." Heyward was worried, too, by a new American opera, Howard Hanson's *Merry Mount*. He heard it performed and was relieved: "From the advance ballyhoo I thought something pretty revolutionary was coming, but it seemed to me to be pretty much the conventional thing."

Heyward would have much preferred that Gershwin come south to soak up atmosphere while they worked together, but he agreed to come north in April and work with Gershwin in his apartment for two weeks. Speeding up the work was important to him because he was again feeling a financial pinch and thus would sooner work with Gershwin in his apartment for two weeks. This he candidly admitted to Gershwin. "I have been letting everything else go," he said, "counting on it for early fall. If it is going to be late, I will have to get something else, myself, to tide me over." And for that he was looking once more in the direction of Hollywood.

The collaboration by letter continued. On March 8 Gershwin had some chatty news for Heyward. He had gone to see Warren Munsell at the Theatre Guild to tell him about progress on the opera. "He seemed very excited about it," Gershwin wrote, "in fact he asked me to come upstairs and tell

some of the other directors what I told him. They all seemed very interested."
All but Lawrence Langner, who made some remarks that struck Gershwin
as "pretty stupid. I shall probably have to ask him in the future to stay out of
my way."

He was still fixed on Paul Robeson for the Porgy role, and Munsell had
agreed to ask about his availability. "I am skipping around — writing a bit
here and a bit there. It doesn't go too fast, but that doesn't worry me as I
think it is all going to work out well." Because he didn't know the rhythm
Heyward had in mind for one of his songs, he said, "I would appreciate it if
you would put dots and dashes over the lyric and send it to me."

A scene in the third act struck him as needing cutting. "You must make
sure," he told Heyward, "that the opera is not too long as I am a great
believer in not giving people too much of a good thing, and I am sure you
agree with this." He had also taken to Heyward's suggestion for the Jasbo
Brown opening. He and Ira, he said, were working on words to the music for
the opening "in Jazzbo [*sic*] Brown's room while the people are dancing, and
I finished it with a sort of African chant."

Meanwhile, Heyward had suggestions for Gershwin. For a song which
Jake (captain of the fishing fleet) would sing, he advised George to "imagine
yourself at an oar and write the music to conform to that rhythm — that will
give you a better idea than anything I can write."

W H I L E   I T   I S Gershwin who understandably and rightfully deserves
much of the glory for the opera's qualities, Heyward's contribution cannot
be overestimated. He had the threefold task of condensing the play so as to
conform to the slower action of the opera, of providing opportunities for
arias and choruses, and of finding the words for the songs and spirituals that
Gershwin would compose.

As Gershwin later said, "When I first began work on the opera I decided
against the use of traditional folk material because I wanted the music to be
all of one piece. Therefore I wrote my own spirituals and folk songs."

There was another reason. The play *Porgy* had contained traditional
spirituals and folk songs. Aside from Gershwin's natural desire to compose
original music, using traditional material would have seemed old hat by the
time the opera was presented. *Porgy* was presented in 1927; in 1930 Marc
Connelly's *The Green Pastures* came along, using spirituals, as, in 1933,
Hall Johnson's *Run, Little Chillun!* did. So, Heyward created quasi-
spirituals and work songs.

Late in the play Bess is heard singing the traditional lullaby "Hush, little baby, don' yo' cry. Mudder an' fadder born to die." Heyward used the first line in another context for the lyric that became the glorious "Summertime." At certain places in his text Heyward would simply insert "song here," and what was needed would be worked out later, sometimes with Ira Gershwin's collaboration.

The solution to working together across a thousand miles of distance came with Ira's entry into the association. "We evolved a system," Heyward said, "by which, between my visits North, or George's dash to Charleston, I could send scenes and lyrics. Then the brothers Gershwin, after their extraordinary fashion, would get at the piano, pound, wrangle, swear, burst into weird snatches of song, and eventually emerge with a polished lyric."

During his visit with the brothers in mid-April, Heyward found inspiration from George's improvising at the piano. He was with them in George's workroom when George suggested there was a spot in the libretto where Porgy might be given something lighter and happier to sing than what he had been given earlier. He went to the piano and began improvising. In hardly any time at all a cheerful melody emerged. "Something like this . . . ?" he said. Both DuBose and Ira thought the melody just what he was looking for, and, about as quickly as George had found a melody, Ira came up with a title for the song. Ira said later that rarely did a title suggest itself so quickly: "Usually I sweat for days." He tried it out on the other two: " 'I Got Plenty o' Nuttin'." He followed that, also on the spur of the moment, with "an' nothin's plenty for me."

DuBose asked Ira if he'd mind his taking the tune and the title back to Charleston and working up a lyric. Previously, George had set his words to music, and here was a chance to write words to fit the music. He was furnished with a lead sheet (the simple vocal line) and two weeks later sent his lyric to Ira, who polished it into the existing song. As Ira explained, it took many years of songwriting experience to know that a certain note cannot take a certain syllable, "that many a poetic line can be unsingable, that many an ordinary line fitted into the proper musical phrase can sound like a million." Yet it is a tribute to Heyward that many of his lyrics sent through the mail to Gershwin emerged in song with rarely a syllable changed. When changes were needed, Ira was there to make them.

GERSHWIN HAD moved in 1933 from his penthouse on Riverside Drive to a fourteen-room duplex at 132 East 72nd Street. There was room for the art he had collected, for his own painting (which he had taken up a few years before), for a gymnasium, and ample working space. Soon enough,

Ira and his wife, Leonore, moved across the street. George's visitors were impressed by the lavishness of the layout. Alexander Woollcott came and afterward described "a great paneled reception hall, three pianos, a bar that was a rhapsody in gaily colored glassware. A private telephone connected the workroom with his brother's apartment." There was a sleeping porch, and "mysterious gadgets designed as substitutes for will power in setting-up exercises. There were flights of stairs that folded up and vanished at a touch."

Woollcott, like many others, found George to be "profoundly interested in himself. But he had no habit of pretense. He was above and beyond posing. He said exactly what he thought, without window dressing it to make an impression favorable or otherwise."

Irving Kolodin, then a youthful music critic, arranged a visit with Gershwin and was invited to come for lunch on a Sunday. He was taken up to the penthouse, with its "suavely modish interior, a view to the west from the large living room with its pianos and pictures and books." Lunch was taken with the café singer Gertrude Niesen, who was seeking lesser known songs for her act from George.

Kolodin noted some of the books on the shelves: Aldous Huxley, Virginia Woolf, Ernest Hemingway, as well as Rudy Vallee's *Vagabond Lover,* inscribed to George. After lunch Gershwin asked his guests if they wanted to hear some of *Porgy,* his work in progress. He played, said Kolodin, a plaintive melody he called "Lullaby from Act One." It was "Summertime," and Kolodin knew they were hearing a Gershwin strain unlike any they'd heard before.

Kolodin came back another day. This time Gershwin was working in a study on the upper level of the duplex at an intricate desk of his own design. It was large enough for oversized orchestral paper and was fitted with ingenious racks, bins, and pigeonholes. Kolodin sat at the keyboard with Gershwin as he unveiled for him more of *Porgy:* "He began with a mood-setting quasi-overture with curtain up on darkened stage, and a solo piano off-stage beating out a rag rhythm to suggest the life of Catfish Row before the characters enter." He found Gershwin most concerned by the contrapuntal scheme by which he wove musical materials together. *Carmen,* Gershwin told Kolodin, was his number one enthusiasm because of Bizet's use of local color. He liked *Boris Godunov* for its dramatic impact and its use of the chorus as an integral part of the play.

The playwright-essayist-biographer S. N. Behrman had long known Gershwin through their mutual friendships with Emily and Lou Paley. Behrman called on him one day with Theresa Helburn of the Guild to hear some sections of the opera. "He played 'Summertime,' he recalled in his memoirs. "Our reaction delighted him; he was in a state of tremendous excitement. 'You know, Terry,' he said, 'they tell me the interest in *Porgy* is so great that just to be sure they'll get good seats, they're subscribing to all that stuff of yours.' As among all that stuff," Behrman added, "was a play of mine . . . I hoped the rumor was true."

Osbert Sitwell had once described Gershwin as "streamlined," and Behrman agreed: "this was so. George was streamlined in all his activities; as a composer, as a pianist, as a painter, as a golfer and tennis player. George stands practically alone for possessing an almost nonexistent quality: joy."

He described what he felt when he first heard George play: "the newness, the humor—above all, the rush of the great, heady surf of vitality. The room became freshly oxygenated, everybody felt it, everybody breathed it."

Gershwin was proud of his wonderful new apartment, and not long after moving in he invited Emily Paley and her friend Mabel Schirmer to lunch. The young women were vastly excited and spent the morning making themselves as glamorous as possible. Promptly at one they rang his doorbell. George had on a new suit, bought in London, and, upon opening the door, said, "Well, girls, how do I look?"

Heyward, too, had descriptions of Gershwin's seeming lack of humility and modesty: "His self-appreciations were beyond modesty and beyond conceit. He was incapable of insincerity; he didn't see why he should suppress a virtue or a talent simply because it happened to belong to him. He was just plain dazzled by the spectacle of his own music and his own career; his unaffected delight in it was somewhat astonishing, but it was also amusing and refreshing."

There was also another side to Gershwin. He could be subject to fits of anxiety and depression, and these, along with his persistent "composer's stomach" (constipation), caused him to consult Dr. Gregory Zilboorg, probably New York's most famous psychoanalyst at the time. During most of the period he worked on the opera he was in analysis, sometimes as often as five times a week. Oscar Levant, his good friend for many years, felt that his year-and-a-half-long bout with psychoanalysis was due less to neurosis than Gershwin's broadening horizon: "His curiosity about things, however, was translated into a curiosity about himself, a need for knowing himself better." The analysis also provided "him with a fresh vein of after dinner conversation."

In an effort to deepen his knowledge of composition and orchestration, Gershwin found time for studies with a musical theorist, Joseph Schillinger, a Soviet expatriate. Schillinger would work on a composer's composition page by page, subjecting it to precise analysis. Was the musical thought "orchestrable"? Did the orchestration interpret the music properly? Shifts in sonorities gradual or sudden were examined in terms of the best projection of the music.

Vernon Duke (born Vladimir Dukelsky), on visiting Gershwin, would find his piano and writing table cluttered with Schillinger's exercises. "Now," Duke remembered, "he had found a toy that was real fun and would also yield great dividends, an unheard-of combination." Duke, confronted with pitch scales and other exotic musical formulas, was skeptical. "You just don't understand," Gershwin told him. "I used to do all kinds of things— harmony and counterpoint, I mean—I thought they were just parlor tricks. They always went great at parties. Now they'll go right into my music."

Levant, who also studied with Schillinger, found evidence of his influence in the working out of "the rhythmic patterns, the planning of such episodes as the fugal background for the craps game scene and in some of the choral passages." Schillinger's mathematically based system extended, Levant claimed, "George's resources considerably" in so ambitious an undertaking as the opera.

Kitty Carlisle saw Gershwin frequently during her early days in New York. She remembered, "George was studying with Schillinger and would come over to see me after his lesson. I was living at the Ritz Tower then, and he would come running up with all his notations, of which I didn't under- stand anything. He would want to repeat what he had just learned to someone else because that is how you remember. I was very flattered."

She, too, was one of the visitors to his 72nd Street apartment. "I used to go there often when he was orchestrating *Porgy and Bess.* He would orchestrate after dinner and I would sit there very admiringly." Now and then George would say, "Sing this for me so I can hear how it sounds."

"I realized later," she said, "that this is what George would use as blandishments for ladies. I wasn't helping him a bit." Gershwin once played for her a little waltz he said was written just for her; later she found it was the same waltz he had written for several other ladies.

Anne Brown, while studying at Juilliard, wrote Gershwin requesting an audition.
She won the role of Bess.
(Theatre Collection, Museum of the City of New York.)

7

WHEN IN MID-JUNE George Gershwin set out for Folly Island, ten miles off Charleston, the trip had the air of a major expedition. With him was a companion, Henry Botkin, his artist cousin, who was then painting Negro subjects. They left from New York's Pennsylvania Station surrounded by well-wishing friends. Earlier, Gershwin's all-around man, Paul Mueller, had loaded a touring car with baggage and easels and would be waiting in Charleston to drive them to the island. Their destination was a small cottage facing the beach, where Botkin would paint and Gershwin would do concentrated work on the opera.

Heyward had found the cottage for them, rented from Charles T. Tamberg. It might today be something of a shrine if it had not been destroyed in a hurricane a few years later. Heyward's nearby cottage is still kept much as it was when he was there working with Gershwin. The Tamberg cottage offered few amenities. It had only four rooms and a sleeping porch, and water had to be transported in five-gallon jugs from the city. Gershwin's room was furnished only with a small iron bed, a wash basin, hooks for hanging clothes, and a rented upright piano.

Gershwin was not in the least dismayed to trade his luxurious circumstances in New York for the spartan conditions here. In fact, he took it as an adventure, as indeed it was, for he planned to absorb the atmosphere of the locale and gain inspiration from the Gullah blacks who inhabited the sea islands. Four days after his arrival, he wrote his mother, telling her, "The place down here looks like a battered old South Sea Island. . . . Imagine, there's not one telephone on the whole island—public or private. Our first three days have been cool, the place being swept by an ocean breeze. Yesterday was the first hot day and it brought out the flies and gnats and mosquitoes. There are so many swamps in the district that when the breeze comes in from the land there's nothing to do but scratch."

When on his fifth day on the island a reporter by the name of Frank B. Gilbreth (later the author of *Cheaper by the Dozen*) showed up from the Charleston *News and Courier,* Gershwin told him he had already changed from his New York sleeping and working habits. At home he slept until noon; here he got up at seven, well, seven-thirty, in the morning. Gilbreth noted that he was dressed as though at a polite summer resort, with a light Palm Beach coat and an orange tie. Two weeks later, Gilbreth came for another interview. This time, he noted, Gershwin's hair was matted and uncombed, his beard was an inch thick, he was bare from the waist up, and he was darkly tanned.

Not that Gershwin had gone completely native. He composed mornings and worked with Heyward on the libretto in the afternoons. From the screened porch he watched the giant turtles laying their eggs on the beach; in the swamps there were alligators and he could hear them roaring. Walks along the beach were possible, but swimming was dangerous because of the sharks offshore. Botkin, in writing of his own experience on the island, told of bugs and insects striking the screens in their flight and the loud cheeping of crickets keeping George awake at night.

With Heyward as his guide he visited close-by James Island, populated predominantly by Gullah blacks who had maintained their customs and preserved their traditional songs. It was like a laboratory, Heyward said, "in which to test our theories, as well as an inexhaustible source of folk material." They watched groups of blacks around cabins and country stores and listened to their spirituals. For George it was more like a homecoming than an exploration, Heyward said. "The quality in him that had produced *Rhapsody in Blue* in the most sophisticated city found its counterpart in an impulse behind the music and bodily rhythms of the simple Negro peasant of the South."

One custom the Gullahs practiced while singing their spirituals they called "shouting." This, Heyward explained while describing his visits with George, "is a complicated rhythmic pattern beaten out by feet and hands as an accompaniment to the spirituals, and is indubitably an African survival." One night at a Negro meeting on James Island, George started "shouting with them," and, said Heyward, "to their huge delight stole the show from their champion 'shouter.' I think he is the only white man in America who could have done it."

He was composing rapidly now, excited by the new ideas he was receiving. Yet he was still able to take time out to paint, and for some social life—on Folly Island and in Charleston. Some of the city's life proved helpful. Heyward, through his Charleston connections, arranged for an evening at the aristocratic South Battery home of Mr. and Mrs. Charles Hagood. Twenty members of the Charleston Society for the Preservation of Negro Spirituals gathered there and performed for Gershwin several of their Gullah interpretations.

From then on, of course, it was another "Gershwin evening." He took over the piano and rocketed through one hit tune after another, on and on until after one in the morning. Neighbors, too, were entranced by the music coming from the Hagood house; the next-door neighbors came out on their porch to hear it better.

Gershwin even found time for what looked suspiciously like a bit of romance. He met, during one social occasion, Mrs. Joseph Waring, a young widow chaperoned by her mother. They kept a cottage on nearby Sullivan Island, and one evening Gershwin invited mother and daughter over for dinner at his cottage. After dinner he played at the upright for them and suddenly announced he would play a just composed section from the opera. "This one is great," he told them. "No one, not even DuBose, has heard it before. You can remember later I told you it would be a classic." The song he played was "A Woman Is a Sometime Thing." The mother thought his remark about the song was conceited and impudent, not realizing that Gershwin was merely telling the truth—quite accurately, as it turned out— as he saw it.

He and the pretty widow walked together on the beach occasionally, and he would ask her to hum certain spirituals she had heard from the time she was a baby—in order, he said, that he could remember them better. "He did talk in a romantic vein from time to time," she confessed, "but no more than you might expect from any boy that far from home." Nothing serious came of the relationship.

To Gilbreth (who signed his articles "Ashley Cooper" after the names of Charleston's two rivers) Gershwin not at all bashfully confided that "the production will be a serious attempt to put into operatic form a purely American theme. If I am successful it will resemble a combination of the drama and romance of *Carmen* and the beauty of *Meistersinger,* if you can imagine that."

"It will be something never done before," he went on. "*Green Pastures?* This will be infinitely more sophisticated. I am trying to get a sensational dramatic effect. I hope to accomplish this by having the few whites in the production speak their lines while the Negroes, in answering, will sing."

After five weeks on the island, Gershwin and Botkin headed back north, stopping off at Hendersonville for a two-day visit with the Heywards, who had returned there. On one of the evenings Heyward took Gershwin to a cabin being used as a meetinghouse by a group of Negro Holy Rollers. They were about to enter when George suddenly stopped Heyward and held his arm. Heyward had attached no special significance to the singing, but seeing Gershwin's excitement he listened more carefully to the dozen or so voices lifted in prayer. "The odd thing about it," he recalled, "was that while each had started at a different time, on a different theme, they formed a clearly defined rhythmic pattern, and that this, with the actual words lost, and the inevitable pounding of the rhythm, produced an effect almost terrifying in its primitive intensity."

In New York, Gershwin had two full months before his radio chores were due to begin again in October, and he was able to continue his work on the opera with full energy. Meanwhile, Heyward, once more needing income, accepted a Hollywood screenwriting job, to tinker, as he put it, on the film to be made from Pearl Buck's *The Good Earth*. When he arrived on the lot he was curious enough to ask why he, in particular, had been chosen for the assignment. "It was made perfectly plain to me. Negroes were not a Caucasian people. Neither were Chinamen. It was obvious then that I would understand the Chinese," he recalled. The man who had hired him was no one less than Irving Thalberg.

Heyward asked for and received permission to do his work wherever he pleased, so he chose the top floor of the Beverly Wilshire Hotel. He was there alone and spent three months "living in solitary like a sixth tier man at Alcatraz." He worked rapidly, much to his agent's chagrin, since the salary was on a continuing weekly basis. But Heyward was anxious to get back to *Porgy*, and the production which now loomed. After he left Hollywood, twenty other writers followed him on the script. When the film finally appeared in 1937, Thalberg was dead and the major writing credits went to others, although the final script closely resembled Heyward's. He had done a surprising thing; he had read and followed the book.

Early in November 1934, he learned from Gershwin, via letter, that the production had been set for the Guild's next season and that plans were being made for auditions and rehearsals. Gershwin liked to throw himself into every detail of a production; as Levant said, he would willingly have designed and set up the scenery, directed, trained the singers, and conducted the orchestra. In thinking of directors, the name of Herman Shumlin was still alive, as was that of John Houseman, who had produced and directed *Four Saints in Three Acts.*

Gershwin by this time was close to completing the piano score. He told Heyward that he wanted to finish it as soon as he could, then go over "the whole thing for any possible changes. I am off to Emil Mosbacher's place in the country this afternoon to get some work done on Scene 2, Act 3."

Film director Ernst Lubitsch paid him a visit at his apartment around this time, and, as with most other visitors, Gershwin played him some music from the opera. Lubitsch made some suggestions: the settings should be "just a bit off realism" and to enhance dramatic effects a very free use should be made of lighting. Gershwin liked the ideas.

"Incidentally," he said in his letter to Heyward, "I start and finish the storm scene with six different prayers sung simultaneously. This has somewhat the effect we heard in Hendersonville as we stood outside the Holy Rollers church."

Ira wrote most of the prayers for this scene. DuBose, in the libretto, had included a prayer which began, "Oh, Doctor Jesus, look down on me wit' pity . . ." When George decided he needed five more prayers, and Heyward was busy with his screen work, Ira wrote them for him.

Eventually, as the songs from the opera achieved enormous popularity, questions arose about just who, between DuBose and Ira, had created the lyrics. Each was generous toward the other in offering credit. When the songs were copyrighted separately, Heyward received full authorship for "Summertime," "My Man's Gone Now," and "A Woman Is a Sometime Thing." With Ira he shared the rights to "I Got Plenty o' Nuttin'" and "Bess, You Is My Woman Now." Ira received sole credit for "It Ain't Necessarily So" and "There's a Boat Dat's Leavin' Soon for New York."

Ira also wanted to put Heyward's name on "It Ain't Necessarily So" so he would have enough songs to his credit to become a member of ASCAP and thereby have a yearly revenue from them. Heyward wouldn't allow it. "You're very sweet, Ira," he said, "but no one will ever believe I had anything to do with that song."

"DuBose was a poet," Ira recalled long after about his work on the opera, "which I am not. He could do something like 'Summertime,' which is poetry. DuBose wasn't much good on a rhythm number, though, like 'It Ain't Necessarily So.' He would turn in his poetry and George would set it to music. With me it worked the other way. I cannot read music. I have to hear a tune before I can write lyrics. My job was to sit and listen to the music that George created and then set words to it."

At one point George played Ira a sixteen-bar tune that he thought could be sung by Sportin' Life in the picnic scene on Kitiwah Island. The first words of a dummy lyric that came to his mind were "It ain't necessarily so." For two days he mulled over what Sportin' Life might reasonably sing, then decided that the rascally fellow might well startle his pious neighbors with a cynical and irreligious message. He came up with such rhymes as "Bible" and "li'ble" and "chillun" and "villun," but still had no song until it occurred to him to go back to the dummy title, using the notion that some Bible accounts were not entirely believable. Of course, all this was sweated out with George improvising on the piano.

George's contributions to the welding of words and music were more subtle but of exceeding importance. The alterations he made in the lyric for "Summertime" seemed minuscule, but the changes resulted in the right number of words and syllables for the notes he had in mind. Often he reshaped scenes as written by Heyward by tightening and cutting lines, and he could strike out a whole scene if he felt it was neither musically nor dramatically important. As the work proceeded toward its finish, he was firmly in control and his collaborators could only go along with him willingly and with admiration.

Toward the end of 1934 Gershwin met frequently with the Guild people on the planning of the production. In discussing directors with Gershwin, Heyward had objected to the logical choice, Rouben Mamoulian, perhaps because of what he had earlier called "conventional Negro vaudeville stuff" and "not my idea of good art." His preference was John Houseman.

But here the Guild asserted itself. Warren Munsell, its production manager, wrote Heyward: "The matter of the director has been discussed at some length and while we were considering John Houseman, the feeling here is that this is a very big show for Houseman to undertake. We would all be very much better satisfied if Mamoulian were to do it. . . . I know you had some minor misunderstandings with Rouben, but I really believe that the values of the present version will be brought out far better by him than by Houseman, and it would be greatly to your advantage, as well as ours, to have him produce the play. . . . We want to close the arrangements now, so that he will hold the time open for us."

Heyward withdrew his objections when a letter from Gershwin made it clear that he, too, strongly favored Mamoulian.

GERSHWIN, FOR several months, had been keeping a lookout for singers suitable for the major roles in the opera, especially for the baritone to sing Porgy. While doing his radio show he had run across a young man at the station, Robert Wachsman, who was the producer of a radio program, "John Henry," which he admired. "What are you doing for the next year and a half?" Gershwin asked Wachsman, then invited him to his apartment to hear what he had composed of *Porgy and Bess*. Wachsman, impressed with what he heard, volunteered to assist Gershwin and stayed with him through the talent search and staging of the opera. He claimed the credit for locating Todd Duncan, thirty-two, who taught music at Howard University, and brought several other singers to Gershwin's attention. Olin Downes also claimed to have told Gershwin about Duncan; he had heard him sing in an all-black production of *Cavalleria Rusticana* at the Mecca Temple on 55th Street. Gershwin was doubtful that a university professor would be right for Porgy, but he gave Duncan a call at his home in Washington and invited him to come sing for him in New York.

"Here is an exciting piece of news," Gershwin wrote Heyward a few weeks after the meeting. "I heard about a man singer who teaches music in Washington and arranged for him to come and sing for me on Sunday several

Todd Duncan, the Howard University music teacher, was "just not very interested" when Gershwin called him for an audition as Porgy in the opera. (Wachsman Collection, Lawrence and Lee Theatre Research Institute, Ohio State University.)

weeks ago. In my opinion he is the closest thing to a colored Lawrence Tibbett [a leading and popular baritone with the Metropolitan Opera] I have ever heard. He is about six feet tall and very well proportioned with a rich booming voice. He would make a superb Crown and, I think, just as good a Porgy. He is coming to sing for me again during Christmas week. I shall ask the Guild to take an option on his services."

Duncan wasn't overly excited by the call. "I just wasn't very interested," he said in retrospect. "I thought of George Gershwin as being Tin Pan Alley and something beneath me." Gershwin had wanted him to come on Sunday, a few days away. Duncan told him he would be singing at a local church on that day, but could come up the following Sunday. He was at Gershwin's apartment promptly at 1 p.m., as had been specified, to be asked, "Where's your accompanist?"

Duncan wasn't aware that it was customary in New York to bring along an accompanist for a musical audition. "Can't you play?" he asked George Gershwin, who blinked. Duncan offered to be his own accompanist.

"I'll try to play for you," Gershwin said. "I'll try."

Duncan placed on the piano rack the music he had brought along with him and selected "*Lungi dal caro bene,*" by Secchi, a little-known Italian composer. He carefully explained to Gershwin that it was a classic and translated the Italian for him. As he said in recounting the incident, "I was just naïve enough to do all the right things and not to know that I was doing them." Gershwin told him that every other singer he had heard had sung "Glory Road," or "Gwine to Heaven," or "Old Man River." After Duncan sang several bars, Gershwin asked him if he knew the song well enough to sing without the notes. He wanted to see him full face. Duncan sang again, this time from the bow of the piano, astonished that Gershwin had already memorized the music. Gershwin stopped him after another eight bars and said, "Will you be my Porgy?"

"Well, I don't know," Duncan said. "I'll have to hear your music."

Gershwin laughed and said he thought he could arrange for him to hear some of his music, suggesting Duncan come back the following Sunday; he could hear his music then, and others would be there to hear him sing. Duncan protested that he couldn't afford to keep coming to New York, train fares being what they were. His teaching salary was not large, and the producers of the opera at the Mecca Temple had decamped without paying his fee. "Would you accept my check for the train fare?" Gershwin asked him. Duncan agreed, and Gershwin wrote out a check for forty dollars— sufficient for a trip that could include his wife this time.

The following Sunday, Duncan and his wife went up in the elevator with a man wearing striped trousers and carrying a cane, and a woman. They were

Lawrence Langner and Theresa Helburn. "Are you this damned genius George has got us all coming to hear?" the irascible Langner asked him.

"I beg your pardon," Duncan said.

"You'd better be goddamned good. George is pulling me out of the country. Woke us all up and got us here to hear you."

"I certainly hope you like my singing," Duncan said.

Most of the Guild's board members were there, and so were Ira and his wife. Duncan had supposed he would sing three or four songs, but Gershwin ran him through a repertoire of some thirty, ranging from opera to spirituals to German lieder. After singing for more than an hour, Duncan and the others were served food, then brought upstairs to Gershwin's workroom. With Ira, George played and sang most of the opera's score, Duncan's first hearing of the music. As the brothers began, he was appalled by their "awful voices," but soon the beauty of the music overrode the vocal deficiencies: "I was in heaven. Those beautiful melodies in this new idiom—it was something I had never heard."

At a point in the second act, Gershwin turned to Duncan and said, "This is your great aria. This is going to make you famous."

"Aria?" said Duncan. The opening bars of "I Got Plenty o' Nuttin'" sounded to him like a banjo song, but its infectious spirit soon caught him. It was a song that Todd Duncan sang all over the world for the next forty years. By the time the Gershwins finished the session with "I'm on My Way," Duncan was weeping.

Finding a cast was a quite different matter than it had been for the original stage production of *Porgy*. The situation had improved somewhat for black performers during the intervening years; agents to represent them had cropped up, and they contacted the Guild casting office on behalf of their clients; the magic name of Gershwin attracted many. During the protracted casting process, as many as a thousand people were interviewed at the Guild, along with those by Gershwin, who for many months scouted the types and singers he wanted in Harlem and wherever he traveled.

Soon after the announcement that George Gershwin was making an opera of *Porgy*, Anne Wiggins Brown, a student at New York's Juilliard Institute (now School), wrote him and asked if he would hear her sing and consider her for a role. She was twenty, the daughter of a Baltimore physician, and, aside from her boldness in writing a letter to the admired composer, shy and withdrawn. Gershwin asked her to his apartment, as he did many others, listened to her, said her voice was fine, but could she act? She had no professional stage experience, but she told him she was sure she could do whatever was needed in that line.

Gershwin had other singers in mind for Bess, including the talented and more experienced Etta Moten, but he chose Anne Brown because of her greater voice range. As he continued to write and orchestrate he would invite her to his apartment to sing his creations. "He would telephone me and say," she remembered, " 'Come down. I want you to sing something.' I'd go down [from Harlem] and sing it and he sang with me, especially the duet roles."

During this period of several months he spent orchestrating his score, he arranged for Brown to go to London, where *Blackbirds* was running. The producer, Lew Leslie, as a favor to Gershwin, gave her a small role in the show to provide her with stage experience.

Another singer, Ruby Elzy, a graduate of Juilliard, was referred to Gershwin by Heyward, who remembered her from a small role she had played in the film *The Emperor Jones*. Horatio Alger might have written her personal history.

Born in a Mississippi village, abandoned by her father, Elzy was brought up and schooled by her mother, who sent her for further education to Rust College, in Holly Springs, Mississippi, a school run by a Methodist Missionary Society. She washed dishes to work her way through and liked to sing while she worked. She happened to be heard by two educators making a survey of Southern schools, one being Dr. C. C. McCracken, then president of Ohio State University. He offered to bring her to Ohio State, and there she was placed under the tutelage of the head of the music department, and, for her keep, worked in Dr. McCracken's home.

As a soprano, she was so promising that an anonymous trustee of the university put a thousand dollars a year in a bank account to see her through school. From there the Chicago Rosenfeld Fund took over; money was provided to send her to the Juilliard Institute in New York. There she came under the tutelage of Lucia Dunham, who believed strongly in acting skills for singers. By the time Ruby Elzy auditioned for Gershwin, she was so well prepared to take to the professional stage that one hearing was enough for him to offer her the role of Serena.

Cab Calloway claimed over the years that the characterization of Sportin' Life came directly from his own performances at the Cotton Club during the mid-thirties. True enough, Gershwin often came to the so-called club that occupied the second floor of a two-story building at 142nd Street and Lenox Avenue, as did just about every other celebrity in New York. The gangster Dutch Schultz (before he was caught by a burst of bullets) could be sitting at a table near Mayor Jimmy Walker. They all came: Jack Dempsey, Irving Berlin, Clara Bow, Bing Crosby. The shows were magnificent by the standards of the day, and Cab Calloway was the star act for several years, too busy, making too much money, he said, to accept the offer of the role.

*On her way to the role of Serena
in* Porgy and Bess, *Ruby Elzy washed
dishes to work her way through a
missionary college. (Theatre Collection,
Museum of the City of New York.)*

But Gershwin's choice for Sportin' Life was, from the beginning, the dapper John W. Bubbles (as the Guild eventually billed him, though his real name was John William Sublett) from the vaudeville team of Buck and Bubbles. The latter's dancing was vastly admired by Fred Astaire, and it was to Bubbles's talents, not Calloway's, that the role was shaped.

As a boy he hung out and exercised horses at a Kentucky racetrack, where he became friends with another boy, Ford Lee Washington, who was nicknamed Buck. John had a habit of talking so fast that he was nicknamed Bubbles. Buck played the piano, and Bubbles liked to improvise dances while he played. While ushering in a Louisville vaudeville theatre they would take the stage after the audience left and practice an act. The manager saw them, gave them a spot on the program, and they clicked at once. By the time Gershwin saw them they had traveled the vaudeville circuit throughout Europe and most of the United States. Gershwin hired both for his opera, Ford Buck, as the Guild named him, to play a small role. Bubbles presented a problem, though; he could not read music, and it was questionable whether he would survive through the rehearsal period.

But rehearsals were still months away when in January of 1935 Gershwin left New York for Palm Beach, where his friend Emil Mosbacher had rented a large house. During the month he spent there he worked away at the difficult task of orchestration. He also fretted about sour estimates from the Guild that the budget for the opera's production might run as high as $75,000 or $100,000 and that this amount (a very large one at the time) would be beyond the Guild's resources.

"I'm afraid the Guild might not go through with *Porgy*," he said to Mosbacher one day.

Mosbacher, a shrewd businessman, counseled Gershwin: "George, handle it my way. Go to the telephone and tell the Theatre Guild lawyer that I, Emil Mosbacher, will put up half the money for the show. George, I bet you a hundred dollars I won't get any part of it, because as soon as they hear I'm ready to come in on that scale, they'll go ahead with the show and do anything to keep me out."

The budget problem was worked out after the Gershwins offered to put up approximately a quarter of the needed money, an early estimate being $40,000. As George informed Ira from Palm Beach, "I wrote [Warren] Munsell of taking 25% of the opera and told him how it would be split, namely four thousand for me, four thousand for Emil, and two thousand for you. Just received his answer in which he says he'd rather not have any outside money in the property, meaning of course, Emil's interest. The cost may go higher in which case I think if we took 15% between us it would not be risking too much and we'd have a good interest in the undertaking." Later, Heyward agreed to buy a 5 percent interest, which he assigned to his mother.

In the same letter, Gershwin wrote about the orchestration: "It goes slowly, there being millions of notes to write."

8

ROUBEN MAMOULIAN, now an eminent film director, was in Hollywood when he heard that *Porgy* was to be an opera by George Gershwin. The news at first shocked him. The play he had directed and shaped, that had had so signal an effect on his subsequent career, was for him pure, complete, and so strong in its simplicity that he feared giving it operatic form would spoil it. But Gershwin's name and talents were so potent an argument that when the Guild asked Mamoulian to direct the production he accepted without hearing a single note of the score. It couldn't be sent to him because Gershwin was still orchestrating it.

Mamoulian had had only one previous meeting with Gershwin. That was during his opera-directing days in Rochester. Some friends asked him to a gathering of musicians at a local club where Arthur Rubinstein and the conductor Eugene Goossens were being entertained, and also a slender young man, George Gershwin. When Gershwin was asked to play, he seemed shy—after all, the great Rubinstein would be hearing him. His playing of his songs, though, provided such enjoyment that he tried out a new composition. Mamoulian was among the first to hear portions of a work that Gershwin said he thought he would call *Rhapsody in Blue*.

That was in 1923, and both men did very well over the next dozen years. After *Porgy*, Mamoulian directed several plays for the Theatre Guild and other organizations, including Eugene O'Neill's *Marco Millions* and Ivan

Turgenev's *A Month in the Country*. Then, in 1929, he made film history. With the entry of the sound era, and the need for actors to be able to speak passable dialogue, stage directors were in great demand by film producers. Walter Wanger and Jesse Lasky of Paramount lured Mamoulian to the Astoria studios in Queens to direct a talking picture, *Applause*, starring Helen Morgan in a sob story of vaudeville life. The camera and the potential in sound recording immediately fascinated him. Ignoring what he was told could not be done, he innovated the use of "mixing"—two separate sound channels mixed into one—and was among the first to make use of a mobile camera, which would move freely in and out of a scene.

Soon he was in Hollywood, where he directed the by-now classic 1931 version of *Dr. Jekyll and Mr. Hyde*, with Fredric March and Miriam Hopkins; *Love Me Tonight*, the racy musical with Jeanette MacDonald that out-Lubitsched Lubitsch; and another film of near-mythic dimensions, *Queen Christina*, with Garbo and Gilbert. When the offer of *Porgy* came he was once more making film history with *Becky Sharp*, the first feature film in Technicolor.

Gershwin kept him abreast of his progress. "I have about five months work left," Gershwin wrote him in the spring of 1935. "It is really a tremendous task, scoring three hours of music." Mamoulian finally arrived in New York and was invited to an evening at George's apartment to hear the score. Ira was there and, as Mamoulian later wrote, "All three of us were very excited. George and Ira were anxious for me to like the music. As for me, I was even more anxious. I felt about *Porgy*, the play, the way I imagine a mother feels about her first-born."

He was handed a highball and given a comfortable leather armchair. Ira stood over George at the piano. George hesitated and turned to Mamoulian. "Of course, Rouben, you must understand it's very difficult to play this score. As a matter of fact, it's really impossible. Can you play Wagner at the piano? Well, this is just like Wagner!" Mamoulian assured him he understood. But the apology, if that was what it was, was unnecessary. Mamoulian was caught at once by the color and provocative rhythm of the music. George played, Ira sang, and then George joined in and sang an approximation of the orchestra parts, while Ira sang the vocals.

"It was touching to see how Ira, while singing, would become so overwhelmed with admiration for his brother that he would look from him to me with half-open eyes and pantomime with a soft gesture of his hand, as if saying, '*He* did it. Isn't it wonderful? Isn't *he* wonderful?'" It was late at night before they were finished with the opera, and for Mamoulian it was, "in a way, the best performance of it I ever heard." He was touched, too, by the brothers' devotion to each other.

Rehearsals did not begin until August. Meanwhile, the Guild gave Gershwin a virtually free hand in adding to his production ensemble. For his musical director he chose the Russian-born Alexander Smallens, the conductor of *Four Saints in Three Acts* and an associate conductor of the Philadelphia Orchestra. Gershwin went backstage after the opening of *Four Saints* and told Smallens he was writing an opera and would like him to hear it. Like others, Smallens went to Gershwin's apartment and was impressed with what he heard, although he was not enthusiastic about the use of recitatives. Nevertheless, he accepted the assignment.

Another musician of Russian-American origin, Alexander Steinert, was at a Town Hall reception for Igor Stravinsky when he felt a tap on his shoulder. It was Gershwin, who was aware that Steinert had been coaching the singers of the Russian Opera Company. Would he be interested in coaching the singers of his new opera, *Porgy*? Steinert indeed would, and he signed a contract with the Theatre Guild the next day.

Eva Jessye was the leader of the Eva Jessye Choir, a black group with high musical standards that earlier had been used by Virgil Thomson for *Four Saints in Three Acts*. The troupe of twenty ordinarily barnstormed through several states without earning much more than needed for train fare. Back in Harlem after one of those tours, Jessye came across a notice in a show-business paper about a need for a black choir. She took her ensemble to the theatre for an audition, and, as she remembered it, "People from the Theatre Guild were there. We did the shout 'Plenty Good Room' and danced all over the stage. George Gershwin jumped up and shouted, 'That's it! That's what I want!' After the audition he invited me up to his penthouse on 72nd Street. I remember a glassed-in flower conservatory and the three Steinways in the apartment. But the first thing I noticed was a long table with several copyists busily working on the score of *Porgy and Bess*."

By this time, with rehearsals approaching, the name had been changed. The Guild's publicity department was worried that *Porgy* on the marquee might strike people as a revival of the original play. Discussing the problem with Gershwin, Heyward came up with the new title. "There had been, of course," he wrote wryly in explanation, "*Pelléas and Melisande, Samson and Delilah, Tristan and Isolde.* 'And so,' said Heyward, with the humility characteristic of those who draw their sustenance from the theatre, 'why not *Porgy and Bess*?' To which Gershwin replied, with the detachment which could not possibly be mistaken for conceit, 'Of course, it's right in the operatic tradition.'"

The managers of the Guild were also worried about excessive use of the word *opera* out of fear that it would scare off Broadway audiences. Dorothy Heyward later said that Gershwin fought the Guild on this point, finally agreeing to a compromise: "folk opera." Even then, she said, he wasn't entirely happy about it.

In mid-July of 1935, with two of the three acts orchestrated, Gershwin was able to hear, for the first time, his music with cast members and an orchestra. This was done through the good offices of William Paley, the head of CBS, who financed an orchestra of forty-three pieces and provided a company recording studio. Gershwin himself conducted the orchestra, and CBS engineers recorded some portions of the session, a recording which still exists and which has Gershwin's voice on it. Six weeks later the final act was orchestrated with the help of a battery of copyists working in Gershwin's penthouse. At the end of the full score of nearly six hundred pages Gershwin noted: "Orchestration begun late 1934—finished Sept. 2, 1935." By this time, rehearsals, which began on August 26, were already under way.

Morning on Catfish Row, with fishermen preparing their nets. Cleon Throckmorton designed a more elaborate set for the opera. (Lawrence and Lee Theatre Research Institute, Ohio State University.)

Heyward, who had come north again, could only marvel at the way Steinert, at the first rehearsal, had the cast ready to read the score from beginning to end.

Steinert had been working with Gershwin nearly every day for months. He would sit for hours, listening to hundreds of auditions, marking down types, and noting which of the voices were satisfactory. Eva Jessye's group was augmented to forty. The musical equipment of the large cast varied. Among the principals the musicianship was high: Of Todd Duncan's qualifications there was no doubt. Anne Brown and Ruby Elzy had fellowships at Juilliard; Abby Mitchell (Clara) had studied with fine teachers; Warren Coleman (Crown) was a graduate of the New England Conservatory of Music in Boston. Others were unable to read music and had to learn their roles by ear.

The principals and others, well before Mamoulian's arrival, had reported daily to Steinert for coaching, before advancing to the bare stage of the Guild Theatre for rehearsals. Few of the singers, born and educated in the North, had any trace of Southern speech patterns and they had to familiarize themselves with the dialect. Gershwin amazed them often by demonstrating how they were to interpret their parts.

Mamoulian quickly became aware of the monumental nature of his task — welding the different elements of the production into a cohesive shape. "The first day of rehearsing a play," he complained in retrospect, "is always difficult. It is like breaking mountains of ice." He was staying at the Navarro, an apartment hotel on Central Park South; exhausted and depressed, he was already in bed when the phone rang and Gershwin was announced. Feeling badly in need of encouragement, he was pleased to get the call.

"Rouben," George exclaimed, "I just *had* to call you and tell you how I feel. I am so thrilled and delighted over the rehearsal today." Mamoulian at once began feeling better.

"Of course," George said, "I always knew *Porgy and Bess* was wonderful, but I never thought I'd feel the way I feel now. After listening to that rehearsal today, I think the music is so marvelous, I don't believe I wrote it." Mamoulian had to do without his needed encouragement, but, as rehearsals continued, he grew more understanding of Gershwin's attitude toward himself and his work. He had, he said, "this faculty to look at himself and his work in just as detached a manner as if he were looking at somebody else. Whatever he liked, he praised. He happened to like his own music, too, so he praised it without any self-consciousness or false modesty." Admittedly, Gershwin had these traits in larger quantities than most. Mamoulian, who was a celebrity in his own right, and had been so greeted when he arrived in New York to begin rehearsals, could only be amused. On one occasion, late for dinner with George and some of his friends at a restaurant across the street from the Guild Theatre, he apologized for his unshaven appearance.

"Don't apologize, Rouben," George said. "Personally, I love you when you're unshaven." Mamoulian wondered why. "Because when you're unshaven you look like me." Whether this represented an attempt at humor or an abundance of self-love is hard to say.

Todd Duncan, too, was aware of Gershwin's "incredible love for his own score." He told of an occasion during which, in the midst of a rehearsal of the wake scene in Serena's room, where the people of Catfish Row gather to pray and mourn the death of Robbins, Gershwin came in and disappeared quietly into the back of the dark theatre. Mamoulian worked energetically with the actors, setting entrances, positions, coordinating music and action. (Having played the violin in his youth, he was able to read music and worked with the score.) The singers became tired, which worked well for the silent atmosphere needed for the prayer.

Ruby Elzy went down on her knees as if she actually felt a need for prayer. Then, as described movingly by Duncan, "there rose the most glorious tones and wails with accompanying amens and hallelujahs for our sick Bess that I ever hope to experience." The scene stopped there as if of its own accord instead of carrying over into the next, as did the piano accompaniment. The actors came to the edge of their seats; Mamoulian's face bore an expression of sheer delight at what had taken place. "Then, George Gershwin like a ghost from the dark rows of the Guild Theatre, appeared before the footlights. He simply could not stand it. He knew then that he had put down on paper accurately and truthfully something from the depth of the soul of a South Carolina Negro woman who feels the need of help and carries her troubles to her God."

There were times, too, when Gershwin was less than pleased with the way his music was treated. If someone sang a wrong note or wasn't able to sense a rhythmic pattern, he would race to the footlights and ask for the correction. When one of the singers, during an entire rehearsal, kept singing the wrong words, Gershwin couldn't bear it. After pacing up and down, he finally called to his chauffeur to take him home. It was Duncan who calmed him the next day by telling him he would take the fellow in hand himself.

Most trying of all was Bubbles, who was unaccustomed to the rigors and complexities of rehearsing an opera, or indeed just what the score of an opera represented. He had received the score while performing in Texas and was bewildered by it, not only by being unable to interpret it but because he thought all of the several hundred pages was his part. Steinert took on the task of coaching him, hitting on the idea of getting him to tap-dance the rhythm of "It Ain't Necessarily So"—a happy inspiration as it turned out in performance. But he was often late for rehearsals, and this caused Smallens to toss away his baton on one such occasion and shout at Mamoulian, "I'm sick of this waiting! We'll have to throw him out and get someone else."

This brought Gershwin out of his seat and down the theatre aisle. "Throw him out?" he cried. "You can't do that. Why, he's the black Toscanini." The description was anything but accurate, other than the fact that Bubbles conducted himself in his part according to whim or will—changing rhythms and notes, with disastrous results on others in the cast, who would miss their cues, and on Smallens's temper. One day, after several unfortunate repetitions of the same scene, Smallens left his chair, slammed his fist on the score, and shouted out the correction to Bubbles, then told him the number of times he had already corrected him. Was there, perhaps, he asked, something at fault with his conducting?

Bubbles was contrite. "Mr. Smallens," he said from the stage, "if I had the money of the way you conduct I'd be a millionaire."

Gershwin was there to protect Bubbles and took great pride eventually in his performances.

Mamoulian, while rehearsing and staging, always kept his copy of the score before him so as to adjust movement with the measures and accents of the music. He instructed the cast to "regulate your movements by the rhythm and character of the music at the moment" and told the chorus not to "stand around like a chorus—break the formality of it all."

At one point during the craps-game scene, as Crown's ugly temper and animosity toward Robbins grows toward the eventuality of a fight between them, Mamoulian directed the members of the chorus forming the crowd to group themselves closer about the principals. The chorus members kept their eyes on the conductor to get the cue for the chord. Mamoulian counseled: "Move forward on the accent, but pay no attention to the music—make it spontaneous. You don't move forward because I want you to—you move closer because you want to hear what they're saying."

His method was close to choreography, and he would make changes in the libretto to suit his sense of what was appropriate in blending words and music, not hesitating at times to add a clarifying line of dialogue. He would tell the cast, "Do the thing that comes to your mind—if I don't like it, I'll tell you." For one of Bess's moments with Porgy in the prayerful wake scene in Serena's room he wanted a gentle swaying movement from Anne Brown as the couple sit back to back on the floor. Here he adopted musical terminology, saying, "You're the accompaniment, not the melody. What we want here is an obbligato."

For the staging behind Porgy's singing of "I Got Plenty o' Nuttin'" Mamoulian provided a colorful accompaniment: cast and chorus members

Crown warns Robbins not to touch the money he has won.
(Theatre Collection, Museum of the City of New York.)

shook dishrags, feather dusters, and bedding from the set's windows; they blew soap bubbles, wielded hammers and knives, and even some empty rocking chairs responded to the rollicking singing.

Gershwin did not object to this kind of embellishment of his score. "In my opinion," he said after the opening, "he has left nothing to be desired in the direction."

Mamoulian's attention to detail made unusual demands on the Guild's production staff, including Serge Soudeikine, the set designer. Mamoulian wanted the shadow of the buzzard in one scene to appear as if it were flying overhead and in a later scene to have the same shadow fall across Porgy's door as though it was perched on the roof. Howard Wicks, the technical director, somehow had to work this out, simple enough in Hollywood, but not so easy on the stage. Mamoulian also wanted the authentic sound of the chimes of Saint Michael's Church in Charleston. The out-of-town opening in Boston, set for September 30, was looming, and the Charleston Public Library was hastily asked to provide an authority on the chimes. Mrs. Martha Laurens Patterson was contacted and commissioned to listen to the striking of the bells and to take down the tempo and pitch. After listening to the chimes she hurried home, dreading that someone might stop her before she was able to write the tones down exactly from memory. In her letter to Wicks she cautioned him to pay particular attention to the flatness of the lowest note, E.

Gershwin, too, made Wicks's life difficult. A production of an African drama, *KyKunker,* had been given at the Chanin Auditorium in New York City the previous year. Gershwin, presumably, had been present, because he asked Wicks to locate the authentic native drums that had been used in the production so he could add them to his own orchestra.

A few days before leaving for Boston, Smallens gave a full-scale concert

The quarrel turns to tragedy. Crown attacks Robbins with his cotton hook.
(South Carolina Historical Society.) Overleaf: Serena over
the body of Robbins, her husband. Bess tells Crown to flee. (Theatre
Collection, Museum of the City of New York.)

run-through of the show in Carnegie Hall, where he had been rehearsing the orchestra, while at the Guild Theatre Mamoulian continued working with the cast. The two groups came together before an audience made up of family and friends. "Until then," Ira remembered, "only George knew what it would sound like. I couldn't believe my ears. That wonderful orchestra and the full chorus on the stage. I never realized it would be like that. It was one of the great thrills of my life."

Many years later it was claimed that George Gershwin had never heard his orchestral and vocal score performed in its entirety. He did on that day. But Mamoulian, who was present, warned him: "If you want to have success with your opera you may have to make some harsh cuts." Some cutting was already in process by the time the show arrived in Boston.

FOR BOSTON it was the season's most notable music and drama event—the world premiere, at the Colonial Theatre, of an opera by the famed composer George Gershwin. "The opening," reported Betty Alden, society

The shadow effect in this prayer scene from the opera was created accidentally when a stagehand left a footlight on during a rehearsal. (Theater Collection, Museum of the City of New York.)

editor of the Boston *American,* "recaptured the glory of those now almost legendary days, before the advent of the motion picture; when the green room and the theatre were the focal point of social attention." She reminded her readers that "though a tale of work-day-Negroes," *Porgy and Bess* was written by a world-famous composer, staged by a world-renowned director, and was the first American opera indigenous to American soil. And it was presented to an audience "which sparkled with theatrical, musical and social luminaries."

Actress Colleen Moore, she also reported, wore "a diamond tiara in her burnished locks, and an ankle-length velvet wrap with ermine sleeves." Albertina Rasch, of the dance world, was in a green chiffon tunic dress, while tall, slim Gloria Braggiotti, with her black hair in a simple knot low on her neck, was attired in a tight-fitting black velvet gown sweeping into a train. Everyone there deemed the occasion worthy of their finest feathers, or rather, jewels, furs, and lavish gowns.

A large group of debutantes and postdebs were recruited to usher for the premiere, a benefit for what was then the New England Hospital for Women and Children. In attendance were the presidents of Harvard, Radcliffe, M.I.T., and Wellesley; Serge Koussevitzky and Sigmund Spaeth, among other prominent members of the musical world; and a large cadre of the Theatre Guild's subscribers.

J. Rosamond Johnson was the assistant conductor of the chorus and also played the part of Lawyer Frazier, who sells divorces for a dollar or two. In Boston, at the close of the performance that lasted some three and a half hours, he watched George Gershwin acknowledge fifteen minutes of thunderous applause. Mamoulian and Smallens came out on stage, too. They were embraced by the main members of the cast, and after the audience excitement had died down, friends and colleagues joined the group onstage. "As he stood there on the stage," Johnson wrote, "I was amazed at the modest manner in which he received many warm and hearty congratulations. Finally, when I got a chance to grasp his hand, I whispered to him, 'George, you've done it—you're the Abraham Lincoln of Negro music.'"

The remark meant a great deal to Gershwin, so much so that he thanked Johnson for it again the next day. However, in spite of the congratulations by such as Koussevitzky, Spaeth, and S. N. Behrman ("It should be played in every country of the world," he said, "except Hitler's Germany—it doesn't deserve it"), he was aware that he had problems before the production could go on to New York. His theatre experience told him what Mamoulian and the Guild's managers had told him—that the show as it stood was running much too long and would have to be cut substantially before it could open in New York. Mamoulian marveled over Gershwin's equanimity: "George, who loved his own stuff as much as he did, never hesitated to make any cuts that were necessary." A change had been made prior to Boston — the elimination of the atmospheric opening that had been suggested by Heyward — Jasbo Brown playing the dance-hall piano. Warren Munsell told George the simple scene would have to be cut in the interest of economy; he said it needed a completely different set. George didn't object. "Okay," he said, "that means we start with the lullaby ["Summertime"], and that's some lullaby."

Gershwin made a cut of his own when he realized that Todd Duncan's voice might buckle under the strain of singing three songs in a row night after night. Duncan had no understudy, so Gershwin took out the tragic aria the "Buzzard Song." As he explained to Ira, "If we don't you won't have a Porgy by the time we reach New York. No one can sing that much eight performances a week."

After the tumultuous opening, Gershwin, Mamoulian, Steinert, and Kay Swift walked the Boston Common until three in the morning, discussing and arguing over more cuts. Steinert said, "Very few composers would have stood by and witnessed with comparative calm the dismemberment of their brainchild until it had been reduced by nearly a quarter! He was quite philosophical about it." The six prayers that had resulted from Gershwin's visit to the little church in Hendersonville had to go, and George fought only to keep a third-act trio that he loved, although agreeing to a change; it became Porgy's solo "Where's My Bess?"

The Boston critics, of course, knew none of this. And the opera they reviewed was considerably longer than that which went to New York. Moses Smith wrote in the Boston *Transcript,* "It is unique. Is there another American composer for the lyric stage who exhibits at once such eclecticism and individuality? He has traveled a long way from Tin Pan Alley to this opera." In the same paper, Edwin F. Melvin was most impressed by the theatrical qualities, saying that while "the orchestra approaches operatic proportions . . . in the staging, the lighting, the liveliness of the acting, the quality of the characterizations and the idiomatic flavors of the lyrics, there is more the feeling of the theater at its best than that of the more stylized opera house." But Ann Ames of the *American* claimed, "When the cries of genius subside, George Gershwin's *Porgy and Bess* will take its place indubitably as the 'first' American opera." Her drama colleague George Holland was even less restrained: "For a symphony in stage movement, with colors, actions, music, synthesized as never before in an attempted American opera, it reaches the ultimate in theatrical production."

Only the out-of-town correspondent for *Variety* sounded a note of commercial caution. Gershwin, he said, justly deserved praise for his "sincere effort to create a form of opera . . . but it looks as though the cash customers may let him down." He thought it fine for "musical students, novelty seekers, and the opera crowd," but feared "the dose too heavy for one evening and apt to swerve the masses past the door."

In Boston the warning proved baseless. In fact, the Guild ran into heavy criticism from many of its subscribers, who were unable to get tickets because of the immediate sellout of the one-week run.

In spite of the cuts, the opera that opened on October 10 at the Alvin Theatre in New York was trimmed rather than changed drastically, as later accounts have had it, and the trimming was done mainly for effectiveness as operatic theatre and to keep the evening from becoming too long for Broadway. Nor had Gershwin bowed in the direction of musical comedy; his principals, with the exception of John Bubbles, would have been in opera houses if the opportunities had existed. As it was, their voices and musicianship were several cuts higher than the standards of Broadway.

Even so, a touch of Broadway was in the score—what Irving Kolodin described as "good old-fashioned Gershwin"—as in the chorus number "Oh, I Can't Sit Down." And Gershwin himself preferred to call the solo numbers songs rather than arias. "Bess, You Is My Woman Now" and "It Ain't Necessarily So" would have made a classic out of any Broadway musical. But for Gershwin, it was an opera, fashioned and blended from classical sources, spirituals, jazz, blues, and yes, Broadway—and its originality and vitality, the fertility of the invention would finally become clear many years later.

The cuts made for the first production gave rise to questions and controversy in later years. Was this version, shortened for practical reasons, true to Gershwin's conception of his opera? Did he intend all those missing forty minutes from what became known as "the full score" to be performed in the future? One thing is certain: after *Porgy* opened in New York, Gershwin made no further changes.

Mamoulian always maintained that it was as the composer wanted it. A birthday party on the stage of the Alvin was given for the director two days before the opening. Gershwin had a gift for him—some rolled-up pages of the score, tied with a red ribbon. According to Mamoulian, Gershwin said: "This is my thank you for making me take out all that stuff in Boston."

PERHAPS THE expectations in New York had reached too high a pitch from the huzzahs in Boston and the advance publicity. Or, just as likely, since Gershwin had taken on a creative challenge that would force

J. Rosamond Johnson is Lawyer Frazier.
(Theatre Collection, Museum of the City of New York.)

comparison with Europe's musical titans, critics were careful and serious about their responsibility to evaluate. At the gala first night the glittering audience was as demonstrative as in Boston. But after the festive all-night party at Condé Nast's apartment, the reviews had a sobering effect. Not that there was any lack of praise, but with it came a certain suspiciousness about whether Gershwin had really created an opera.

Lawrence Gilman, for instance, immediately brought the matter up in his review: "Whether *Porgy and Bess* is or is not a blown-in-the-bottle opera seemed of no concern to any one at all last evening. But that is little reason why one should not call it that. Mr. Gershwin thinks it is, and the music critics present will surely agree with him."

Olin Downes, the music critic of *The New York Times,* was friendly, judicious, and reasonably warm toward the work, but hardly overawed by it. "He has not completely formed his style as an operatic composer," he said of Gershwin. "The style is at one moment of opera and another of operetta or sheer Broadway entertainment." But he also said that "when it came to sheer acting last night certain operatic functionaries should have been present. If the Metropolitan chorus could ever put one half the action into the riot scene in the second act of *Meistersinger* that the Negro cast put into the fight that followed the crap game it would be not merely refreshing but miraculous."

In the adjoining cubicle at the *Times,* as Downes tapped out his review, Brooks Atkinson, the paper's drama critic, was allowing that "whether or not Mr. Gershwin's score measures up to its intentions as American folk opera lies in Mr. Downes's bailiwick." To his ears, "Mr. Gershwin's music gives a personal voice to Porgy's loneliness when, in a crowd of pitying neighbors, he learns that Bess has vanished into the capacious and remote North . . . and adds something vital to the story that was missing before."

But Atkinson turned grumpy over the recitatives. "Why commonplace remarks that carry no emotion have to be made in a chanting monotone is a problem in art he [the reviewer] cannot fathom. Turning *Porgy* into opera has resulted in a deluge of remarks that have to be thoughtfully intoned and that annoyingly impede the action. Why do composers vex it so? 'Sister, you goin' to the picnic?' 'No, I guess not.' Now why in heaven's name must two

Gershwin during fifteen minutes of applause after the Boston opening, with principal cast members and, on his left, Mamoulian, and just over his shoulder, Heyward. (Lawrence and Lee Theatre Research Institute, Ohio State University.)

Picnic time for Catfish Row in the Theatre Guild production, 1935.
(Theatre Collection, Museum of the City of New York.)

characters in an opera clear their throats before they can exchange that sort of information?" Obviously, he would have had the same objection to *Aida*.

Samuel Chotzinoff, music critic of the New York *Post*, took up the matter of the recitatives and admitted that all through the performance he found himself wondering "why Mr. Gershwin continued to impose the recitative on matter that did not require it." The paper's drama critic, John Mason Brown, advocated cutting about half an hour, but otherwise thought *Porgy* contained some of the loveliest music the composer had ever written and that it was "compellingly dramatic" and "one of the most notable feats in virtuoso direction our modern theatre has seen."

The last statement gathers more force when placed in context with what was going on in drama that year, when Clifford Odets galvanized audiences of the Group Theatre with *Waiting for Lefty* and also delivered *Awake and Sing* and *Till the Day I Die*. Maxwell Anderson's stark and poetic *Winterset* starred Burgess Meredith and Margo, and Leslie Howard and Humphrey Bogart inhabited Robert E. Sherwood's *The Petrified Forest*.

Brown paid a good deal of his tribute to Mamoulian, whose production "is filled with a visual music of its own, unforgettable in the ever-changing beauty of its groupings, extraordinary in its invention, and amazing in the

*"It Ain't Necessarily So," sings John Bubbles—the Kitiwah Island
setting for the Theatre Guild production. (Lawrence and Lee Theatre Research
Institute, Ohio State University.)*

atmospheric details it employs to recreate the whole pattern of life in Catfish Row." He pointed to the shutters and doors that slammed whenever a white man appeared on the scene, the shadows on the walls of Serena's room (a touch taken from the play production), the excitement of the crap game, and the departure of picnickers for Kitiwah Island.

Brown joined in the near-universal admiration of the cast, singling out Todd Duncan, Anne Brown, Warren Coleman, and John W. Bubbles. And he was one of those who made sure to point out the "melting pot" aspect of "the most American opera that has yet been seen or heard: it is a Russian who has directed it, two Southerners who have written its book, two Jewish boys [*sic*] who have composed its lyrics and its music, and a stageful of Negroes who sing and act it to perfection."

But as reviews continued to drift in from sources other than daily papers, the chorus seemed to be neither full approval nor entire disapproval, although some of the darts drew blood. Most wounding was Virgil Thomson's comment that the opera was "crooked folklore and halfway opera." With a pen dipped in acid, he wrote, "Gershwin's lack of understanding of all the major problems of form, of continuity, and of straightforward musical expression is not surprising in view of the impurity of his musical sources and his frank acceptance of them." What were these impure sources? "At best a piquant but highly unsavory stirring-up-together of Israel, Africa, and the Gaelic Isles."

Joseph Wood Krutch in *The Nation* sneered that "admiring it will be one of the Things Being Done," and in *The New Republic* Stark Young wondered if the "trouble with the whole thing" was that it was "neither black nor white." He thought that most of the cast members needed "to be darker or made up so."

Gershwin's faith in his work remained unshaken. He defended it, however, in an article for the *Times*'s drama section, which appeared ten days after the New York opening. He wanted to make clear why he had called it a folk opera. "*Porgy and Bess* is a folk tale. Its people would naturally sing folk music." He had decided against the use of original folk material because he had wanted the music to be all of one piece: "Therefore I wrote my own spirituals and folksongs. But they are still folk music—and therefore, being in operatic form, *Porgy and Bess* becomes folk opera."

He said, too, that it brought to the opera form "elements that have never before appeared in opera and I have adapted my method to utilize the drama, the humor, the superstition, the religious fervor, the dancing and the irrepressible high spirits of the race. If, in doing this, I have created a new form, which combines opera with theatre, this new form has come quite naturally out of the material."

The authors of the opera, following the Boston premiere.
(Lawrence and Lee Theatre Research Institute, Ohio State University.)

Cover of the sheet music for "Summertime," published in 1935.
(Theatre Collection, Museum of the City of New York.)

9

Within a matter of days after *Porgy and Bess* opened, it became apparent that there would not be a run at the box office comparable to that of the first stage version. In fact, it may have been the very popularity of the original *Porgy* that dampened interest in the opera, especially in view of the muddled perspective the critics gave it. Nor were black performers any great novelty now on Broadway. The early to mid-thirties saw a surge in plays about Negroes. In 1930 *The Green Pastures,* a biblical fantasy accompanied by the spirituals of Hall Johnson, was highly successful. Soon came *Singing the Blues,* conducted by Eubie Blake, and Hall Johnson's *Run, Little Chillun!* (the story of a conflict between a pagan cult and a Negro Baptist church in the South), in which the playwright conducted his own beautifully disciplined choir. The burgeoning left-wing theatre movement of the early and mid thirties brought attention to the Negro's place in American life and labor. *They Shall Not Die* focused attention on the case of the Scottsboro boys. *Stevedore, Mulatto,* and *Hymn to the Rising Sun* dealt with the Negro in a social context. And the previous year, the stylized, nonsensical, but successful *Four Saints in Three Acts,* with its fine Negro cast, was given.

The reaction to *Porgy and Bess* by blacks was mixed, but the grounds were different from those of white critics. "The times are here," said Duke Ellington, whose own music was being taken more and more seriously, "to debunk Gershwin's lampblack Negroisms." He complained that "the music does not hitch with the mood and spirit of the story. It does not use the

Negro musical idiom." On the other hand, he thought it "grand music and a swell play, but the two didn't go together."

Ralph Matthews, music critic for *The Afro-American*, agreed that "it most certainly isn't Negro." The music, he said, had none of "the deep-sonorous incantations so frequently identified with racial offerings. The singing, even down to the choral and the ensemble numbers, has a conservatory twang. Superimposed on the shoddiness of Catfish Row they seem miscast."

Hall Johnson contributed a long and measured essay on the opera to the Negro magazine *Opportunity*. "After having sat through four performances," he wrote, "I am now certain that I do like it and that it is a good show. Nobody should have expected it to be a perfect Negro opera. That would have been miraculous." But it was to the cast that he gave the largest degree of credit. "It is only as good as it seems to be because of the intelligent pliability of the Negro cast. They are able to infuse enough of their own natural racial qualities into the proceedings to invest them with a convincing semblance of plausibility. This is true even in the musical and dramatic moments most alien to the real Negro genre." Johnson had much more to say about what a really good Negro opera must be. In sum, it had to be in an authentic Negro musical language and sung and acted in characteristic Negro style. He had strong doubts that any white composer had the requisite knowledge or experience for the task.

J. Rosamond Johnson, aside from his role as Lawyer Frazier in the opera and assisting the coaching of the chorus, could hardly have disagreed more. He said the opera's "musical influence will live through the ages." While not "one hundred percent negroid, at least eighty percent of its musical idioms are."

Yet through the welter of criticism and comment could be seen a general recognition, even at the time, that *Porgy and Bess* was the high point in attempts over the years to weld the Negro musical idiom with a dramatic Negro theme and at the same time to create an important native opera. Its peckish put-down by Virgil Thomson seems somewhat suspect, when the richness of *Porgy and Bess* is compared with the playfulness of his *Four Saints*. (To be fair to him, Thomson turned more generous in later years.) When sales at the box office lagged, the Guild lowered its high $4.40 ticket price to the more usual $3.30, but that didn't help much, and so, to lower costs, it tried dickering with the Musicians' Union to cut down the size of the orchestra. The union said absolutely not. After 124 profitless performances, the show was sent on a tour of four cities in the hope of recouping what was now a $70,000 investment.

Gershwin's enthusiasm for his work remained undampened, and 124 performances of an opera in a single season was something hitherto unheard of. The last performance at the Alvin played to a full house, and Gershwin was there at the end to cheer his cast. Meanwhile, Victor had made a recording of several excerpts with the orchestra of the Metropolitan Opera and with Lawrence Tibbett and Helen Jepson singing the lead roles, their names deemed to be of more drawing power than those of Todd Duncan and Anne Brown. Several of the opera's songs were sweeping the country—heard on radios, played on phonographs, and sung in stage shows and in concert halls. No fewer than four, "Summertime" and "It Ain't Necessarily So" among them, were on the list of the year's top hits, on their way to becoming American classics.

The show's tour began in Philadelphia on January 27, 1936, from there moved on to Pittsburgh and Chicago, and was to finish with a week's run in Washington in March at the National Theatre, the city's only legitimate playhouse. The manager of the theatre, S. E. Cochran, kept in force a long-set policy of segregation. When *The Green Pastures* had played there a few years before, he had broken his rule only to the extent of allowing black patrons to inhabit a roped-off section of the second balcony. This caused some heated protest, and he compromised with a special Sunday performance for a black audience.

Todd Duncan, a Washingtonian, was well aware of the National's policy and, as soon as he learned that *Porgy and Bess* was scheduled for his city, was determined to do something about it. He announced he had no intention of playing at a theatre he himself would have been unable to attend. When Anne Brown took the same position, a crisis confronted the Theatre Guild and Cochran. Duncan kept it boiling by hiring a secretary and dashing off letters to such personages as Eleanor Roosevelt and Ralph Bunche. Cochran called him, finally, and made a compromise offer. Negroes, he said, could attend Wednesday and Saturday matinees. Duncan said that wouldn't do. The manager made another offer: Negroes could sit in the second balcony at every performance. That wouldn't do either, Duncan said.

The managers of the Theatre Guild tried to convince Duncan to accept a compromise. His position, they told him, would affect the whole company. The Musicians' Union entered the fray by threatening to fine him $10,000 and suspend him for a year, and still Duncan held firm. Nothing would do, he said, other than that black people be allowed to buy tickets for any seat in the house. Finally, Cochran gave way. Hundreds of blacks attended the performances with no dire result (Cochran was amazed that not a single white asked for money back), and the National, for the first time in its history, was desegregated, blacks and whites seated in the same rows all over the house, a significant early step in the movement toward racial equality.

With the finish of the run in Washington, Gershwin and Heyward's opera appeared to have reached a dead end. George, Ira, and DuBose each lost his $5,000 investment. George received some royalties, but they went to pay the copyists' fees for the orchestration. Heyward had hoped to buy a house in Charleston with his royalties, but they were so minuscule he gave up the idea. Still, at the Guild, for all its renowned penny-pinching ways, there was pride that something new, vital, and important had been brought to Broadway under its aegis.

After all the time and work that had been put into the undertaking, it was understandable that the Gershwins would welcome offers from Hollywood. In August 1936 they closed down their New York apartments, put most of their effects in storage, and planed westward, as *Variety* might have put it.

MERLE ARMITAGE, a concert and opera manager whose projects had brought him to the West Coast, was keenly interested in George Gershwin's presence in California. He was a fervent admirer and proponent of Gershwin's music. In *Porgy and Bess* he saw and heard a music drama stripped of the customary artificialities of operatic convention. Instead of grandiose scenery, interpolated ballets, arias designed to give a prima donna or a tenor opportunities for vocal pyrotechnics, he found music that didn't break with the story being told, that was a valid expression of breathing, singing, working, playing, living people. The critics, he felt, had missed the point; they had been prejudiced against Gershwin because he came from the theatre and made only sporadic entry into the concert halls. It might have been easier for him if he had been altogether unknown. Armitage also believed in jazz as an authentic expression of the American spirit of the times and felt it was Gershwin who had done the most to give it validity as a sound musical form. In October of 1936 he wrote Gershwin a letter proposing two concerts of Gershwin music using the Los Angeles Philharmonic.

The Gershwin brothers had been hired to compose the score for an RKO musical starring Fred Astaire and Ginger Rogers and eventually titled *Shall We Dance*. Samuel Goldwyn had also lined up for their services, so it looked as though the Gershwins would be working in Hollywood for at least a year and probably more. The Depression had put Broadway into retreat. Not only had *Porgy and Bess* lost its investment, but the previous Gershwin musical, *Let 'Em Eat Cake,* had also closed in the red. After some haggling between agents and producers, George and Ira signed their contracts and were given a send-off by family and friends at Newark Airport before boarding their transcontinental sleeper plane. Among the well-wishers was Kay Swift, who had agreed with George that it would be best to be free of each other while he was away; later on they could decide whether or not to have a future together.

Ira's wife, Leonore, did the house-hunting in Beverly Hills while the Gershwin ménage stayed temporarily in a suite at the Beverly Wilshire Hotel. Two weeks later they were installed as a family in a large, cream-colored Spanish-style stucco house, complete with swimming pool and tennis court, on North Roxbury Drive, above Sunset Boulevard. When George reacted positively to the idea of the concerts, Merle Armitage became a frequent visitor at the house, which was almost always full of friends. The Gershwins had been taken up with enthusiasm by the creative crowd, many of them in exile from New York. Oscar Levant was probably the most frequent guest, constantly peppering the others with his sardonic jibes. Harold Arlen was there often; so were Lillian Hellman, Dashiell Hammett, Rouben Mamoulian, E. Y. Harburg, Moss Hart, Arthur Kober, and Edward G. Robinson. Arnold Schoenberg was usually to be found on the tennis court, while Paulette Goddard would be lying in a scanty bathing suit by the side of the pool. The talk was endless, full of wit, often argumentative. These were Easterners mostly, people of liberal political ideas, and some later on would suffer because of it.

Full as the house was of conviviality, of informal leisure, Armitage saw another side of George. Arriving there to discuss the proposed concerts, he would often find the composer upstairs in a room with an easel; he liked to get away from the tumult below to paint.

The two decided to hold the concerts early the following year, 1937. George would be piano soloist, with Alexander Smallens conducting *Rhapsody in Blue* and *Concerto in F.* But with George's enthusiasm increasing, they decided to add some selections from *Porgy and Bess,* with a black chorus. They went to a Negro district to recruit the members, and after holding auditions selected thirty men and women with fine voices. At George's invitation, Todd Duncan agreed to participate.

The concerts were held in Philharmonic Auditorium in February. The two performances were not only sold out, but hundreds had to be turned away. It was at the second of the concerts that Oscar Levant, in the audience, noticed that George stumbled on a very easy passage in the first movement of the *Concerto.* Then, in the slow second movement, he made another blunder, missing a few bars entirely. Smallens covered the lapse well, and George was once more in full control. After the concert, backstage, he admitted the slips to Levant and also mentioned that he had experienced a curious burning odor and a dizziness that had left him with a headache. Neither Levant nor anyone else took the complaints seriously in a man who was so obviously the personification of vitality and vigorous good health. Levant could only be amazed by a man who each day took a six-mile walk through the hills of Beverly.

The concerts were a huge success, socially as well as musically. (A critic for the *Musical Courier* commented with inverse snobbery: "It was obvious that a large number had never been in the auditorium before. Anyway, they saw some movie stars.") During a celebration held at a night spot on Sunset Strip, Armitage in a flush of enthusiasm proposed performing *Porgy and Bess* on the West Coast and then taking it across the country for another run in New York. George cautioned him by telling him about the Theatre Guild's loss of investment in the first production. He had been hoping for a European tour of the opera, certain that it would be well received in London and Paris, but the Guild's Warren Munsell had put a damper on the idea by saying that the opera would fail again unless the cast took cuts—highly unlikely—in salary. Not only that—Munsell thought the only way to realize any gain from the opera was to sell it to the movies.

"Do you dare?" George asked Armitage.

Armitage replied in the affirmative, and he promised Gershwin that he would produce it during 1938.

Gershwin wrote a thank-you note (dated March 16, 1937) to Duncan for his appearance at the concerts and in it said, "I hope Merle Armitage can manage to bring the entire opera out next season. He is definitely a superior impresario who does things well and I would love to hear my opera as it was originally sung." It was an implied request, which Duncan would eventually honor.

THROUGH 1936 and the first half of 1937, George and Ira worked on three films, two for RKO (*Shall We Dance* and *A Damsel in Distress*) and, for Samuel Goldwyn, *The Goldwyn Follies*. During the spring of 1937 friends noticed in George an increasing restlessness and bouts of depression. The general feeling was that his sour moods could be attributed to a disaffection with the Hollywood life-style. It would be hard not to be aware that while the film colony basked in the sun and their lofty salaries, dust storms were still sweeping the midlands, floods were menacing the Northeast, and 17 percent of the nation was still unemployed. George had his own socially liberal viewpoint. And he did not take cordially to Sam Goldwyn's blunt way of treating those in his employ. "Why don't you write hits like Irving Berlin?" Goldwyn asked him at one point. The real cause of Gershwin's distress was far more serious, however.

Two months after the concerts he had another episode of dizziness and again was aware of the curious smell like burning rubber. An examination showed nothing wrong, but in June the dizzy spells became more frequent, occurring almost daily during the early-morning hours; with them came headaches and fatigue. Furthermore, very much unlike him was his sudden desire to marry and settle down, and not in New York, but in Los Angeles. He went so far as to propose to Paulette Goddard, who was already married to Charles Chaplin and not about to break up that valuable relationship. Another of George's fancies was the French actress Simone Simon, who had presented him with a gold-plated key, initialed G.G., to her home.

An unusually severe headache early one Sunday morning caused Ira and Leonore to insist that George get a thorough physical checkup. A doctor and a neurologist came to the house and examined George in his bedroom. Oscar Levant was there for lunch, and when George came down in bathrobe and slippers, Levant asked him what the doctors had said. George gave a laugh of relief and said, "Before they told me anything they wanted to rule out the possibility of a brain tumor." Psychoanalysis proving of no help, he went to a hospital and had X rays taken. They revealed very little, and although a spinal tap was proposed to check for the possibility of a brain tumor, George refused to spend the necessary time in the hospital to have it done.

By the first week of July, George's deterioration was strikingly evident. A nurse was now with him; doctors came daily. The house that had been so full of talk and laughter grew morosely silent as his attempts at work ended in long periods of fatigue. His behavior became more strange. When a box of chocolates was sent to him by an admirer he squeezed the entire contents into one gooey lump and spread the mess over his body. He had to be taken to the bathroom and washed.

During the late afternoon of Friday, July 9, he took a nap that deepened into a coma. He was rushed to Cedars of Lebanon Hospital, and a call was sent to Dr. Walter Dandy, a prominent brain specialist at The Johns Hopkins Hospital in Baltimore. Dandy got as far as Newark Airport, where he was notified that a spinal tap indicated a brain tumor, with immediate surgery the only possible intervention. A team of four surgeons performed the delicate operation late Saturday night, and into early Sunday, removing portions of a cystic tumor in Gershwin's right temporal lobe. Ira remained in the operating room during the entire four-hour procedure. Five hours later, at 5 a.m. on Sunday, July 11, George Gershwin died without regaining consciousness.

Assuming the best possible result of the operation, he might have survived longer, but any recovery would have meant, in Dandy's opinion, a progressive and hopeless deterioration.

GERSHWIN'S DEATH shocked the world. Eulogies came from everywhere. The loss was especially poignant in view of his age, only thirty-eight, with the full flowering of his gifts seemingly ahead of him.

On Monday, July 12, at 2 p.m. EST, the Mutual network presented a nationwide memorial broadcast in which Irving Berlin, Cole Porter, Richard Rodgers, Larry Hart, Leopold Stokowski, Frances Langford, and Bing Crosby participated. An orchestra played a selection of Gershwin's best-known and best-loved song compositions. On that same day his body was put on a train bound for New York. Ira followed the next day by plane. Funeral services were held simultaneously on Thursday, July 15, in Los Angeles and New York.

In Los Angeles, a memorial committee led by Berlin, Moss Hart, and Sigmund Romberg issued the invitations to attend the service at B'nai B'rith Temple. The turnout was composed of the luminaries of the music, film, and theatre worlds: a partial list includes Adolph Zukor, Oscar Hammerstein II, Jerome Kern, Arnold Schoenberg, Dashiell Hammett, Eddie Cantor, Ernst Lubitsch, Harry Cohn, and Charles Chaplin. Oscar Hammerstein read the eulogy.

In New York, at the services held in Temple Emanu-El on Fifth Avenue, the list of honorary pallbearers was equally impressive: among them Mayor Fiorello La Guardia, Governor Herbert Lehman, Walter Damrosch, W. C. Handy, Felix Warburg, and Condé Nast. More than two thousand mourners crowded the temple to its capacity to hear two rabbis, Nathan Perilman and Dr. Stephen Wise, conduct the services. The temple was banked by floral pieces sent from the capitals of the world. Inevitably, Rabbi Wise, in his eulogy, stressed the Americanism of Gershwin and his ability to capture the spirit of his land, his interpretation of it in song, and made contrast with the somber events occurring in Europe. Outside, where more than a thousand others had gathered and remained standing, rain fell.

UNDETERRED BY Gershwin's death—in fact, spurred by his promise to him—Armitage went ahead with his plans to produce the opera. Arrangements first had to be made with the Theatre Guild; scenery had to be built and props acquired. To mount so expensive an opera only for Los Angeles and San Francisco would be a financial risk, so bookings were made for a tour that would take the company to several Western cities. Most of those in the cast that had played in New York were willing—indeed, some turned down other engagements for the opportunity to come to the West Coast. The first to arrive for rehearsals was Todd Duncan. Rouben Mamoulian, back in Hollywood, took on the direction for no pay and Alexander Steinert the conducting.

John Bubbles was willing to perform Sportin' Life again, but the fee he asked was too rich for the budget. Armitage looked elsewhere and soon found Gershwin's own second choice, Avon Long. As it turned out, he was a find indeed, stylizing the part in a way that gave him a long career in the American theatre.

By the time rehearsals were in progress, news of the new production had spread and demand for it mounted. Concert managers all over the West Coast asked for it, and so did others in cities as far afield as Kansas City, Detroit, and Cincinnati. For Armitage and the company it looked as though a national tour would prove successful.

The first-night performance was in Pasadena before an audience made up of top Hollywood personalities and socialites from the gilt-edged bedroom communities of Beverly Hills, Holmby Hills, and Bel-Air. The reception was such that phone operators had to be hired to handle the calls for reservations for the eleven subsequent performances at the Los Angeles Philharmonic Auditorium. Some tickets for the final performance there went for more than ten times the amount of the box-office price. Those who had also seen the New York production thought this one more exciting and satisfying. As Armitage said, "Motivating our efforts was my desire that we not let George Gershwin down. That feeling was shared by every person in the cast."

Three more weeks were scheduled at San Francisco's Curran Theatre, after which the plan was to move on to other Western cities. But during the last week of the San Francisco run the rains came in devastating force, followed by some of the most disastrous floods in California's history. For seven days no trains moved. Residents of outlying communities who would have attended performances remained at home, and Armitage, who was hoping to break even in the succeeding engagements, found himself unable to meet the final week's salaries.

The truth was told to the cast, gathered on the Curran's stage. Armitage explained that receipts were way down because of the floods and not only was he short of funds for salaries, but the other engagements had to be canceled. In plain language, he said, "I'm completely wiped out."

He was profoundly touched by the response. "It was *my* misfortune," he said, "which concerned them. Before I could leave the stage that night, completely surrounded by the company, dozens of them diplomatically and generously offered loans from their meager savings."

As it turned out, though, cast members were able, through the intervention of Actors Equity in Hollywood, to reclaim some of their lost pay. Armitage had hired New York concert manager Charles L. Wagner to locate and gather members of the original production. Equity's position was that Wagner was responsible for the pay of those he had recruited, some of them stranded on the West Coast. These performers had been provided with return transportation, but many had sold their tickets on the assumption they'd be coming east with the opera. Wagner paid up on the implied threat that otherwise performers under contract to him would not work for him.

As the cast of *Porgy and Bess* straggled back to New York, it was a sad ending to Armitage's hopes for nationwide recognition of the Gershwin work.

10

G E O R G E   G E R S H W I N wrote his last letter to DuBose Heyward six months before his death. On RKO Pictures stationery, he told DuBose about the two concerts he would be giving in two weeks with the Los Angeles Philharmonic. He was hoping, he said, that the concerts would "whip up some enthusiasm for picture possibilities on the part of the studios who, as you know, are keen about it, but slightly afraid on account of the color question." He said, too, that he was anxious "to start thinking about a serious musicale. How about planning another opera or operetta for the future? So put your mind to it, old boy, and I know you can evolve something interesting."

Heyward, at the time, had an idea for a novel that would be set in the Virgin Islands and that might well serve as the basis for an opera. The novel, his last, later appeared under the title *Star Spangled Virgin*, and, after Gershwin's death, an effort was made to get a musical version of it under way, with Arthur Schwartz as the composer and Ethel Waters proposed as the star. The collaboration with Schwartz never got very far; Heyward's fragile health, and the frequent postponements because of it, was the main obstacle.

It is not certain how much Gershwin knew of Heyward's efforts or whether Heyward was aware of the composer's deteriorating condition. But evidence of his continuing closeness with Gershwin came in a letter sent him by Ira, three weeks after his brother's death.

"To the end of my days," Ira wrote him, "I shall never forget the exciting and thrilling period of *Porgy and Bess.* George had, not only a great respect for you, but also a deep affection, and I assure you, though I believe you must have known, I felt the same way about you and considered it a great honor to be associated with you, however small my contribution." Heyward had admired a silver tankard of George's, and Ira said it would go to him once the estate matters were settled. "My mother will need no convincing," he added, a reference to the fact that George had died intestate and that their mother was now George's sole heir.

The Heywards were active that year on another project, which would have had to take precedence over a new collaboration with Gershwin. This was a dramatization of DuBose's novel *Mamba's Daughters,* written expressly with Ethel Waters in mind. DuBose and Dorothy had thought of dramatizing it soon after the book's appearance in 1929, but they couldn't think of a black actress for the leading role who had the requisite distinction and star power.

The Heywards met the famous Broadway musical star and comedienne Ethel Waters in New York in 1935 soon after the opening of *Porgy and Bess.* She was invited to a party given by her friend Georgette Harvey, who had sung Maria in the opera, for Rouben Mamoulian. The Heywards were there, too, and Ethel Waters happened to be sitting with them on a couch, unaware of who they were. She mentioned to them that she preferred the opera to the play because "the performers express themselves more honestly and freely." In the play, she said, she had the feeling that the characters kept apologizing for being themselves. "I've known a great many bitches and whores in real life. They never apologize for what they are." As for the players, it was as though they were implying, " 'I'm not really like this in private life. I'm just acting here tonight.' "

Dorothy delicately made it clear that she was talking to the authors, so Ethel changed the subject to *Mamba's Daughters,* not knowing that DuBose had also written that novel. She had been struck by how much Mamba's family was like her own, she told them, but of the three generations of the story it was Mamba's daughter Hagar who had impressed her as the book's most important character, much like her own mother, and like "all Negro women lost and lonely in the white man's antagonistic world." The astute Dorothy Heyward mentioned that her husband had written the novel and then promised Ethel Waters that if they were to dramatize the novel she would have first chance at the lead. Two years later the play was written and they sent the script to her. She not only agreed to play the role of Hagar, around which the story was now built, but refused other commitments that would tie her up if a production was imminent. The Heywards made severe changes from the novel, eliminating the white characters of the plot and making of it a play in which, except for a few subsidiary roles, all the characters were black and centered around Hagar.

Getting the play onstage, though, was difficult. The Theatre Guild turned it down, as did several other producers. Some felt the play was too melodramatic; others did not think Ethel Waters—on whom the Heywards were insistent—was accomplished enough as an actress to carry it. Frustrated by his inability to get the play produced, Heyward took it to a friend, Guthrie McClintic, the director husband of Katharine Cornell, for an opinion. McClintic not only agreed to put the play on his schedule, but championed Ethel Waters for the key role of a strong, devoted, generous woman, yet one capable of the violent rage which would cause her to kill the vicious seducer of her daughter, Lissa (changed from an opera singer to a radio vocalist). DuBose included spirituals as he had in *Porgy* and also wrote the lyrics to a song for Ethel Waters, set to music by Jerome Kern. Heyward insisted, "There must be music in an all-Negro play."

Only Brooks Atkinson desisted from the general chorus of praise for Ethel Waters; he liked neither her nor the play. The show ran for six successful months and, after touring the country, returned to New York in March 1940 for a two-week reprise. As with *Porgy,* several new performing careers resulted for black actors. Most phenomenal of all was the subsequent success of Ethel Waters onstage and in film.

The Heywards were now living well. Although *Porgy and Bess* had failed to produce any substantial royalties, the constant playing of its songs produced a continuing flow. He was thus able to purchase a house near prestigious South Battery, overlooking the harbor. Busy with writing activities, he nevertheless made himself part of the Charleston cultural scene, much as he had done before creating *Porgy.* He was helpful in bringing about a replica of the historic Dock Street Theatre, became its resident dramatist, and served on the board of the Carolina Art Association. He became the first South Carolinian to be elected to the National Institute of Arts and Letters. He and Dorothy became the leaders of a group that met twice weekly (much as in the early days with John Bennett and Hervey Allen) to discuss and criticize its playwriting efforts.

One of the members of this group was Frank Durham, who later wrote a biography of Heyward: "With all of us he was unfailingly patient and unfailingly understanding . . . half reclining in a Windsor chair in the spacious drawing room of the Dock Street Theatre with its Adam mantels and ancient paneling. Though his body was relaxed, his head was always thrust a little forward as he listened intently to our readings and occasionally jotted down a comment. . . . Sometimes we met in the upstairs sitting room at 24 South Battery, its windows looking out on White Point Gardens and the blue expanse of the harbor. And there was an occasional gathering, more social than literary, at the Heywards' rambling house on Folly Beach. It was as if a wheel had come full circle for DuBose Heyward, as if he were living again in the early days of the Poetry Society."

As always, when the hot, humid weather came to Charleston, the Heywards retreated to Dawn Hill in the mountains of North Carolina. On June 16, 1940, prior to leaving with Dorothy for their beloved MacDowell Colony, DuBose went to nearby Tryon for a checkup in its hospital. After the examination he started for Hendersonville, but suffered a heart attack and was brought back to the hospital, where, soon after, he died. Fifty-five at the time, he was buried in the graveyard of Charleston's Saint Philip's Church.

A local obituary recorded the fact that he was "perhaps the most famous writer ever produced by this city," but much of the article—in fact, most of it—was taken up with an account of the writing of *Porgy* and all that happened following its appearance. Much was made of how the supposed presence of Catfish Row had brought tourists by the thousands to Charleston. In a sense, honored with Heyward was the humble Negro beggar who had first struck his imagination and had brought him fortune and fame.

Gershwin's reputation soared ever upward after his death. Not so Heyward's. Critics in succeeding generations have not taken him seriously as either a writer or a dramatist. Such fame as still accrues to his name comes almost solely because of his association with Gershwin and *Porgy and Bess*.

There is some unfairness in this. He should also be seen as one of the most important influences in opening up the American stage to black participation. The large casts for *Porgy* as both play and opera gave great opportunity to a host of black performers, made new black stars, and gave white and mixed audiences a new appreciation of the talents of black performing artists. As will be seen, it is a contribution that lives on.

What is not fully appreciated yet is the precision and poetry of the libretto for *Porgy and Bess*. A reading of it without the accompanying force and power of the music reveals writing of a quality far beyond that of the run-of-the-mill Broadway musical and of most classic operatic librettos, too.

From a latter-day perspective, Heyward's view of the South, and of the urban Negro's place in it, seldom includes any great moral outrage at white exploitation, but there is nevertheless truth and realism in his portrait of life in Catfish Row, and with it always a great sympathy. This was new, and even bold, in his time. It is an irony that his name lives on through *Porgy,* but, gracious gentleman that he was, he would undoubtedly have seen this as fitting.

GEORGE GERSHWIN and DuBose Heyward died without having an inkling of what further adventures their *Porgy and Bess* would encounter. George had been cocksure enough to guess that his music would still be around in another hundred years, and fifty years after his death he was proven to be at least half right. As it turned out, it was only a little more than a year after Heyward died that *Porgy and Bess* took the stage once more.

The angel of rescue was Cheryl Crawford, who with John Wildberg, a theatrical lawyer, took over in 1940 a large old movie house in Maplewood, New Jersey, and turned it into a thriving home for summer stock. Crawford's career had undergone several changes since her job as assistant stage manager for the Theatre Guild's 1927 production of *Porgy*. She had come to the Guild from Akron, Ohio, as a student actor in its fledgling school and found a job there when she decided her talents were more useful behind the scenes. As she put it, "The *Porgy* company and I had a long love affair." She was entranced by the exuberance and sense of fun of the cast. Each week she joined a bunch of them and went to Small's Paradise in Harlem, or the Lenox Club, or a rent party.

When *Porgy* closed down in New York, she stayed with Mamoulian as his assistant and in 1929 took the production to London. During the thirties she joined the Group Theatre as one of its managers, was involved with several of its productions, and, on its decline, produced on her own, but with more prestigious than financial success; her backers invariably lost money. The Maplewood Theatre attracted her as a place where she could present a play a week, and the size of the house was large enough to allow for modest ticket prices. The theatre was easily accessible, just opposite the railroad station, and close enough to New York so the actors could return home after rehearsals.

The theatre, with its twenty-week season, was a rousing success from the start. Crawford was able to get Broadway shows to spend a week in Maplewood after their close and to persuade stars of her acquaintance to perform: Ethel Barrymore, Paul Robeson, Helen Hayes, and Tallulah Bankhead. Tickets were kept to a top of $1.65. Audiences came from New York and the surrounding New Jersey suburbs, and the theatre flourished into the 1942 season, when wartime gas rationing drastically cut the number of people who had formerly driven from New York. Meanwhile, Crawford had decided to close the 1941 season with something truly big, and her choice was *Porgy and Bess*.

She was well aware of the sorry economics of the original production. It

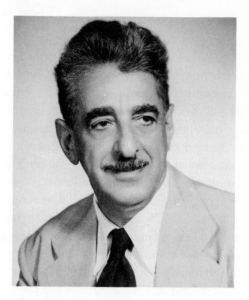

Alexander Smallens, music director for the opera.
He didn't favor the recitatives. (Lawrence and Lee
Theatre Research Institute, Ohio State University.)

had taken in an average of $20,000 a week, but had cost at least that much to keep going, to say nothing of recouping the original investment. Crawford envisaged a sparer but nevertheless first-rate production. When she viewed the original show she felt the recitatives had impeded the opera's pace and may have contributed to its early closing. This notion found a sympathetic ear in conductor Alexander Smallens, who agreed to take on the musical responsibility only if the recitatives could be eliminated in favor of spoken dialogue.

Smallens had made no secret to George Gershwin of his dislike of giving musical settings to mundane lines, essential only to move the plot along, and felt he was committing no sacrilege by throwing them out while retaining the words. In justification he cited Mozart, Weber, and Beethoven as having used spoken words instead of recitatives. At the same time, he felt the opera was a greater work than it had been regarded in 1935 and that its songs had already demonstrated their imperishability. No one at the Theatre Guild, or Ira Gershwin, presented any obstacle to the "streamlining" of the opera. Crawford felt the forty-four-piece orchestra scored and used by Gershwin unnecessary; Smallens, through reorchestration, was able to cut the number of musicians to twenty-seven. "The big orchestra was too heavy for the singers, anyway," said Crawford. The size of the cast was cut, too; a lot of people running around the stage in Mamoulian's lively production, she thought, had complicated the staging. All in all, as she sat with Smallens in the theatre with score in hand during the rehearsal period, they were able to reduce the length of the show by thirty-five minutes.

She was able to find most of the principals of the original production. Todd Duncan came from the West Coast, where he had just completed working in MGM's *Syncopation,* a history of jazz since 1906. Anne Brown was concertizing in New York. Georgette Harvey, fresh out of *Mamba's Daughters,* came back in her third appearance as Maria; she was a veteran of *Porgy,* both play and opera. Bubbles was sought for Sportin' Life, but was not available, and in his place Avon Long was recruited from the Merle Armitage production.

In its new incarnation the show moved swiftly along. Overflow audiences were enchanted by it, and tickets for the one-week run became impossible to obtain. It had not been far from Cheryl Crawford's mind that a Broadway run and a following road tour were possibilities. To that end, Lee Shubert, of the Shubert theatres, was invited to see the show. Wildberg also invited several Wall Street financiers. All were impressed, the Wall Streeters enough to pledge some $25,000 for a Broadway opening. Lee Shubert offered a theatre, the large Majestic.

Tears sprang to Crawford's eyes. "Please," she begged, "don't put us there. That big old barn has been a jinx house for years." The big house turned out to be an advantage, though; the number of seats made it possible to keep the best seats to a low price of $2.50. After three weeks in Boston, *Porgy and Bess* arrived at the Majestic on January 22, 1942.

During its week's run the previous October, Virgil Thomson, in his role as critic for the New York *Herald Tribune,* had paid a visit to the Maplewood Theatre. Now he revised his original estimate of the opera, attributing much of his change of heart to the diminished instrumentation and to the "elimination where possible of the embarrassments due to Gershwin's incredibly amateurish way of writing *recitativo.*" He had found Mamoulian's scenery and stage movements ponderous; not so in this production. He heartily approved of all the changes. "It seems to me," he wrote, "that kind of [textual and instrumental] correction, carried out by a skillful musician who knew the composer well and respected his genius, is exactly what the work needs right now. . . . Gershwin would not have minded, I am sure."

But aside from these not-so-gentle slaps, Thomson decided that in spite of its "numberless faults, its inspiration is authentic and its expressive quotient high" and, after six years, it was "still a beautiful piece of music." His mood eventually turned patriotic. It was a work which "America might well be proud to honor and happy to love."

There were far fewer qualifications from critics who covered the New

York opening. The reception now was all that Gershwin or Heyward might have wished for. Olin Downes of *The New York Times* decided that "in his own way Gershwin has taken a substantial step and advanced the cause of native opera." Drama critics Richard Watts, Jr., and Wolcott Gibbs awarded it the status of "classic." Brooks Atkinson, who by this time must have been familiar enough with the story to recite it by heart, ascribed the reception of the new production to the fact that "when a composer stops writing new music, his old music has a better chance to become appreciated." He did not mention that there were no recitatives to annoy critics, as he had in 1935. Most everyone agreed that this, along with other trimmings, had hastened the pace of the show and made it more accessible to audiences. In shape it was now less of an opera and closer to Broadway expectations for a musical show.

In a symposium on black theatre in *Theatre Arts,* Edith J. R. Isaacs wondered what "among its many virtues, it is that keeps *Porgy* fresh and alive in all its forms," since the pattern of the action was no longer novel and

Successful as the Cheryl Crawford version was, some Gershwins called it "the bargain basement production." (Lawrence and Lee Theatre Research Institute, Ohio State University.)

exciting and its high moments often imitated. "Perhaps," was her conclusion, "it is because a poet gave *Porgy* its life that *Porgy* lives today. Perhaps because the actors knew something of the sordid life and the characters, both bad and beautiful, that peopled it and because there were poets among them, too." She was alone, though, in giving credit to Heyward for its survival.

There was one unfortunate lapse that required correction. Crawford, to trade on the composer's increasingly hallowed reputation, advertised the production as "George Gershwin's *Porgy and Bess*." This caught the vigilant eye of Dorothy Heyward, whose request for a change was quickly granted. Heyward's name was added to the authorship.

The run of 286 performances from January until the end of September was the longest theatrical revival on Broadway then, and from New York the heralded show immediately went on tour for another eighteen months, playing in forty-seven cities in the United States and also in Toronto. When it returned to New York, it played to sold-out audiences for two weeks at the New York City Center. Todd Duncan by that time had sung the role more than a thousand times. Anne Brown had left the show in June 1942, and a new Bess (and a new Broadway star) took her place in the person of the attractive Etta Moten.

Gershwin, as mentioned earlier, had rejected her for the role because her voice range was not high enough. After several seasons of concert work around the country she was in New York just at the time Anne Brown was signifying her intention to leave. Alexander Smallens contacted Moten and told her he was sure she could sing Bess. Having added some high notes to her register, she tried out and found she could sing the role after a few notes were transposed in the fiercely sensual Kitiwah Island scene when Crown reappears and quickly seduces Bess. She sat out front for twelve days watching the performance, then with director Robert Ross's help and Duncan's generosity with rehearsal time, went onstage to great praise and a long run.

The superbly trained and educated young woman balked, however, at the use of one word in the libretto—"nigger." She refused to sing it, and the word was eliminated. In 1951, when Goddard Lieberson produced the first full-length recording for Columbia Records, he became concerned about the word running through the libretto. "Sometimes, happily," he explained, after it was excised from his recording, "times change, and with the times, ethical values. It seemed proper to eliminate certain words in the lyrics which, in racial terms, had proven offensive, and the first person to join enthusiastically in the making of these changes was Ira Gershwin himself, who has supplied new lyrics when they seemed desirable." But this was only the first of the irritations to black sensibilities caused by the opera. With increased black militancy, *Porgy and Bess* was attacked on more grounds than a few offensive and outmoded words.

As Ira Bell expressed in *Ebony,* the 1942 revival was more tolerated by blacks than accepted. He described its black critics as divided into three camps: "Those who like it, those who do not like it—and the cowards who confine their reviews to the indisputable excellence of talent and to technical perfection."

A year after the Crawford revival, *Porgy and Bess* made its first appearance across the ocean. Danish Royal Opera premiered it in Copenhagen, in Danish, on March 23, 1943, with an all-white cast. In spite of white actors playing black roles, the opera was an extraordinary success, so much so that the Nazi occupiers suggested strongly to the opera managers that an American work of any kind was not to its liking and that this one be withdrawn from the repertory.

Nevertheless, the opera was given and sold out twenty-one more times, with the theatre surrounded on each occasion by a cordon of Danish police. Finally, the Gestapo lost patience and said if *Porgy and Bess* were given one more time the opera house would be bombed. The opera's managers decided to end the run.

But the banning of *Porgy and Bess* had the unlooked-for effect of stimulating the Danish spirit of resistance to its occupiers and soon became a symbol of this spirit. When the Nazis broadcast communiqués over Danish radio citing their victories, the Danish underground would cut in with a recording of "It Ain't Necessarily So." When the war ended, *Porgy and Bess* was quickly reinstalled in the repertory.

PART TWO

AN OPERA FOR
EVERY MAN

Cab Calloway had doubts about playing Sportin' Life in the
Breen-Davis production. But it resuscitated his career. (Lawrence and Lee
Theatre Research Institute, Ohio State University.)

11

WHEREVER Robert Breen, general director of the American National Theatre and Academy (ANTA), went that spring of 1950, it seemed to him he heard people on the streets whistling tunes from *Porgy and Bess*. It happened in London, in Frankfurt, and again in Paris. Breen, a high-minded theatre visionary, was, among other activities, making arrangements for the first European tour of the Ballet Theatre—in fact, the first such by any American ballet company. International cultural exchange was on the rise during these post–World War II years, and art and theatre festivals were springing up in country after country; Breen was one of those most actively involved in fostering American participation. Although he had never seen a production of *Porgy and Bess,* he was well aware of its audience popularity through his association with Cheryl Crawford, his partner in some of ANTA's experimental stage productions. It struck him that the American folk opera, featuring a first-rate black cast, would be an ideal production for European audiences.

Breen mentioned to festival directors, theatre managers, and impresarios the possibility of bringing over *Porgy and Bess* and found the response invariably enthusiastic. He was so caught up by the idea of a grand tour of the Gershwin opera in such great cities as London, Paris, Berlin, and Vienna that he cabled his wife, Wilva (his assistant at ANTA), to look into the rights situation, to put a hold on them if possible, and also to pick up whatever recordings were available.

For some years, Breen, a lithe, graceful man of forty-one, with a gaunt and yet oddly handsome face, had been a dynamo of theatrical ideas and projects. His almost boyish liveliness was balanced by a not unattractive self-assurance. His mind bubbled with ideas, and once he was convinced they were valid he pursued them forthrightly. In 1945, he had developed a plan for a national theatre foundation. Its avowed purpose, through endowments, government, industry, and foundations, was to stimulate theatre as art, recreation, and education, and to establish a training institute. (The plan later became one of the cornerstones of the National Endowment for the Arts.) ANTA, always in search of a mission for itself, seized on the ideas in the plan and appointed Breen to its newly established post of executive secretary. When UNESCO was formed, Breen lobbied hard to have its arts program include theatre, at that point neglected. It took time, but he was successful.

ANTA sprang into wispy being in the mid-thirties when Congress gave some idealistic theatre-struck Philadelphians a national charter for their organization, a not very magnanimous gesture, since no funds were voted by the government. Few such charters existed: the Boy Scouts of America had one, so did the Red Cross, the Smithsonian, and the Federal Reserve Bank. For ANTA from the very beginning the vexing question was, Just what was an American National Theatre? Board members met infrequently to define their purpose; most clung to the pattern of subsidized "national theatres" in Europe. But in the United States there was little backing for the establishment of a state-supported national theatre such as the Comédie-Française in Paris or the Burgtheater in Vienna, although it was generally agreed that something was needed to rescue theatre from a decline caused by the movies, radio, and the dwindling number of touring companies.

Matters were set back further when Congress authorized funds for a Federal Theatre Project, which was notably energized by its administrator, Hallie Flanagan, then decided the ideas in the plays presented were too dangerously liberal. The Dramatists' Guild came along and joined with ANTA, by then little more than a charter in need of a defined purpose; before their notion of sending cheaply priced plays on tours could be developed, the war intervened and Robert E. Sherwood, president of the guild and ANTA, became the administrator of the Office of War Information in Washington. ANTA lay moribund until 1946, when its board took note of Breen's ideas for a national theatre foundation and decided these would become its basic principles of operation. Breen was appointed to become its activator.

With his wife, Wilva, Breen organized round-table discussions on what to do. Regional theatre was high on the list in that era of postwar enthusiasm and so were repertory and experimental theatre. Margo Jones's Theatre-in-the-Round was helped into being in Dallas. ANTA found funding for Margaret Webster and Eva Le Gallienne for their repertory theatres, which were about to fold. And, with Breen as general director, ANTA established its Experimental Theatre, with a range of productions that would include *Galileo* with Charles Laughton, and a presentation of the Martha Graham Dance Company. At the ANTA Playhouse Katina Paxinou would appear in Lorca's *The House of Bernarda Alba* and John Garfield in a curious production of Ibsen's *Peer Gynt* directed by Lee Strasberg.

Breen was an indefatigable organizer: for the State of Utah Centennial he arranged productions of Katharine Cornell's *The Barretts of Wimpole Street* and Orson Welles's *Macbeth;* Welles, incidentally, took his company of players to the West Coast and made his film of *Macbeth* with them. With the Barter Theatre of Virginia he staged and acted the lead in a touring production of *Hamlet.* It was this that brought him into close contact with Blevins Davis, a wealthy theatre enthusiast. Through Breen, Davis became a member of ANTA's board of directors. When Denmark invited the Barter Theatre to bring over Breen's *Hamlet,* Davis sponsored its highly successful presentation. And, in turn, Breen organized for Davis, the president of the Ballet Theatre Foundation, the ground-breaking European tour of its ballet company.

Breen found a way to get the Ballet Theatre to several cities in West Germany by offering performances to Occupation G.I.'s in return for Army Air Force transport. What was Ballet Theatre, a general wanted to know. "It's just a lot of pretty girls in pink tights," Breen told him. The general supplied the transportation.

Davis, then forty-seven, had grown up next door to the Truman home in Independence, Missouri, and was among the intimates of the president and Mrs. Truman. Out of Princeton and the University of Missouri, he took postgraduate work at the Yale Drama School. After a spell of teaching English and drama in high school and a junior college, he moved into radio and was selected by the National Broadcasting Company to be a commentator at the coronation of King George VI in Westminster Abbey. Soon after, he was appointed by NBC to supervise its educational programs, among which was the Great Play series, which traced the development of drama from the Greeks to Broadway. Robert and Wilva Breen listened to the series avidly long before they knew him.

Davis's fortunes improved noticeably when in 1946 he married the widow of James Norman Hill, son of James Jerome Hill, the railroad magnate. She was considerably older than Davis, and left him a widower not much more than a year after the marriage. While on a train journey from the West Coast, she became violently ill and died soon after being taken from the train and moved to a hospital. Davis became a multimillionaire and purchased Glendale Farm, a baronial estate outside Independence, where he entertained the Trumans on several occasions. Homosexual, he never quite lived down rumors that he had married the matronly lady principally for the life of ease she afforded him.

But Davis was very much an idealist, according to those who knew him, very enthusiastic, not very deep. "He loved to see good things happen," said one, "or rather, things he considered good." A man of charm, widely acquainted in important social, cultural, and political circles, he was strongly attracted to causes that would widen the scope and impact of theatre, both nationally and internationally, and he used his windfall fortune in their behalf. Ballet was a favorite. Breen had talent, fantastic energy, and no money; Davis had money and important connections. While Breen was managing the European tour of the Ballet Theatre for Davis he suggested they form a partnership to produce *Porgy and Bess,* not necessarily through ANTA. Davis thought it a great idea. It was a time when anti-American rhetoric was thundering out of the Eastern European bloc, and some of this propaganda was based on what the Communist countries regarded as America's virtual "enslavement" of its black population. Here was an opportunity to show how blacks were rising in the cultural firmament and at the same time to nullify propaganda about their lack of opportunity.

"From the very beginning," said Wilva, who was Breen's loyal associate in all his endeavors, "those factors were uppermost in their minds. It was an essential element of the project."

Even so, when they first began dealing with the Gershwin and Heyward interests for the rights they needed, they were unaware that they were about to make theatrical history of a magnitude even they could not have imagined.

PORGY AND BESS, as Breen and Davis discovered, had made its reappearance in Europe hardly a week after the Nazi surrender. In Moscow, the Stanislavsky Players performed the opera without benefit of orchestra, the singers accompanied only by piano and drums. Dimitri Shostakovich, in attendance, deemed the work "magnificent" and compared Gershwin to such Russian greats as Borodin and Moussorgsky. The Danish Royal Opera quickly brought back the work and gave it forty-nine performances over the next several years, occasionally with Todd Duncan and Anne Brown re-creating their roles.

Zurich began a long-lived love affair with the opera in July 1945 when it was performed in the city's annual festival of music. One critic called it "a miracle of technique . . . astonishing how this work succeeds in reflecting the emotional, the naive, and the realistic elements of the stage action." In Sweden, in 1948 and 1949, the opera was given in Gothenburg and Stockholm. For the most part, these performances were heavier than the American productions—more operatic, in other words. In Zurich, the orchestra was expanded to sixty-seven instruments. The German translation was unable to cope with the Charleston vernacular, and the white European singers played in blackface. Opera audiences were not bothered, though. They were accustomed to seeing stout Italians costumed as Japanese in *Madama Butterfly.*

In England, in 1947, Covent Garden began negotiations with the Theatre Guild for a production. The Guild would assemble and rehearse the cast and arrange for its transportation. Covent Garden would pay those costs and be responsible for scenery and costumes and some quite hefty royalties—10 percent to the authors and another 10 percent to the Guild. Smallens, if available, would handle the music direction and Mamoulian, if available, the staging. The difficulties of coordinating all this, along with the expense, caused the opera company to lose its enthusiasm.

Breen and Davis were not alone in seeking the rights to a new production. The Theatre Guild was actively interested in a revival, but it was by now less an organization dedicated to originality and excellence in theatre than a group of managers, led by Langner and Helburn, in commercial competition with other Broadway producers. During the war the Guild's fortunes were so precarious that it took the unexpected success of *Oklahoma!* to give it renewed life. It no longer gave a full season of plays. It was now more interested in solid returns on investment, and in the case of *Porgy and Bess* it was entitled to a hefty percentage in the event of a film production. Langner and Helburn would be the principal beneficiaries of such a sale. In 1942, Ira Gershwin had suggested to Dorothy Heyward that he thought the film rights might bring as much as $25,000. A few years later, amounts ten times that much were being discussed.

The rights were complicated because George Gershwin had died intestate, with his mother, Rose, his sole heir. Ira Gershwin had a share of authorship, and Dorothy Heyward had inherited her husband's interest. Each had a right to percentages of royalties from *Porgy and Bess* productions and a share of film rights, along with the Guild, as the original producer of the opera. In 1948 Rose Gershwin died, leaving her estate in trust to her children, which meant that the interested parties now included Ira's younger sister, Frankie, and his younger brother, Arthur. There was also something called "infants rights"—the children of children. All of these parties were represented by lawyers and agents. Dorothy Heyward counted twenty-seven participants at one meeting of the group.

The Guild had earlier fended off John Wildberg and Cheryl Crawford when they had claimed a share of film rights on the ground that they, as producers of the revival, then still running, were so entitled according to Dramatists' Guild rules. With Ira's and Dorothy's consent, the Guild played a waiting game, holding off any sale of the film rights until the show ended its run, at which time the Dramatists' Guild's rule would no longer apply. Wildberg and Crawford's insistence on having their share of the pie, however, did not endear them to Ira, Dorothy, or the Guild managers.

Ira, in his devotion to George during his lifetime, had taken to managing his accounts and, after his death, became a watchdog over the Gershwin finances. George's works continued to produce a sizable amount of income, much of it involving Ira's own lyrical contributions. This was the case with *Porgy and Bess*. Ira's share here was small, but because of his watchdog role anyone interested in the opera's stage, film, or recording rights had to contend with him.

Rose Gershwin's estate provided for several trustees—her three children and two lawyers. Her son Arthur had done less well than the other two remaining offspring, and to him she left a stipend of $25,000 a year and, in addition, 40 percent of George's royalties. Frankie also received a 40 percent share, but Ira was left with 20 percent, which would lapse at his death. This nettled Ira; it left his wife, Lee, out in the cold, a reflection, perhaps, of the East Coast Gershwins not getting along well with Ira and Lee on the West Coast, where they had remained after George's passing.

Not that Ira and Lee were in dire need. In 1941, Ira teamed with Kurt Weill and Moss Hart on the highly successful *Lady in the Dark,* starring Gertrude Lawrence and the effervescent Danny Kaye. And he continued writing lyrics for films and other stage works. But the electric charge on his energies that George had supplied was not there. He was more than comfortable in his Roxbury Drive home in Beverly Hills. "As long as I have ASCAP," he once said, "I won't have to pass cap."

During the time it took to settle Rose Gershwin's estate, the terms of her bequests changed. The three heirs finally managed to agree among themselves that Ira was entitled to an equal share and that his share could go to Lee in the event of his death. But it was during this period that Breen and Davis had to contend not only with Rose Gershwin's trustees, and Dorothy Heyward, but other bidders, which now included the Guild. Merely getting all the lawyers, agents, and principals together in one meeting at one time was a problem; after this came the problem of making up their collective minds. Dorothy Heyward was sympathetic to Breen and to his ideas for presenting the opera. Moss Hart, a friend of Breen's, was enlisted to get Ira's approval. Rose Gershwin had made a trustee of a lawyer friend who raised everyone's hackles. He had a 5 percent stake in the trust he had helped set up and therefore had a motive and a voice. In fact, a few years before, he had attempted to produce the opera himself, until Ira stepped in.

After a year of frustrating negotiations, a serious sticking point developed when Breen, not yet all that familiar with the opera or those who might perform it, thought it a good idea to bring in Cheryl Crawford, his former production associate at ANTA, as an overall adviser and consultant. But as soon as her name came up, the negotiations were suspended. It came out now that the Gershwins (and Dorothy Heyward, too) had been unhappy with Crawford's *Porgy and Bess* in spite of its long run and box-office success. They took to calling it the "bargain basement production." Assurances were sought that Crawford not be organically involved in this one and that none of her ideas would be imposed. She had not only whittled down its running length, she had dispensed with George's recitatives, cut several of the characters, and drastically scaled down the size of the orchestra.

Breen had a long-standing and friendly association with Crawford, now the vice president of ANTA. He was anxious not to offend her and, in fact, felt she would be valuable on casting and other aspects of the production. The copyright owners demanded that he give a pledge in writing about Crawford's noninvolvement. Breen drafted a letter and sent it to all concerned parties on September 14, 1951:

"I feel certain that this whole matter of Cheryl Crawford's possible function in our projected production has been exaggerated and enlarged to unreal proportions. As we all know, Miss Crawford will not be a part of Mr. [Blevins] Davis' contract in any way. He has always felt that since she has once been through the business of producing the opera, that we would want to call on her for help and advice on various aspects of the production. It is not in any way a foregone conclusion that any of Miss Crawford's suggestions or ideas would be put in force willy-nilly. As you know, I have certain definite ideas about the nature of this new production and it will in no way, I assure you, be a re-production of any past presentation."

The Gershwin people still were not satisfied. They wanted additional assurances that Robert Ross, the director of Crawford's version, would not be employed for the new one. Breen talked to Dorothy Heyward and Ira Gershwin about their preferences, and inevitably the name of Rouben Mamoulian came up.

"Gershwin would like to have Mamoulian," Breen told Davis, "but every time he starts talking about him he begins to talk himself out of it. He says what a nice, charming fellow Mamoulian is, but 'whenever he gets into a theatre he thinks he invented the stage and that he superseded the Greeks.' He said Mamoulian signified his willingness to direct, but he had film commitments to take care of first and he would require Alexander Steinert as his conductor." Breen at this point was talking to, and was much taken with, the more experienced conductor Alexander Smallens. For a time he considered José Ferrer as director, then contacted Orson Welles, but without success.

While these nettlesome matters were being worked out, Breen was busy with other projects. Working with the State Department and the air force, he brought *Oklahoma!, Medea,* and the Hall Johnson Choir to the Berlin Festival in the summer of 1951. (He had hoped to bring *Porgy and Bess* instead of *Oklahoma!* and felt vindicated when the superbly trained Hall Johnson Choir proved to be the big hit of the festival.) Later in the year, through ANTA, he arranged the American visit of the famed French actor Louis Jouvet and the company of the Théâtre de l'Athénée from Paris. With *Porgy and Bess* and the grand tour he envisaged for it now his prime interest, complications with the ANTA board caused him to resign his post.

This internationally minded man of the theatre had his beginnings and training in the heart of the American Midwest. He was born in Hibbing, Minnesota, on December 26, 1909, to a grandniece of "Buffalo Bill" Cody and to Henry Breen, an Irishman related to the Dublin revolutionary Daniel Breen. Robert was a stutterer and, while in the Catholic schools he attended, had a leaning for the priesthood. In one of these schools, a priest helped conquer his stutter through the reading and reciting of Shakespeare.

From his father, too, he developed a feeling for theatre. One of Henry Breen's undertakings was an impressive hotel he built in Saint Cloud, with a winter garden that attracted traveling stock companies. A theatre lover, he also built a fine theatre next to the hotel that boasted an inventive air conditioning system. (The theatre still stands and is in the process of becoming a Saint Cloud community center.) At age seventeen, Robert was in a University of Iowa stage production that toured through the Midwest; back at the University of Minnesota, a year later, he joined the Minneapolis Repertory Company and took on roles as diverse as Captain Hook in *Peter Pan* and Baptista in *The Taming of the Shrew.* At age eighteen he was directing for the College Art Theatre and played Hamlet under his own direction.

During the next few years he was a whirlwind of acting and directing. A

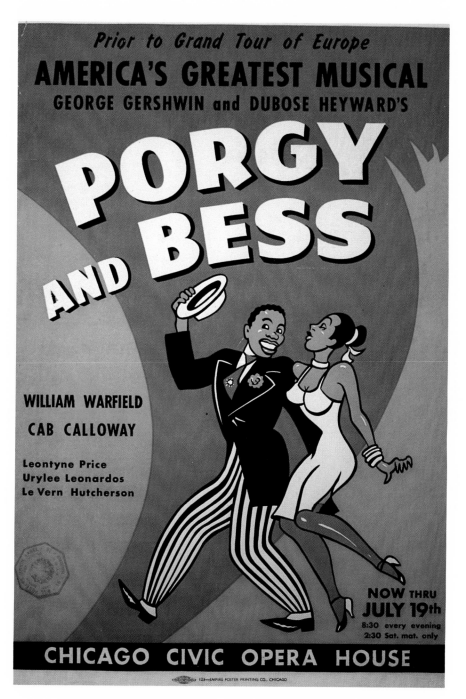

After the Dallas opening, the tour begins—Chicago, 1952.

(Institute on the Federal Theatre Project and New Deal Culture, George Mason University)

Conquest in Berlin—1952.

(Institute on the Federal Theatre Project and New Deal Culture, George Mason University)

Opposite: From Berlin to London—1952.

(Institute on the Federal Theatre Project and New Deal Culture, George Mason University)

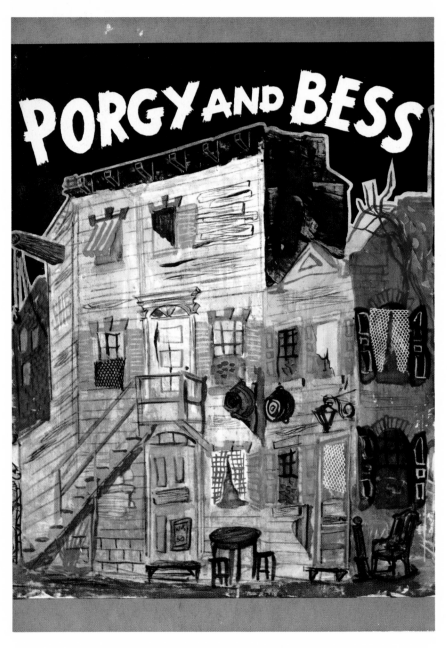

Painting for the program cover—New York, 1953.

(Courtesy of Wilva Davis Breen)

A triumph in Athens — 1954.

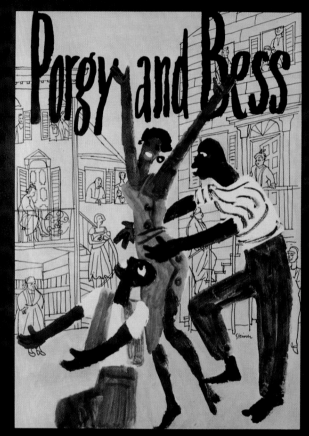

Zurich — 1954.

(Institute on the Federal Theatre Project and New Deal Culture, George Mason University)

Musical history made at La Scala—1954.

(Institute on the Federal Theatre Project and New Deal Culture, George Mason University)

Behind the Iron Curtain—Warsaw, 1956.

(Institute on the Federal Theatre Project and New Deal Culture, George Mason University)

fellow student, Wilva Davis, married at the time, became his companion and eventually his wife. The pair formed a traveling repertory company that performed several plays, including his *Hamlet,* and ended its tour in Chicago. It was here, in 1935, that they were located by Hallie Flanagan, who, as the recently appointed administrator of the Federal Theatre, asked them to survey Chicago's theatre needs. Early the following year they became directors and administrators of Federal Theatre No. 1, which served the Chicago area.

Not for long. Mayor Edward J. Kelly was known for protecting his citizenry from the evil that plays could do and had already banned several, including *Tobacco Road* and *The Children's Hour.* One of the first plays sponsored by the Federal Theatre in Chicago was Meyer Levin's *Model Tenements,* which more than hinted that changes were needed in social and economic systems. This caught the mayor's vigilant eye, and he appointed a priest to clean up the play. Breen was unable to stomach this sort of interference and left his post. It was at this time that he came up with the idea of a U.S. Public Arts Foundation, which would replace the already politically raddled WPA arts projects.

During his hectic careering, he caught the attention of John Barrymore, who invited him to come out to California to produce and direct him in a *Hamlet* that would be performed in the Hollywood Bowl. Breen remained in Hollywood for two years, during which time the aging and alcoholic Barrymore vacillated between doing *Hamlet* or *Macbeth* (so that his young wife, Elaine, could play the infamous lady) and a dreadful comedy, *My Dear Children,* which Elaine selected as ideal for her Broadway debut. This, too, was enough for Breen. Now in New York, he started an experimental theatre which he called the American Art Theatre. It was in Virginia, acting Hamlet at Robert Porterfield's Barter Theatre, that he and Porterfield drew up a more formal plan for a National Theatre Foundation, which, as it turned out, was Breen's passport to ANTA. The two had met in the army earlier, and even then they were besieging ANTA board members with their theatre ideas.

By the time of his involvement with *Porgy and Bess,* Breen's goals were turning more and more to the internationalizing of theatre communities. He was exceedingly ambitious, but loftily unconcerned about money matters. As Brooks Atkinson noted, "Breen regarded an empty treasury as an inspiration, never worried about his salary, because he drew none, never worried about the landlord, because he and his wife installed the ANTA headquarters in the apartment they occupied over the Hudson Theater." Entered through what looked like a stage entrance, the upper two floors of the cavernous apartment served as living quarters and office, out of which poured a ceaseless barrage of correspondence typed by Wilva, Breen, and a secretary. There was a room for auditioning and another where luncheon discussions could be held free from noise and the interruptions of waiters. Much of the haggling on the rights to *Porgy and Bess* took place here, when Breen was able to get together everyone concerned. It was not until January 24, 1952, that contracts were at last signed for the staging of the opera. Breen also succeeded in getting Ira to go along with some of the ideas he had for the new production. Times and styles of production had changed since the opera was first heard, he told Ira. He pointed out that a revival of *The Green Pastures* had failed because it was an exact reproduction of the original.

"I don't mean there is in any way anything major to be done," he wrote Ira. "For instance, as I was telling Dorothy Heyward the other day, I heard that in Cheryl's production some years ago it was very difficult indeed to understand the lyrics." And this was also true, he claimed, of Columbia's full-length recording. Part of this was due to sloppy diction, part to the conductor Lehman Engel's inclination to lean too heavily on the orchestra, thereby blurring the singer. Ira and Dorothy Heyward certainly had no objection to his and DuBose Heyward's lyrics being clearly heard.

Breen went quickly into action. He utilized Cheryl Crawford, who was in Europe, by asking her to negotiate for a booking at a large theatre in London. A European manager was hired to arrange for Continental bookings. Blevins Davis came up with $10,000 of working capital toward an eventual budget of $75,000 to $100,000. Wolfgang Roth, who had designed *Medea* for the Berlin Festival, was brought in to create the settings. But now Mamoulian, when faced with a firm date for rehearsals, bowed out. Breen, unable to find a director with the kind of creative dash he wanted, decided, with the agreement of Ira and Dorothy Heyward, that the solution was to take on the direction himself, although he was already managing the entire enterprise. Blevins Davis was helpful when he could be, but he had his interests in the Ballet Theatre to maintain, traveled widely, and his primary usefulness was financial; he paid the bills, sometimes grudgingly, that Breen forwarded to him.

Breen's theatrical tastes, oddly enough, were opposed to opera in general, unless it was staged in a lively, spontaneous, well-acted way. In one of his letters to an opera manager he confessed, "I'm the sort who got more genuine rest and sleep at English and Continental opera performances than I got in bed. The music is wonderful—but I'd rather just listen to it without being bothered by the cluttering up of perfectly good theatres with them. I think all the opera house subsidies should be withdrawn and I'll wager it would somehow lead to a revitalizing of the musical theatre of the world."

In studying *Porgy and Bess*'s score and libretto he saw opportunities for vividly dramatic movement and color, for acting that would enhance the effect of fine voices. He also noticed that some of the musical material, notably the "Buzzard Song," had been excised from previous productions. Disregarding Cheryl Crawford's advice, he saw places where Gershwin's recitative could be used effectively. By transposing some scenes, more dramatic tension could be built. Later on, after several months of performances, he reformed the three-act opera into a first act of four scenes and a second act of six. It was a fuller version than previous ones, but time was saved by eliminating a second intermission.

In search of the finest singers available, Breen and Smallens traveled to Boston, Philadelphia, Chicago, and Cleveland. They hired Lina Abarbanell, a former Viennese operetta singer and a kind of musical talent scout, to spot other prospects and send them to New York for auditions. Early on, Cheryl Crawford suggested William Warfield for the role of Porgy. He had made a notable concert debut in 1950 and, by the time he was signed, had made a stunning film debut as Joe in MGM's *Show Boat*. But well before this, Crawford had employed him in a small role in Marc Blitzstein's *Regina*, an operatic version of *The Little Foxes*. Warfield's availability was limited, however, because of concert commitments. Breen soon saw that for the kind of tour he was planning, and the voice demands, he would need alternates for the principal roles. Salaries could be kept close to Actors Equity minimums except for that of Warfield, who, through *Show Boat*, had reached star status.

During the search for singers, Breen and Dorothy Heyward went to a performance of Verdi's *Falstaff* at the Juilliard School of Music. In the audience that night was Virgil Thomson, who was on the lookout for singers for ANTA's two-week revival of *Four Saints in Three Acts*, a response, perhaps, to Breen and Davis going independent with *Porgy and Bess*. The twenty-four-year-old Leontyne Price sang the part of Mistress Ford, and, soon after, Thomson gave her the chorus role of Saint Cecilia. During the opera's run, Breen invited her to his apartment office to meet with him and Dorothy.

In her early years in Laurel, Mississippi, Leontyne Price came under the sponsorship of Mrs. Alexander Chisholm, a musician and the wife of a banker. She saw the child (a niece of her maid) as musically gifted and gave her piano and voice lessons. During Leontyne's junior year at Central State College in Ohio, Mrs. Chisholm arranged for her to go to New York and sing for a jury at Juilliard. She was immediately granted a full scholarship.

Breen had not yet decided on his Bess when Price arrived for her audition.

William Warfield came to Porgy and Bess *after a triumph in the film* Show Boat. *(Lawrence and Lee Theatre Research Institute, Ohio State University.)*

Leontyne Price, of the Breen-Davis 1952 production.
"A Bess of vocal glory," a critic raved. (Lawrence and Lee
Theatre Research Institute, Ohio State University.)

Because she was planning to go to Europe to study on a Fulbright fellowship, "I wasn't too excited," she remembered. "They talked with me and I sang 'Summertime' and some other things from *Porgy*." Breen and Heyward were all for using her, but had to talk Ira Gershwin out of his objection that she lacked the stage experience for so exacting a role. She was signed two days after her visit—rehearsals were soon to begin—and Price gave up her plans to study abroad, where she had decided to stay when *Four Saints* went to Paris for a brief engagement.

Breen, confident that he could train Price in whatever acting skills she needed, was inclined to select excellent singers with college and music degrees, with the result that the educational quotient of the company—replete with music and university degrees—was high. He was not unaware of the impression this would make when they went abroad.

Over the years, *Porgy and Bess* was noteworthy for creating careers for its performers, for providing a stepping-stone to greater achievement and fame, and, in some cases, providing rescue. Cab Calloway was on a downhill slide from his glory years when Breen approached him to play Sportin' Life. During the Depression years he was one of America's best-loved entertainers and a musician greatly respected by jazz aficionados. Starting out from the back streets of Baltimore, he made his way through the jazz clubs of Chicago to Harlem's Savoy Ballroom and to Broadway in the revue *Hot Chocolates*. With the band he formed he spelled Duke Ellington at the Cotton Club.

Ellington had the star name then, but when Cab Calloway wrote a song called "Minnie the Moocher" and sang it in a piercing tenor, dancing and cavorting around the stage, the patrons went wild. He became one of the kings of the big band era and flourished right through World War II until the big bands lost their popularity. Jazz had turned cool, the big nightclubs and dance palaces faded away, and the movies and television took over. Cab called in his musicians, told them the band couldn't get bookings, and kept only a few members for a small combo.

During the good years he was profligate with his high earnings. During the bad years, after 1947, he made matters worse with his passion for horse racing. He traveled the country with his seven-piece group, then cut that down to a trio. He was at one of his lowest points when he received a letter from Breen in March of 1952 asking if he would be interested in playing Sportin' Life in *Porgy and Bess*. "I didn't pay any attention to it," he said. "A few days later, in Denver, I got a long-distance call from Breen, who convinced me this was a serious proposition."

"Cab had a lot of mixed feelings about it," his wife, Nuffie, revealed. "He had been away from the stage since *Hot Chocolates* in 1929, and he didn't know if he could do it. Finally he agreed to try it. God bless Robert Breen. He was fantastic, and he knew how to get the best out of Cab."

It was Lina Abarbanell who spotted a handsome, burly young man, an imposing six feet six inches tall, in a production at Cleveland's Negro Karamu Theatre, famous in the area for its productions that mixed first-rate amateurs and professionals. John McCurry had spent six years in the army, rising from private to captain, and was now in college, getting language and music degrees, and driving a bus and sometimes working in a steel mill for income. Acting and singing for him was fun, but not something he thought of as a moneymaking career. He became theatre-struck when he found himself applauded in Shaw's *Androcles and the Lion*. Lina Abarbanell heard of him when he sang the Escamillo counterpart in the theatre's production of Oscar Hammerstein II's *Carmen Jones*, a contemporary *Carmen* with a black cast.

He had never heard of *Porgy and Bess* when he was told he was wanted for an audition. " 'Summertime,' you know." "Oh, sure," he said. He was brought to New York and auditioned with fifteen others in a hotel room across the street from Breen's apartment. The accompanist was Samuel Matlowsky, the assistant conductor to Smallens. When Smallens arrived, Matlowsky pointed McCurry out to him. To his own amazement, McCurry was immediately taken on for the role of Crown and learned that he would actually be paid for singing and acting. Henceforth, his life and living would be as a performer.

Rehearsals began on May 5, 1952, in a Harlem second floor studio at 116th Street and Lenox Avenue, Breen having made up his mind only a few days before to take on the direction. Plans had been made, changed, made again; now the starting place for the projected tour was the auditorium of the annual state fair in Dallas, Texas.

IN THE EARLY stages, especially while the contract for the rights was being worked out, plans about where and when the company would perform were fluid. There were several options, most of them assiduously explored by Breen, his wife, and his assistant, Warner Watson.

From his European manager, Anatole Heller, came word that the Maggio Musicale in Florence wanted the production and that La Scala in Milan was also expressing great interest. Appearances in West Berlin and Paris seemed certain, and there was every likelihood of a lengthy run in London. While developing the projected European tour, Breen and Davis also talked with the managers of the New York City Center and the Metropolitan Opera about a run long enough to pay the way to Europe. The pockets of Blevins Davis were, after all, not boundless. The City Center negotiations fell through because the dates Breen wanted would conflict with its own opera season.

Breen, in mid-February of 1952, talked with Rudolf Bing and Reginald Allen, the Metropolitan Opera's general manager and business manager, respectively, about playing in that house before leaving for Europe. Davis was often out of New York on other interests while Breen did the planning and negotiating, but Breen kept him fully informed.

Breen wrote him: "Anthony Bliss came over here on Thursday, February 14th, and reported that the Metropolitan Board is most enthusiastically in favor of having *Porgy and Bess* at the Met, and want to make it sort of a continuing deal for touring here in this country, and playing at the Met first, upon return from Europe. The estimation is that with three weeks of playing time, at popular prices, we could pay off our entire production cost, and make some money. . . . I think you know that if we do the Met thing, part of the agreement is that while the production is overseas, it will have to be billed as 'Blevins Davis, etc. presents the Metropolitan Opera Production of PORGY AND BESS.'"

The Met, however, would be unavailable until after Labor Day of 1952, at which time Breen had hoped to bring *Porgy and Bess* to the Berlin Arts Festival and gain with it State Department backing for a subsequent European tour. Meanwhile, he was being pressed by Charles Meeker, the manager of the Dallas State Fair, to open its summer season. During the spring of 1952, as he gathered his cast together, he still had no firm schedule for a company of sixty-five performers and a production staff of eight others. But he felt he was in a position of strength, mainly due to the power of the name of his show and the Gershwin name associated with it. He was certain that rights he had worked so hard to obtain would prove their value.

12

THE BOARD OF the Metropolitan Opera Association met, and word was relayed to Breen and Davis that it had decided against presenting *Porgy and Bess* because of a long-standing policy that allowed only its own productions to play in its house. And as Reginald Allen further explained to Breen by letter: "The Board felt it was unwise for the Metropolitan Opera name to be attached to any single production which would carry this name for the first time into the major Grand Opera centers overseas."

Breen did not take kindly to "no" as an answer. He shot back a reply pointing out that it was Rudolf Bing who had suggested placing a "Metropolitan" label on the production. As for its policy of exclusivity, he thought loosening it would be a very good idea, "especially in the light of *Porgy and Bess* being a unique case in that it requires Negro artists. We know very well indeed," he went on, "that if *Porgy and Bess* did not require Negro personnel, the Metropolitan would have long since acquired the rights for its repertoire. I can safely say that if last year's experiment in national touring had utilized *Porgy and Bess* instead of *Die Fledermaus*, the financial results would have been more than satisfying. . . . It would have earned itself many thousands of new friends who ordinarily would veer away from anything resembling 'opera.'"

The letter had its desired effect. The board met again and decided that its policy could be relaxed in favor of *Porgy and Bess*. But the date set for the opening—September 3, 1952—was six months off and Breen was already locking up his large cast. This made the offer from Charles Meeker in Dallas doubly welcome. Meeker proposed that the Davis-Breen production open its season on June 9 and play for two weeks. The state fair organization would put up $65,000 of a projected $100,000 production cost, and Davis and Breen would be responsible for the balance. If ticket sales held up, Davis would get most of his money back.

Admittedly, opening in Dallas was not as prestigious as opening at the Metropolitan, but it would allow for the production to be mounted, broken in, and mostly paid for prior to touring in the United States and Europe before going to New York. The affiliation with both the Metropolitan and the state fair organization would benefit from a nonprofit setup, Breen felt. Davis went along with this, albeit reluctantly, since he would not be able to earn any profit from his investment. Any surpluses would have to go into other nonprofit enterprises. The name Everyman Opera was given to the new corporation.

Breen scheduled appearances to follow Dallas. Bolstered by advice from Cheryl Crawford, he booked the show in Chicago, Pittsburgh, and Washington, D.C., the cities that in her experience had shown the most welcome to Porgy and Bess.

Meanwhile, Davis was talking to people in high places, most importantly to the president. Truman's intercession during his last year in office may have been a factor in propelling this revival of Porgy and Bess on a lengthy odyssey. Truman certainly had something to do with the swiftly changing racial attitudes in the nation. It was his directive in 1950 that had ordered integration of the previously segregated armed forces. Cases involving segregation were making their way to the Supreme Court. State Department officials were worrying about America's image abroad, where charges of racial harassment, even oppression, were rampant.

The company had already set out for Dallas when word came that the State Department was now keenly interested in sponsoring appearances in Vienna and West Berlin as part of its international cultural exchange program. It particularly wanted to include the opera in the Berlin Festival in September. This presented a dilemma for Breen and Davis, who wanted the sponsorship because the company's heavy transportation bill would be paid to and from Europe, where bookings were already in negotiation. But it would also mean losing the Met engagement, which they were loath to do.

Mary Stuart French, a State Department representative and a fellow ANTA board member, helped sway them. Idealism was added to practical considerations, though Davis and Breen feared a suit by the Met's manage-

Blevins Davis, Alexander Smallens, Robert Breen: "A sense of cultural mission."
(Lawrence and Lee Theatre Research Institute, Ohio State University.)

ment to fulfill their commitment. The Met, however, never acknowledged that it had been passed over. London's largest theatre, the Stoll, was quickly booked to follow Vienna and Berlin and then another theatre in Paris. The tour was already taking on historic proportions.

Ella Gerber, a young woman who had just staged an Equity Library production of *All God's Chillun Got Wings* with a black cast, received a call from Robert Breen to come and see him. But it was not for *Porgy and Bess*—rather, it was on Dorothy Heyward's behalf. She was seeking a director for the play *Porgy,* scheduled to be performed at Charleston's Dock Street Theatre.

Ella Gerber was recommended for the job, but, to her vast displeasure, she was turned down when the people in Charleston decided they didn't want a woman director. Then, suddenly, another call came from Breen. *Porgy and Bess* was going into rehearsal, and he needed an acting coach for assistance in training the cast, especially for the relatively untrained Leontyne Price.

"The next day," Gerber said, "there I was, in the Harlem studio, at the rehearsal. Mr. Breen never told me anything to do, but it was as though I had a pipeline to his brain. As the rehearsing went on, I sensed what was missing. Breen was talented beyond belief, but he liked working freely, and often it was left to me to do the over and over again drilling of certain of the performers, always with the objective of bringing out the characters and making it all live and vibrate. When he came up with the conceptions I was able to help him put them into practice. When it was time to leave for Dallas he seemed to take it for granted that I would stay with the company. 'You're coming with us, of course,' he said, and I said, 'Yes.' Things were made easier for me when my husband, who was both an actor and a photographer, was cast in one of the small white roles. Breen had to find titles for all of us. Warner Watson was his general assistant, Lina Abarbanell was called 'production consultant.' Dorothy Van Kirk was his secretary—she should have been called 'general secretary.' And there was Wilva, who did just about everything, too, and was always encouraging to everybody. Eventually 'stage manager' was added to my acting coach title, but it was taken for granted that I was the assistant director. Breen encouraged the cast to . . . well . . . go and fly, and they responded instantly."

A good many came from music schools and often were picked more for their voices and suitability to the roles than for dramatic skill. "Helen Thigpen, chosen for Serena," Gerber said, "had a gorgeous voice, but did not know how to use herself emotionally, so I rehearsed her constantly, especially for her aria 'My Man's Gone Now,' which she was to sing while climbing stairs in the set. I helped her make it dramatic. I had her walk up the stairs in the halls outside, crying and sobbing, doing it over and over again, so much that others in the cast told her she'd lose her voice if she kept doing it. She didn't, of course. She had the voice for it and wanted to play Bess, but she wasn't physically right for the part."

Leontyne Price had no such fears. She wanted to learn, and William Warfield, with whom she soon became infatuated, was helpful. "She didn't know upstage from downstage, stage right or left, but when she hit that high B flat in her first line," Gerber said, "you knew you were on easy street. Breen had a bold conception of how to do the seduction scene on Kitiwah Island— bold, because you didn't do those things in those days. He had Crown run his hands over her arms, her breasts, down her thighs. Breen had found the music notes for the action in the score, even though the scene had not been played that way before. A strong note is struck and Bess starts to writhe to the music."

Leontyne Price was either shocked by the physicality asked of her or pretended to be. "What would my Pappy think?" she asked solemnly.

Gerber said, "To accommodate a change of scenery that follows the seduction scene, Gershwin had added two and a half minutes after Crown carries Bess off into the bushes. Samuel Matlowsky, who was at the piano for the rehearsals, came to me one day, and said, 'My God, is that in the score?' He thought the dramatic impact would be lost. So we made the scene end right there. That way the audience realizes that Bess is succumbing to Crown, and immediately after learns she's sick and back in Catfish Row."

Breen's avowed purpose in directing the opera was to make it "good theatre, to wring from it every legitimate value and illusion of the theatre." To accelerate its tempo he telescoped scenes so that the action never stopped except for intermissions. With the time saved he was able to restore three songs cut from the original production: the "Buzzard Song," "Roll Them Bones," and "I Ain't Got No Shame," the last two sung by Sportin' Life. Ira Gershwin was pleased. In New York to witness rehearsals he told a reporter: "This will be fuller than the 1935 *Porgy*. They have figured a way to change sets without waiting. The curtain actually comes down only once between scenes, so we expect to use some of the business there wasn't time for in the original—some of Jasbo Brown at the piano in the very beginning, and maybe even that one section from the storm scene where you have six different prayers going on simultaneously, all in different keys, but without orchestra. I heard it once at Carnegie Hall and it was beautifully eloquent. I don't know why George took it out." He thought Breen found a perfect place for the "Buzzard Song," switching it from the first to the final act so as to create an air of foreboding before the citizenry of Catfish Row admits to Porgy that Bess has left him.

"Robert," his wife, Wilva, said, "although not a formally trained musician, would shorten the music in one section, stretch it out in another, and inject previously unused music, including recitative, making careful notes which he would give to Alex Smallens, who would work it into the orchestration. One day, Alex invited us to lunch, and spent much of it praising Robert for his changes. Gershwin, he said, should have thought of them. Then, turning to me, he raised his voice to a high pitch. 'But if your husband doesn't stop improving the score, I won't be finished, the orchestrator won't be finished, and we won't be able to open!'"

Neither was Breen averse to adding dialogue, which, after discussions with Dorothy Heyward, was taken from the novel.

Wolfgang Roth provided settings to allow for the fluidity that Breen wanted. Before attempting any designs, Roth, a clown in his early days and a painter, saturated himself with Gershwin's music and Heyward's libretto, then, at libraries, pored over pictures of black quarters in Southern towns. With Jed Mace, the costume designer, he went to Charleston and took a look at Cabbage Row. He decided to represent Catfish Row as Porgy would see it.

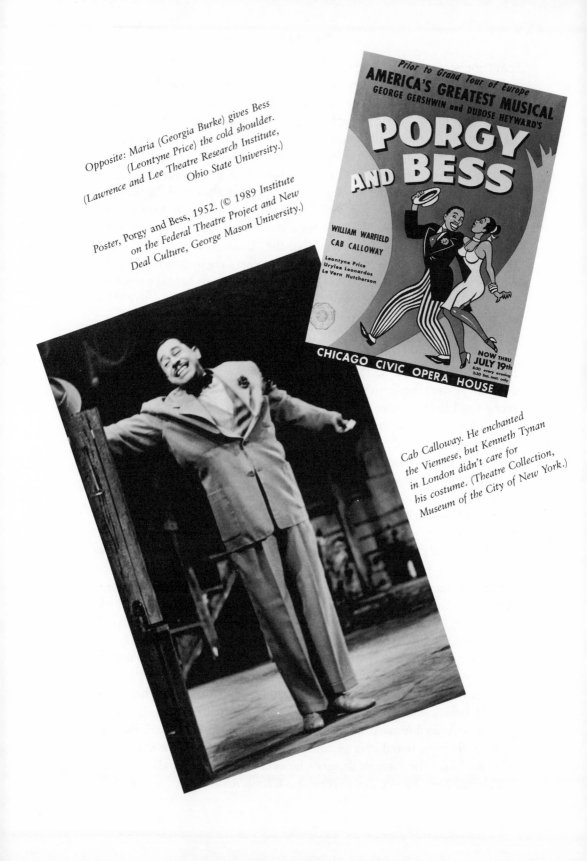

Opposite: Maria (Georgia Burke) gives Bess (Leontyne Price) the cold shoulder. (Lawrence and Lee Theatre Research Institute, Ohio State University.)

Poster, Porgy and Bess, 1952. (© 1989 Institute on the Federal Theatre Project and New Deal Culture, George Mason University.)

Cab Calloway. He enchanted the Viennese, but Kenneth Tynan in London didn't care for his costume. (Theatre Collection, Museum of the City of New York.)

"From his knees," he said, "not as seen by an observer from New York, but a crippled, unsophisticated Negro."

Breen had his own requirements for playing areas and stage levels, which Roth incorporated into his designs. For the hurricane scene, a sizable section of the Catfish Row set was made to revolve so that the action played on the upper level of a small interior set. Breen wanted the effect of much humanity, seeking shelter, huddled in a small space.

He wanted vivid action, too. For the fight scene between Crown and Robbins he provided John McCurry and Howard Roberts (who was also found at Cleveland's Karamu Theatre) with a genuine stevedore's cotton hook and a menacing switchblade knife and made the battle so strenuous that both men were exhausted by each day's rehearsing. Breen asked Roberts to try keeping a bag filled with catsup under his shirt, so that when Crown knifed him, blood would apparently flow. But at the first performance, the gasps and outcries from the audience were so loud that Smallens fumed to Breen, "You're ruining my show!"

Breen worked to give each character part, no matter how small, its

Robert Breen directs new cast members while on tour. Seated, right, is Maya Angelou. (Lawrence and Lee Theatre Research Institute, Ohio State University.)

individuality, naming those left unnamed in the libretto. When Eva Jessye inquired about the placement of her chorus, she was told there was no choral body as such; each member would be part of the general action.

Lillian Hayman, who played Maria, recalled, "Mr. Breen would sit down and watch you in your daily movements and would integrate those into the show—it made it so much more comfortable in what we were doing. There were scenes of playing cards in the show, and we often played cards off the show, mainly while traveling by train. Cab Calloway, John McCurry, I, and a few others had a poker club. One time Mr. Breen bought a tape recorder and set it up in the poker game. Then he took some of the expressions we used and integrated them into the crap game scene. Sayings like, 'Oh, man, go ahead.'

"There were times when we in the cast objected to what he wanted—do this or say that. We were singers most of us, and we didn't want it to be too Uncle Tomish, the stereotype sort of thing."

Breen was careful, Wilva remembered, not to give directions for stereotypical movement or speech. "However," she said, "when he began to detect a certain formality in the speech of some of the cast he called them all together and rose to considerable emotional heights in a little speech. He said, in effect: 'I understand that your backgrounds are not like those in Catfish Row. I know that many of you have Master's degrees in music and fine cultural backgrounds. And I cannot and will not tell you how to get the essential flavor of Catfish Row.

" 'But I know this,' he went on, 'if I were cast in an Irish folk play, I would come up with all the richness of the Irish countryside, all the local color, all the special and individual reactions that would set them apart, I would call upon every bloody Irish ancestor in my heritage, soak myself in Irish literature, and I would revel in it.'"

"After that," Ella Gerber said, "their attitudes toward the story and the nature of the material became more understanding. They accepted it as from another time and place, and they found a way to identify with the characters they played. And above all, they were thrilled to be working, and at the prospect of going to places like Vienna."

"When it was done, those little touches," Lillian Hayman said, "with the singing and the orchestra, it always worked."

A S T I P U L A T I O N that Breen had insisted on before signing a contract with the Dallas manager was that blacks be allowed seating on any level of the state fair auditorium. He followed the letter of the agreement. Blacks

Serena (Helen Thigpen), on stair landing, looks disapprovingly at the
gamblers under Robert Breen's animated direction.
(Lawrence and Lee Theatre Research Institute, Ohio State University.)

were there in both the orchestra and balcony — but far over on the left side.
As a member of the cast remarked: "We been desegregated out there,
sidewise."

But just before the opening performance, a more disturbing incident
occurred. One of the local stagehands made a crude racial remark to a
member of the cast, which was reported to Breen. "He immediately went to
the manager," Wilva related, "and told him calmly that the stagehand must
leave, and that unless he was sent away, the curtain would not go up. The
manager tried to brush the matter off, but Breen was insistent. His own
people, he said, would be patrolling the curtain, and if that stagehand was
still there, it would not go up. And the man was not to be there through all of
the two weeks of performances. The manager finally gave up, and sent the
stagehand away."

John Rosenfeld of the Dallas *News* was there to report on the performance for *The Saturday Review*. The production was impressive, he found, but it was "primarily a sumptuously sung *Porgy*, of which Leontyne Price has been the Dallas sensation. The voice, a bright and focused soprano, has great impact, but this is only half of it. She brought a lively theatrical imagination to the role of Bess, limning the animal passion and the alternating goodness of Crown and Porgy's woman with such vivid detail that the first-night audience lost its composure when she took her final curtain call."

Aside from Price, Rosenfeld regarded the opera as "a curiously de-Africanized *Porgy and Bess* that Breen delivered. A reason perhaps is what has happened to the Negro population between 1935 and 1952. The strut-ting and shouting, the dialect English, the primitive reactions now have to be acquired. Warfield, for example, sang 'I Got Plenty o' Nuttin' as 'I've Got Plenty of Nothing.'" But Rosenfeld also thought "this flavor of operatic impersonation" actually helped. "The Gershwin score is no more authen-tically Negroid than Bizet's *Carmen* is Spanish. The music, like the book, is about Negroes, not of them."

Eva Jessye, a veteran of the first production, contrasted Leontyne Price with Anne Brown, the original Bess. "Leontyne played it blacker," she said, "if you know what I mean. She was from a little town in Mississippi, after all, while Anne Brown was the high-toned daughter of a Baltimore physi-cian." Oddly, Jessye rather regretted the elimination of what she called "the nigger word," at least where a moment in the original production was concerned. When confronted by Sportin' Life's proffer of happy dust to her, Anne Brown gave vent to "Take that stuff away, nigger!"

"She gave it such a gut-bucket quality," Jessye said, "that it just wrenched your heart."

Taking in nearly $100,000 during its two-week Dallas run, *Porgy and Bess* became, the *Times-Herald* reported, "the box-office champion in the history of summer musical shows in Dallas." When it moved on to the huge Civic Opera House in Chicago, it had to contend not only with the summer heat but with the Republican National Convention. Starting slowly, but hailed by the Chicago critics as the best-sung version yet, it gained momen-tum and by the last of its three weeks was playing to standing room. In that city came the announcement that Leontyne Price would marry the thirty-two-year-old William Warfield.

Breen kept Cab Calloway out of the show in Dallas—instead using Lorenzo Fuller for Sportin' Life—and did not bring him onstage until Chicago. Calloway was having problems adapting to stage technique. He was used to dominating a stage and working alone, facing the audience directly. Breen kept telling him, "You aren't one-to-one out there; you are with these other people." Calloway grew depressed and thought of leaving the show. "It worried him," his wife, Nuffie, said, "that he wasn't giving the best that was in him. In a while, Cab's spirits began to lift; he got the feeling of the work and his depression disappeared like magic." Of the many Sportin' Lifes over the years, Cab Calloway's ranks high, perhaps bettered only by that of John Bubbles, who, after all, was coached by Gershwin himself.

After a week's visit to Pittsburgh, where the Pittsburgh *Post* decided that *Porgy and Bess* now belonged to the ages, Breen's company came to Washington and to the newly desegregated National Theatre. (Its owner had closed the theatre in 1949 rather than desegregate it.) Along the route, instead of employing an entire company of musicians, the orchestra was augmented to thirty-six musicians by members of the local symphonies, easy enough to arrange during the summer season. In Washington, most were first-desk members of the National Symphony.

Opening night on August 6 was a gala affair, with members of the

Eva Jessye, the choral director for three productions of the opera.
(Sam Kasakoff photo, courtesy Ella Gerber.)

government, society, and the diplomatic corps braving the August heat. President and Mrs. Truman flew in from Independence to be present. Their special guest was Perle Mesta, home from her chores as U.S. minister to Luxembourg. The British, Chinese, and Philippine ambassadors came, as did several members of the Truman cabinet. Blevins Davis was much in evidence, his long-standing friendship with the Trumans being noted, and, fittingly, so was Clarence Derwent, who had led Actors Equity in fighting and ending segregation at the National. Hotels for the sixty-five cast members were another matter; Breen had his staff search out the best accommodations for them prior to arrival. Breen had asked the white members of his staff to read books on black experiences in order to be better aware of the problems that would be faced as they moved from place to place.

Hanging over the evening was the knowledge that the show would soon go abroad under State Department sponsorship. Jay Carmody of the Washington *Star* declared that "America has grown up at last to *Porgy and Bess.* A superlative cast sang the work to an audience which appreciated and understood its compassionate revelation of Negro life in this alien hemisphere. It was one of the democracy's historic moments, and sharing its richness was a community that registered its delight with an ovation at curtain's fall."

Richard L. Coe, drama critic for the Washington *Post,* dragged out a virtual dictionary of praise for the performance. Of the Gershwin score— "magnificent vitality." Smallens's conducting and Eva Jessye's molding of the chorus "could hardly be better performed." Cab Calloway—"what a perfect Sportin' Life." Leontyne Price—"a Bess of vocal glory." William Warfield "has the voice to match her." Robert Breen—"it is his staging to which this glittering revival owes its brilliance."

President Truman came backstage after the performance to congratulate the cast, which lined up to shake his hand. He may have been surprised by the length of the line. Some cast members, after shaking hands with him once, went around to the back and got in line again. His Secret Service escort got wind of this and laughingly put it to a stop.

Todd Duncan, a Washington resident, also came backstage to congratulate Warfield. He envied the fact that Warfield had a standby (Le Vern Hutcherson) for the matinee performances, but felt that the role of Porgy was less prominent in this production because Breen kept so much happening around him. Warfield mentioned that the little wheeled cart with which he moved around behind the goat (a native of Texas) on the stage was a better-handling model than the one Duncan used.

As the September 1 departure date for Europe approached, more excitement was generated by the marriage of Price and Warfield. The sell-out

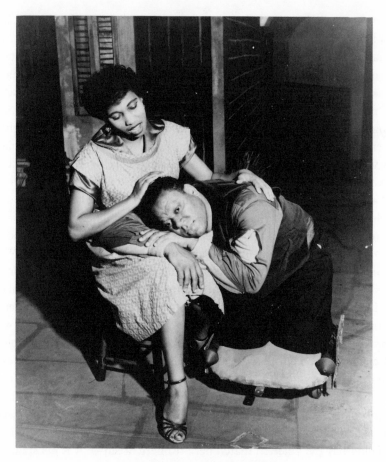

The lovers: Leontyne Price, William Warfield.
(Lawrence and Lee Theatre Research Institute, Ohio State University.)

Washington run ended on August 30, and on the next day, a Sunday, the entire cast went by chartered bus to the Reverend Adam Clayton Powell's Abyssinian Baptist Church in Harlem, where Powell was to officiate. But as he was driving in from Long Island, Powell's brand-new sports car broke down, and he was so upset by this that getting it fixed took precedence over officiating at the wedding. Warfield's father located a substitute, and the wedding took place close to schedule.

Early the next morning, the same bus took the cast back to Washington in time to board a C-54 air force plane bound for Vienna. Three hours out, Warfield noticed something about the sky and the drift of clouds that bothered him. "I went up and talked to one of the pilots," he said, "and they told me they had engine trouble and were heading back, but not to alarm the others. I pretended to be asleep, and when the others found out, too, they thought they were letting me sleep." The plane's trouble, he later learned, was more serious than he had realized. One of the engines had fallen off.

A replacement plane could not be arranged until morning, and no accommodations had been made back in Washington for food and lodging. The army and the State Department were called on to arrange matters. After a long wait at the airport, three buses took the company for what seemed like an endless ride to a suburban restaurant. The white diners in the big, bright room opened their eyes at seeing the stream of blacks pour in. But the maître d' and the waiters ushered them all downstairs to an empty dining room in the basement. Cast members exchanged half smiles and quizzical looks. Soon, though, they got some music and dancing going. The first person to use the toilet facilities came back with the news that there were signs that said WHITE and COLORED, and Cab Calloway asked for a camera. "A picture of this will be valuable soon," he said, "because it's going to be so antique!"

From the restaurant they were taken to the luxurious, then white only, Willard Hotel, near the White House, where the bus drivers were directed to the back entrance. A hotel clerk was waiting with the keys to their rooms, which they all went up and found by themselves.

The flight to Vienna, the following day, was without notable incident.

Although State Department funding was not overly generous and required strict accounting, Breen was imbued with a sense of cultural mission and tended to be above imposed limitations. He wanted the voices to be fresh for all performances, and to make sure they were he carried along three singers for Bess and two each for Porgy and Sportin' Life. With so large a cast there were bound to be illnesses, and he also had to allow for defections during a long touring schedule. So there were substitutes who would be able to fill in for a variety of roles.

The orchestral make-up was less of a problem. A few musicians traveled with the troupe; local talent provided the remainder. Breen was aware of the demands of European opera patrons, so for Vienna and Berlin he specified an orchestra of fifty-two members, more than had ever been used for an American production of the opera.

In addition to the State Department's guarantee of round-trip transportation, its agreement provided for four weekly payments of $15,000 to cover the salaries and housing expenses of cast and crew for the Vienna and Berlin engagements. Neither Breen nor Davis received a fee, and, in fact, the only money Breen ever received was an initial $5,000 for his direction. His living expenses while on tour were charged as a company expense.

Another stipulation was that the money be paid through a nonprofit institution, in this case ANTA (Breen himself had set this avenue up while serving as ANTA's executive secretary), and that Everyman Opera be on a nonprofit basis, which, as it happened, Breen had already anticipated.

When it came to the nonsupported runs in London and Paris, he faced other problems. The value of the dollar was high in comparison to the postwar currencies in Europe, yet Actors Equity insisted that the cast be paid mostly in American dollars. Box-office receipts not only shrank when turned into dollars, but ticket prices were lower than at home. Breen's European manager, Anatole Heller, tended to undersell the show because of the European view that, being American, it was necessarily inferior. When losses occurred, Davis had to make them up.

He found another angel in Herman Sartorius, a former diplomat and businessman, an art lover, and an enthusiastic world traveler. Davis "sold" him a 25 percent interest in the production for $100,000, but somehow neglected to inform him that Everyman Opera was a nonprofit enterprise. Sartorius attached himself to the company when it flew to Vienna and was usually available with ready cash when Breen cried out for rescue. When he realized, through Breen, that his investment would bear no fruit he was furious with Davis, who eventually, after a series of rancorous letters, repaid him.

The way to solve the vexing money problems, Breen decided, was to acquire film rights to *Porgy and Bess,* which he would direct himself and coproduce with Davis. While working out the details of the trip to Europe he was also writing to the Gershwin trustees about his and Davis's desire to make a film on a budget he estimated as a million dollars.

Vienna went wild over the September 7 performance at the Volksoper. "They kept up the applause for half an hour," Ella Gerber said. "They had never seen anything in the theatre like it, the kind of blood, guts, and thunder Breen put into it." The American Embassy turned the opening into a major social and diplomatic event of prewar and bejeweled elegance. Llewellyn Thompson, the Allied high commissioner, invited 550 guests, including the ministers of the Austrian government, and the chiefs of diplomatic missions.

Not to be outdone, Blevins Davis, following the performance, gave a champagne reception for leading theatrical personalities at the Bristol Hotel. At this virtually all-night affair, both Austrian and American singers were prevailed upon to perform. The highlight of the gala night was Warfield, who astonished the crowd by singing Schubert lieder in faultless German. Later on, he gave a recital of lieder for charity at the Mozartsaal of the Vienna Concert House. On another evening, and at another party, Cab Calloway was begged to sing and, after several songs from his repertoire, ended with "Minnie the Moocher" to accompanying "hi-de-ho's" and stormy applause.

The United States Information Service regarded these occasions as important enough to record in a half-hour film. A highlight of the stage performance caught by the film was Helen Colbert's singing of "Summertime," a thrilling performance that has never been surpassed by the many others who have sung it. Colbert, a Juilliard graduate, was a protégée of Marian Anderson's and the winner of the Marian Anderson Award. She remained in Europe after touring with the show, and the only known record of her voice is in the USIS film. Unfortunately, Congress had mandated that U.S. information films be unavailable publicly in this country, and the Vienna negative, if it exists at all, is buried in some government storage place. A print that once belonged to the Breens, however, is in the possession of the Lawrence and Lee Theatre Collection at the theatre institute of Ohio State University.

Vienna had never been very kind to American opera, but the critics now went into paroxysms of praise. "Art becomes life and life becomes art," exulted the *Arbeiter-Zeitung*. "How alive everything is!" exclaimed the critic for *Die Presse;* "What verve, what naturalness!" "This company is the best ambassador for America," claimed another. Crowds lined up at the Volksoper box office to wait for hours for ticket sales to begin. The U.S. Information Center was besieged with requests for seats. One Volksoper attendant shook his head in wonder at the excitement. "Not since Caruso," he said. Viennese citizens stopped any black person they saw on the street, many of them soldiers in civilian clothes, and surprised them by asking for their autographs.

In Berlin, on September 18 at the Titania-Palast, the performance was the principal event of a month-long festival. The reaction was again extraordinary in spite of the audience's lack of understanding of the words being sung and spoken. Applause and shouting continued for twenty-nine minutes; twenty-one curtain calls were counted. No opera lover could remember anything like it having happened in Berlin before. The critical response echoed that in Vienna. "One doesn't know where to praise and where to stop," wrote one who ran out of words. "One sits in the audience amazed, breathless," said a radio commentator, "and again and again surprised how this graceful brown people moves around without any restraints and how completely they live their parts."

Der Tag declared the staging a revelation, an exemplar of how an opera should be played and sung: "Tempo without pause, number after number, unbelievable precision, a feel for rhythm which borders on the fantastic, and voices—voices that take away one's breath with astonishment." Jack Raymond cabled *The New York Times* that it was impossible to exaggerate the acclaim the opera received from the people of Berlin night after night.

One segment of the Berlin press, however, ignored the presence of the American troupe—those in the Russian zone. Strangely, though, Communist marks began to appear in the take of the Titania-Palast box office. Ordinarily, these would have been acceptable only at the rate of five East German marks to one West German. The American State Department quickly ordered that they be accepted at face value, one for one. Soon, East Berliners were coming through the checkpoints in such numbers that news of the show finally made the East Zone's official newspaper.

At the State Department, eyes were opened to the potential good will that such cultural exchanges could foster. Far more than any other presentation, the *Porgy and Bess* success demonstrated the value of subsidizing American entertainment and cultural undertakings for appearances in other countries. And ANTA, because of Breen's initiative, became the umbrella organization for selecting other shows to follow.

The new president, Dwight D. Eisenhower, took notice, too. It was at his urging that an emergency fund was established, with an annual appropriation of $5,000,000, to finance so-called propaganda ventures—half to be used for theatrical productions. As might have been expected from a Congressional appropriation, soon enough politics got into the act.

THE LONDON run was originally set for three weeks. The good word from Vienna and Berlin must have crossed the Channel because a thousand people were turned away from the ticket booths of the Stoll Theatre the first day. Then, because of the large advance sale, Davis and Breen postponed the Paris trip and took the daring step of engaging the Stoll Theatre for several more months. But before the curtain could be raised at the Stoll, a dispute had to be settled with the British Musicians' Union over the conductor. The union threatened to call its members out unless Alexander Smallens handed over his baton to an English conductor after the first three performances. The quarrel went on during the five days of rehearsal, and Breen threatened to open with two pianos instead of an orchestra unless the union gave in. A compromise was reached only a few hours before the premiere. An English conductor would share the baton "as soon as practical."

There was also the problem of the goat, regarded as an important member of the cast and brought to Vienna and Berlin. In Vienna, the Texas native was admitted only on condition he not cohabit with any member of the Austrian breed, and Breen was forced to sign a formal paper to this effect. Because of British health regulations, which specified a long period of quarantine for foreign animals, the original goat was left in Berlin. In searching for a substitute, the company manager supplied a description of the type needed: "A medium sized one, preferably with large horns (either female or castrated male). He must pull a very light cart with an actor on it. We have the harness." A suitable goat was rented from a zoo at a nominal charge.

Kenneth Tynan, the youthful and often acerbic critic for the *Evening Standard,* came fresh to *Porgy and Bess* on the first night and saw it as "something of a hybrid—a cross between a modern morality play and an experimental folk opera. Off our gramophone records it came in the flesh, a breast-beating, heart-pounding show. It remains the fullest exploration of the Negro mind any white man has ever made."

Subtlety of characterization, Tynan went on, was not the opera's strong point, but, at the same time, he wrote, "We never know why Bess takes to the virginal Porgy, except that she is a good girl, nor why she deserts him for Sportin' Life, except that she is a bad girl." Other critics over the years found Bess's behavior more intriguing than puzzling. Breen's direction bothered Tynan: too much "indiscriminate, stomping abandon; too much is happening all the time, all over the stage, and we lose focus."

William Warfield won his praise, as did Leontyne Price's Bess ("a brash high-hipped creature with lots of panache . . ."). Cab Calloway impressed him less: ". . . dives in with a mighty splash, dancing in a wild, strait-jacket torment, athirst for the drug called 'happy dust.' Mr. Calloway's mistake lies in the cut of his clothes; he looks as if he were backing the show, not just appearing in it."

But with the other critics, all was jubilation. By the end of the year, the show was acknowledged as "The Most Sensational Stage Offering of the Year" (*Show Business Annual*) and "Best Musical" (the London Drama Critics).

Not long into the run came one of the classic London fogs. Traffic stopped. Playgoers (and the members of the company) made their way to the theatre flashing lights, ringing bells, and shuffling feet so as not to bump into anyone. In the theatre the musicians could barely make out the conductor, and on the stage a foggy mist did strange things to the lighting. Breen loved the effect; he wished there was some way to emulate it after the fog was gone.

The economics of the run demanded reasonably full houses. But slack periods developed, and after three months or so there were too many empty seats. If they continued playing through the period of the contract the losses would be large. Billy Rose provided a solution. He was seeking a tenant for his large Ziegfeld Theatre in New York, and when he came to see the show in London he thought it would run well back home. And he had another idea for Breen and Davis. He had recently produced *Carmen Jones* and thought that by pairing it with *Porgy and Bess* they could have the spine of a Negro repertory company, with the added benefit for Rose of a long season at the Ziegfeld. After talking over the idea with Rose, Breen wrote Davis: "With *Porgy and Bess, Carmen Jones* and maybe an adaptation of Offenbach's *Orpheus in Hades* we could have a musical repertory company that would keep going 52 weeks a year—either in New York or on the road in U.S. or on the continent. As you know, I have always been in favor of this."

It took some negotiating, but Davis and Breen were able to wriggle out of their contract with the managers of the Stoll and, in February 1953, left for Paris. There the show was greeted by what were now the usual critics' hosannahs. "It is life itself!" "A triumph!" "A masterpiece . . . one doesn't have to say more." Gendarmes were needed to keep those without tickets from crashing the gates of the Empire Theatre.

With the cheers of the Paris audiences still ringing in their ears (the most enthusiastic of all, Leontyne Price remembered), with a sense of triumph and a head full of ideas and plans involving *Porgy and Bess* for the future, Breen and his company flew back to New York, courtesy of the U.S. Air Force, on March 1, 1953. The cast, on arrival, was owed a week of paid vacation, after which this now heralded version of *Porgy and Bess* would have its New York opening at the commodious Ziegfeld Theatre.

13

B REEN HAD studied the reviews of the first production of the Gershwin opera in 1935 and noted the discrepancy of opinion between the music and the drama critics who had jointly covered the premiere. He saw that the music critics, worrying if the work was truly an opera, had given the public muddled impressions of the show. He was determined not to let the same thing happen. The official opening at the Ziegfeld was on March 10, 1953, but on March 9 what was called a "professional performance" was given for an invited audience of theatre people and drama critics. Music critics received tickets for the next day's opening. As a result, the main body of reviews came from the drama critics, and they were sensational. The steam was taken out of the music critics, and, in fact, they received little space for what was already yesterday's news.

Breen made this strategy a policy from then on, and it was a condition in all subsequent theatre contracts. As he wrote one manager, "I am a little weary of seeing all the type-space used up by the so-called music critics in discussing *Porgy and Bess* and whether it meets the specifications of being an 'opera.' We are not selling it as an opera but as a theatre piece." If it had to be labeled he preferred the term "musico-drama."

Blevins Davis also used a bit of strategy to enhance the New York appearance; while still in London, he wrote Billy Rose that it was necessary to get a letter for the Ziegfeld souvenir brochure from the new president,

Eisenhower, praising "this Negro group of artists for what they have done for establishing good will between the countries . . . a direct answer to the communists that will destroy their charges that the Negro is enslaved, etc." Rose contacted Bernard Baruch, who contacted the White House, and the letter duly came: "I have heard reports of the extraordinary success that met your European trip. I cannot emphasize too strongly how serious and enduring this work seems to me. You and your company are making a real contribution to the kind of understanding between nations that alone can bring mutual respect and trust. You are, in a real sense, ambassadors of the arts."

The president's view, however, was not shared by some members of the black community. Protestations, not always from blacks, had occurred earlier when the State Department had announced its sponsorship of the *Porgy and Bess* company's trip to Europe. One member of Congress thought it too ticklish a matter for State Department involvement, complaining that Europeans would assume the squalid life portrayed in the Catfish Row setting had its counterpart in reality and would help feed Communist propaganda about Negro "slave conditions." Of concern to the black protestors was what they called the "negative" picture being drawn yet again by *Porgy and Bess* of the "ignorant, primitive" Negro.

The Washington *Post*'s Richard Coe, a strong proponent of both the show and its European expedition, took notice. He asked: was *Carmen* indicative that all Spaniards were smugglers addicted to free love? Or that because of Gilbert and Sullivan operas the denizens of Victorian England were all assumed to be halfwits and misplaced babies?

"Isn't our most vital contribution to the world our vaunted freedom of expression?" he asked. "How would we look to the people on whom we are trying to impress this very quality if we said, 'No, *Porgy and Bess* shows a side of life we don't want you to know about!'"

Brooks Atkinson said in *The New York Times* that it wasn't easy to dismiss objections that the opera would do more harm than good abroad because it portrayed "the Catfish Row Negroes as poverty-stricken, tattered, superstitious people, and some of them as criminals." He agreed that "from the literal point-of-view *Porgy and Bess* is not a flattering portrait of American life." He invoked *Electra* and *Lysistrata*, however, pointing out that they were hardly flattering portraits of Greek life, ancient or modern.

But detractors of *Porgy and Bess* were not appeased. Lester Walton, chairman of the Coordinating Council for Negro Performers, wrote a letter in reply to Atkinson's analogy. The influence of Greek civilization and culture had been known throughout the world, and the plays mentioned would not have a counteracting effect, he said. He strongly doubted, however, that in most European capitals there was much knowledge of Negro life in America. Because Europeans lacked intimate knowledge of Negro progress, they would be incapable of positive differentiation.

His organization was active the previous year when *Amos 'n' Andy* was brought to television with a Negro cast. It requested, "with success, the elimination of objectionable characters, such as the lawyer whose clowning and ungrammatical language were an insult to the legal profession." The sensitivity of "colored and white Americans" to the prevalent situation was due, he said, "to the addiction of producers to caricatures and stereotypes that fail to give the public an opportunity to see the Negro portrayed in the field of entertainment in a favorable and dignified light. There can be no denying that racial misunderstandings are accentuated by stereotypes which, while true to life, are not subject to generalization."

The mouthpiece of the American Communist Party, *The Daily Worker,* decided that touring *Porgy and Bess* as "a move," in the words of Blevins Davis, "designed to counter Communist propaganda that American Negroes receive no recognition in the arts" was a double-edged sword. Davis's design, said the *Worker,* "was meant to prove a lie." Furthermore it would only "further the vicious fiction of Anglo-Saxon superiority."

The *Worker* brought out some figures to show the lack of black progress in the theatre: from September 1, 1951, to March 15, 1952, 692 players were used in forty-nine Broadway productions. Only thirteen were Negroes, and eleven of these had nonspeaking roles. Television and radio were equally guilty of lopsided use of Negro performers. In grand opera in New York, only five Negroes were employed. What the *Worker* did not bring out was the large increase in off-Broadway and grass-roots theatre. Institutions such as Juilliard, the Cleveland Institute of Music, the New England Conservatory, the Chicago Conservatory, and the American Theatre Wing School were busy developing black concert and operatic artists. The talented cast of *Porgy and Bess* came from a host of schools and institutions. Broadway and the New York opera and concert halls were still the primary lure, but it was a large country out there and its hunger for entertainment and culture provided opportunity for gifted black artists.

But it was not until the Breen-directed production arrived in New York and established itself as a full-fledged hit, with its huge cast bringing black employment on Broadway to a temporary peak, that a more furious attack came, not from *The Daily Worker* but from black writers for the Negro press. In a leading weekly, the Baltimore *Afro-American,* and widely reported in other black media, James Hicks declared the opera to be "the most

"THE MOST EXCITING THING IN NEW YORK"
— WOLCOTT GIBBS, THE NEW YORKER MAG.

"UPROARIOUS" "TRIUMPHANT"
—N.Y. Times

"THRILLING" "GLORIOUS"
—N.Y. Mirror

"SENSUOUS" "FABULOUS"
—N.Y. World Tel. & Sun

"SUPERLATIVE" "IRRESISTIBLE"
—Brooklyn Eagle

"TRIUMPHANT" "THRILLING"
—C.S.

"LUSTY"
—N.Y. Jour.-Amer.

"RAW" "ELECTRIFYING"
—N.Y. World Tel.

PORGY BESS
by GEORGE GERSHWIN
DU BOSE & DOROTHY HEYWARD
and IRA GERSHWIN

"SUPERCHARGED" "RACY"
—N.Y. Herald Trib.

"HILARIOUS" "IRRESISTIBLE"
—N.Y. Mirror

"ENCHANTING" "DYNAMIC"
—N.Y. Post

"THRILLING" "TRIUMPH"
—Morning Telegraph

"DAZZLING"
—Christian Science Monitor

"MAGICAL"
—Wall St. Journal

"PRIMITIVE" "DARING" "TERRIFIC"
—N.Y. World Tel. & Sun

"MAGNIFICENT . . . PASSIONATE"
—BROOKS ATKINSON, N.Y. TIMES

AIR-CONDITIONED

ZIEGFELD THEATRE
6th AVE. AT 54th ST.   MATS. WED. & SAT.

Porgy and Bess *wows the critics in New York (1953), after returning from its first tour abroad. (© 1989 Institute on the Federal Theatre Project and New Deal Culture, George Mason University.)*

insulting, the most libelous, the most degrading act that could possibly be perpetrated against the Negro people.

"This disgraceful felony, against a race of people which is struggling to hold its head high, is further compounded by the fact that our U.S. State Department selected *Porgy* as a show to which it gave its blessings."

His diatribe, however, did not discourage black attendance at the Ziegfeld and caused Hicks to wonder why "forward-looking Negroes who are indignant when they are identified with brawls and cutting in crap games will sit beside white people and rock the rafters with cheers when whites hire Negroes to do just those things."

He saw disgrace in the fact that "the full beautiful voice of Leontyne Price as Bess" was not being heard in the Metropolitan nor were other black voices "second to none in the nation. Instead they are intermingled with the rattle of dice which roll across the stage throughout *Porgy.*"

Hicks was quickly challenged by H. Hayes Strider, head of the music department at Morgan State College in Baltimore. Professor Strider had sung in the Fisk University Choir with Le Vern Hutcherson, who was singing Porgy in the absence of William Warfield, who was on concert tour. He had seen the 1935 and 1942 productions of the show and felt that *Porgy and Bess* had come of age in the Breen version, that it was more vibrant and vital. "It is life itself!"

Duke Ellington took sides when he reversed himself in his earlier opinion of the opera and telegraphed Breen: "Your Porgy and Bess the superbest, singing the gonest, acting the craziest, Gershwin the greatest." When a black reporter went backstage to interview members of the cast he found sharp disagreement with Hicks's point of view. "They stir up controversy to sell newspapers," John McCurry claimed. Urylee Leonardos, a native of Charleston, who alternated with Leontyne Price as Bess, said she knew from personal experience that Catfish Row had its truth in the experience of a large segment of black people. "You can find Catfish Row," she said, "in New York and Chicago." So, for a time, the controversy died down to a simmer.

Warfield was taking plentiful advantage of opportunities on his Columbia Artists concert tour, but he was aware of prevalent attitudes in the black community, to the extent that he hesitated to sing "I Got Plenty o' Nuttin'" in his concerts. "The black community wasn't listening to anything about plenty of nothing being good enough for me," he commented recently. "There was now another feeling in the community about being black—I'm a black man and proud. And with that attitude came a lot of negation and turning your back on things. Hattie McDaniel was accused of Uncle Tom-ism because of her playing of those servant roles in movies.

"But those of us in *Porgy and Bess* saw ourselves as playing only roles, and in no way did we play them as ordinary black stereotypes. It was art, and we were artists. At the same time I have to say there was a fine line as far as my own sympathies were concerned; I could agree with the need for blacks to play roles that would provide more respect.

"One thing the European tour did was to blast away the notion that foreign audiences would misunderstand the show in terms of its black content. They had an intelligent understanding of the real situation in America, and loved the show for its real qualities."

Warfield did not appear in the Broadway run and was upset about it. His contract had allowed him to leave the company in London at the end of December 1952 and rejoin it the following May. He had not expected the New York run to begin so soon. When he completed his concert tour he asked for a raise, and Breen, under firm strictures from Davis to keep costs down, refused. Nor did Davis like the idea that stars such as Warfield and Leontyne Price were intent on advancing their concert careers at the expense of the show. Warfield refused to sign a long-term contract, but indicated his willingness to appear in the movie, if and when it was made. "It was a painful situation for me," he said, "and my relationship with Breen ended, but not with *Porgy and Bess*." He would sing Porgy in two later City Center Opera versions and several more times when the full-length and orchestrally augmented opera went into the repertory of the Vienna Volksoper.

But Warfield or not, *Porgy and Bess* looked to be well established at the Ziegfeld, helped by notices such as that of Walter Kerr: "I am surprised that Berlin, Vienna, Paris and London are still standing. For this is surely the most restless, urgent and shatteringly explosive production of the Gershwin masterpiece we have yet had. . . . As the lights come up slowly on the splintered stairways and sagging shutters of Catfish Row, and as the first strains of 'Summertime' cut across the sultry silence of a South Carolina evening, DuBose Heyward's world of frenzied gayety and passionate violence begins to take on sinuous, insistent life. Hands, bodies, and laughing voices unite in a driving, relentless, and finally irresistible rhythm. The theatre is supercharged with an almost animal fury, and a flaming Bess strides into a Charleston back alley that teems with a raw and racy vitality. Leontyne Price was the Bess and it would be lunacy to ask for a better one. She makes the second act seduction fiercely exciting, and the rueful self-knowledge which she brings to her reunion with the dismayed cripple is honest and haunting playing. . . . In Robert Breen's production, *Porgy and Bess* is an almost uninterrupted series of musical and choreographic detonations, one following the other with the velocity of the hurricane which brings the second act crashing to its climax."

Soviet ambassador Andrei Vishinsky was one of those at the Ziegfeld and suggested to Breen, "Why not bring it to Moscow?" Breen and Davis were already discussing this possibility, and Davis sent word of Vishinsky's casual suggestion to the State Department, causing a ripple of analysis in Washington. Was this a sign of change and thaw toward things American on the part of the Soviet Union? A new line, perhaps? Breen and Davis were told that if a formal invitation came from the Soviet Union, permission for the trip would be granted. Meanwhile, the State Department had other plans for *Porgy and Bess*. Not only was Breen's show regarded as an important musical and theatrical achievement, it was now seen as a potent propaganda weapon in the cold war.

With praise still pouring in for the show at the Ziegfeld, Breen continued tinkering with it, not willing to let well enough alone. The changes sometimes annoyed cast members; they couldn't depend on doing it the same way every performance.

Until New York, audiences had seen a three-act version. Now he changed it to two acts. He wrote to Dorothy Heyward in London: "Remember the old idea about having the show in two parts with only one intermission? As a matter of fact, that is why I had the Serena house designed to roll out—so that it could roll *back*. Well, a week ago we decided to try it and watch the audience carefully for its reactions during the long (1-hour 23-minute) second half. It works very nicely, and saves the 15 minutes used by the second intermission.

"The amusing thing about some of the reaction here to the many changes we've made is that they assume that is the way 'it was written originally.' They talk about how wonderful it is that we 'restored the beautiful dirge' for the transition from scene 1 to scene 2 to scene 3, and about the 'Greek choral effects' in the Buzzard scene—which we added in Paris but which they think was written that way but not used originally."

Meanwhile, it was as though he had to make certain that every moment of the show was charged with energy. Shutters banged open and closed. Everyone on the set was occupied with doing something at all times. The one New York critic to complain about this was the veteran George Jean Nathan, who, while regarding *Porgy and Bess* "as the best achievement thus far in distinctive American opera," regretted what he called "the continual stage hysteria." "Exciting the stage movement," he decided, was characteristic of some modern directors of a "too ambitious ilk."

Breen had his ambitions, all right, and they were far-flung. He wanted to take his production to as many corners of the world as possible, he wanted to enshrine it as a motion picture, and he wanted to make *Porgy and Bess* the cornerstone of a permanent Negro musical theatre.

Soon after the New York opening, Davis and Breen made a determined effort to acquire the screen rights to the work. They made what they considered a generous offer of $200,000, plus profit incentives. But the success of their stage production aroused interest from others and raised the stakes. Several meetings with the various concerned parties took place, and out of these came agreement—or at least so it seemed—that $350,000 was a fair price for Davis and Breen to pay for film rights and that they should make the film for not less than a million dollars.

Breen's relationship with Dorothy Heyward was cordial and she trusted him enough to grant him a five-year option to obtain all her film and television rights in *Porgy* as both novel and play and the opera made from them. This was a ploy by Breen, whose position would thus be stronger in dealing with the Gershwin clan.

In December 1953 all seemed settled. Breen was notified by Emanuel Alexandre, a trustee and attorney for the estate, that he and Davis would receive a ten-year lease on the film rights for *Porgy and Bess* and that Breen would be "solely responsible for the artistic decisions of the production," a statement that Breen took to mean he would be the director. Davis, though, would have to pay $50,000 down and $300,000 more over the next ten years.

And now Davis objected. In essence, he was tired of paying out money; indeed, he thought it time *he* should be paid, having bankrolled the production to its current high prestige. Large sums were owed him; he would never see a profit from the theatre production and didn't expect to, but he thought he should at least be repaid to the extent of his investment. Davis was a peripatetic traveler—to London, Washington, Kansas City, where he had financial interests, and Independence. Because Davis constantly seemed to be somewhere else, it was difficult for Breen to reach an understanding with him. He gathered, though, that Davis would be satisfied with an arrangement that would not cause him to lay out any more advance money—a free option, in other words. Whereupon Breen ventured right into the lion's den, where Ira's agent, Irving ("Swifty") Lazar, was the keeper. Breen flew to California to present a new plan.

But now there were new players in the ball game and the offering price had grown to half a million. Otto Preminger was nosing around the property, as were Joseph Mankiewicz, William Goetz, the producer-director team of William Perlberg and George Seaton, and even that feisty entrepreneur Mike Todd, who saw the opera as ideal for his new Todd-AO process. Ira Gershwin later said that as many as ninety offers were received, including another from the ever faithful Al Jolson, who still wanted to do Porgy in blackface.

In his meetings with Gershwin and Lazar, Breen pointed out that the present value of *Porgy and Bess* as a screen property was directly related to the great acclaim for and popularity of his stage production. He was willing to set a fee for the rights at half a million if Gershwin would recommend to the copyright owners that he be given a year's option on the film rights. "An option for nothing?" Lazar interjected. Obviously this was contrary to all Hollywood law, at least as practiced by agents.

Breen explained that Blevins Davis was not willing to pay for the rights until a production was set and ready to go. He added, however, that if the option were given him in his own name, he would be able to go out and raise the money, or guarantees, for the $500,000. Unfortunately, he had no money of his own for an option.

Lazar offered an alternative, to trade off the advance on an option in exchange for 10 percent of his and Davis's share as producers. Breen readily agreed. He flew back to the company, which by now had left New York for a cross-country tour, buoyed by assurances that the trustees as a body would undoubtedly approve the arrangement. Davis was happy, too; he didn't have to dig further into his pockets for the time being.

After 305 performances at the Ziegfeld, the company opened in Philadelphia on December 1, 1953, and from there headed once again to the National in Washington, then ventured south as far as Richmond, Virginia. Segregated seating, not to mention other discomforts for the cast, made it unfeasible to head deeper into Southern America. In all, the tour took in nineteen cities in the United States and Canada.

In the midst of the tour an invitation came from Venice for a week of performances during its Festival of Contemporary Music. Everyman Opera's European representative, Anatole Heller, was already arranging for a revisit to Paris. From Milan and its famed La Scala opera came a request for

Oscar Levant entertains the cast during its 1953 appearance in Los Angeles. Helen Colbert (Clara) and Lorenzo Fuller (Sportin' Life) look on. (Sam Kasakoff photo, courtesy Ella Gerber.)

the company to perform there early the following year. Musical history would be made, since this would be the first American work and company to be invited to what was generally regarded as the world's premier opera house. The problem for Breen was how to fill gaps in the schedule. The salaries and expenses of the seventy-three-member company had to be paid during off weeks as well as on. Providentially, the State Department now regarded *Porgy and Bess* as an instrument of international good will and proposed (through ANTA's International Exchange Program) a tour of the Mediterranean and Near East that would include stops in Zagreb, Belgrade, Cairo, Athens, Tel Aviv, Casablanca, and Barcelona.

The U.S. government's largesse would hardly enrich the coffers of Everyman Opera; its sponsorship and contribution would amount to no more than providing travel expenses and a guarantee against losses, which would have been inevitable in Yugoslavia, where the price of a ticket came to about sixty cents in American currency.

While the American tour was in progress, Dorothy Heyward was about to see her dream come true: the play *Porgy* would be performed for the first time in her late husband's home city, Charleston. Under the aegis of the Dock Street Theatre, the local production, with a Negro cast (except for two whites) was scheduled for four performances in April 1954, at the County Hall. What was most remarkable, even historical, was that this would be the play's first performance in the Deep South.

Then trouble arose. The Dock Street management had gotten together with the Stagecrafters, a local Negro dramatic organization, for cooperation in casting and—more important—seating arrangements. South Carolina law required "no mixing of the two races in places of amusement" for what were called "historic reasons of compatibility." As a compromise, the president of the Stagecrafters, A. J. Clement, specified that the auditorium be split exactly in half from gallery to orchestra—one side for whites, the other for blacks.

This segregation-by-aisle arrangement caught the attention of the black national weekly magazine *Jet,* which sent up the first rocket. "*Porgy,*" it reported, "will play in Charleston for the first time, twenty-seven years after its birth there. The audience at the County Hall will be segregated for the performance by a predominantly Negro cast." After this the NAACP, which at first had not objected to the seating arrangement, changed its collective mind and demanded no racial separation of any kind; otherwise it would boycott the play and demonstrate actively and aggressively in the city.

Rather than fight, the board of the Dock Street Theatre decided to cancel the production, much to the chagrin of the cast and production staff, who had all worked without pay. And an opportunity was missed to challenge the state statute. Attorneys, both black and white, had been ready to take on the case at a most timely moment: the Supreme Court had just ruled against segregation in public schools.

M O N T R E A L   W A S   the last stop on the North American tour of *Porgy and Bess,* and there a new member joined the company. Maya Angelou was found singing and dancing at a popular night spot, the Purple Onion, when the company had performed in San Francisco.

Angelou was twenty-five, tall, slender, and attractive, recently divorced, and the mother of a small boy. Breen, urged by members of the cast, came to see her and suggested she audition for a vacancy that would soon be coming up: a woman of the chorus who could dance as well as sing. Before joining the company, however, she was offered a more important part in a new Broadway musical, Truman Capote's *House of Flowers.* "There really was no contest," she later wrote. "I wanted to travel, to try to speak other languages, to see the cities I had read about all my life, but most important, I wanted to be with a large, friendly group of Black people, who sang so gloriously and lived with such passion."

She was in Montreal only four days before the members of the company were bused to the Montreal airport, where they boarded a plane bound for Milan. After a nine-hour flight, another bus took them to Venice, with a luncheon stop on the way at the fabled city of Verona. Maya Angelou was in near-ecstasy.

Her true discoverer was a diminutive, pretty soprano of twenty-four, Martha Flowers, who had seen her at the Purple Onion and had brought others there. She had not been long with the company herself. Breen was always on the lookout for replacements. He knew he would soon be losing Leontyne Price, who was anxious to embark on a new phase of her career. He, Wilva, and Ella Gerber took in a student performance of *Così fan tutte* at Juilliard and there came upon Martha Flowers. "Her voice," said Ella Gerber, "was every bit as good as Leontyne's."

Flowers was not only on scholarship at Juilliard but the recipient of the Marian Anderson Award and several others that enabled her to pursue her career. But would she be suitable for Bess, who was usually played by someone tall and willowy? Martha was only five-feet-two, dainty and ladylike (her friends called her "Miss Fine Thing"), the daughter of a Baptist minister in Winston-Salem, North Carolina. She was taken on for the small role of the Strawberry Woman, whose hawking of strawberries to the Catfish

Martha Flowers—"a voice every bit as good as Leontyne's." (Courtesy of Ella Gerber.)

Row residents is in the form of a quite arresting song; then nursed along, singing Clara, until she was deemed ready to move on to Bess. Breen and Gerber were her patient coaches, and the cast members were invariably supportive. Even so, she had no idea that one day she would sing the leading role at that dream goal of all opera singers: La Scala.

But in Venice she sang the Strawberry Woman, and was an alternate for Clara. She, like Maya Angelou, shared none of the attitudes expressed by black critics toward the story and its characters, and fully appreciated its historic and folk origins. Angelou wrote: "I found myself more touched by the tale and more and more impressed by the singers who told it." In the rococo, gilded Teatro la Fenice, the singers, she said, "sang with fresh enthusiasm as if they had been called upon to create the music on the spot and were equal to the challenge." When Helen Colbert as Clara sang the last note of "Summertime," the theatre seemed to explode with the rush of applause. Irene Williams sang Bess that night and was rewarded with so many flowers brought to the stage that they obscured her face. The cheering audience would let neither her nor Le Vern Hutcherson, as Porgy, go before taking a lengthy series of curtain calls. "When the curtain closed for the last time," said Maya, "we hugged each other and danced with ecstasy. They loved us. We loved them. We loved ourselves."

The young woman made a discovery that would be further verified in Paris: in Europe, "more often than not, blacks were liked, whereas white Americans were not." An extreme statement perhaps, but indicative of an acceptance different from her encounters in her home country. During that week in Venice the stars of the opera were continually feted. Onlookers crowded around on the streets, curious but cordial. Gondoliers gave members of the company free rides on the canals and sang the songs of *Porgy and Bess.*

The Blue Train took them to Paris, where they were scheduled for three weeks at the Théâtre de l'Empire; the demand for tickets kept them there an additional seven weeks. But it wasn't only in the theatre that they made their presences felt.

Several members of the cast supplemented their incomes with other jobs. Helen Thigpen was a soloist with the Paris Symphony and Chorus in a presentation of Handel's *Messiah*. Others appeared on radio and television, in films, and made recordings of spirituals. Lorenzo Fuller danced and sang, after hours, as did the indefatigable Maya Angelou, at the Mars Club near the Champs-Elysées, a smoky room that featured black entertainers. When others in the cast dropped by, Maya would introduce them to the audience. Martha Flowers had a fine sense of theatre, and when she was introduced, Maya wrote, "she stood up slowly and solemnly. She inclined her head, first to the right, then to the left. Only after she had bowed did she smile . . . her teeth glimmering like a row of lights, she snapped her head back and laughed, the high sound tinkling like chimes." She at last assented to the audience demand that she sing. To a piano accompaniment she sang her Strawberry Woman song. When she finished there was no sound at first. Then came applause, and people crowded around her table. "She coyly accepted the attention," Maya said, "as if she hadn't worked hard for years to earn it."

Part of the enchantment of *Porgy and Bess* for Parisian theatregoers was the novelty of seeing and hearing a supremely talented, meticulously chosen black cast, and much of it was due to their love of the Gershwin melodies that swept through the opera, but Martha Flowers thought it was also Breen's staging. "I happen to believe he was a genius," she said long after, "and I was always amazed that he was not put among the great stage directors of all time.

"No one had ever done *Porgy and Bess* that way before, with the subtleties, the touches that were so natural and beautiful. These dramatic touches added to its interest. And he staged it in such a way that audiences abroad, not knowing the language, nor having the libretto, clearly understood what was going on at all times."

From Paris, the show, now under State Department auspices, moved on to Zagreb, where the members of the company were assembled and advised that the State Department wished them to know that they were the first American singers to be invited behind the Iron Curtain and certain discretions would be in force. One was that they were to walk within a radius of only four square blocks of the hotel, another that they were not to mingle with Yugoslavians. The advice soon went out the door. The triumph was such and tickets were so in demand that families, unable to get tickets for everyone, would divide them up. One saw the first act; another saw the second. During intermission there would be a crush in the lobby as seat occupants came out to give their ticket stubs to those waiting outside for act two.

Several of the women cast members received love-smitten proposals from Yugoslav men. Martha Flowers and Maya Angelou, besieged to the very doors of their hotel rooms by persistent courtiers, found the courtship methods both alarming and hilarious. By the time they reached Belgrade, supposedly a more sophisticated city, Tito had cut the red tape, and the company was given a welcoming banquet attended by a gaggle of high officials. Invitations to parties flowed in. At one of these, Flowers was asked to sing, and, forgetful of an unspoken rule that no one sang in public a song that properly belonged to another artist, she sang "Summertime."

Helen Colbert was there. It was *her* song. She stood up and sang the song again—but, to the astonishment of the Yugoslavs present, in Serbo-Croatian. On her arrival in Zagreb, she had found an instructor who taught her the words in the local language, and she made it a practice from then on to do the same wherever the show traveled. So successful was this that Wilva Breen had accurate translations of "Summertime" made in several languages and checked them out with a somewhat nonplussed Ira Gershwin, whose linguistic ability was confined to his own language.

But Yugoslavia struck most in the company as a dreary place, especially after the charms of Venice and Paris. The weather had turned cold and gray; the atmosphere of their hotel, the Moskva, was grim and heavy with cooking odors; the city's inhabitants wore heavy clothes lacking in style. They all looked forward to their next destination, Egypt, where it would be warm and the North African sun would shine.

As though the tour were not enough of an adventure, the train the company boarded at Belgrade was the fabled Orient Express, which took them to Athens. The State Department had booked them there, too, but not before their appearances in Alexandria and Cairo.

On embarking for Egypt at the Greek port of Piraeus, they were given cabin assignments on a steamer bound for Alexandria and invited to a champagne party on board hosted by Lee Gershwin, who was traveling with the company as "authors' representative." For her, the tour was a welcome travel opportunity; Ira preferred staying home in Beverly Hills. Her party was not very successful. Winds and high seas sprang up soon after departure, and seasickness gripped most of the cast members.

After debarking at Alexandria and arriving at their hotel, Maya Angelou and others in the cast were eager to look at genuine Africans. "It took less than five minutes to discover," wrote Angelou, "that the bellhops, porters, doormen and busboys were black and brown and beige, and that the desk clerk, head waiters, bartenders and hotel manager were white. As far as we knew, they might all have been African, but the distribution of jobs by skin color was not lost on us."

Aboard ship, bound from Athens to Alexandria, December 1952. Left to right:
Joy McLean, stage manager James Hagerman, Ella Gerber, Leslie Scott, Martha Flowers.
(Lawrence and Lee Theatre Research Institute, Ohio State University.)

Breen rehearsing a new Bess, Ethel Ayler.
(Lawrence and Lee Theatre Research Institute, Ohio State University.)

14

WHILE THE *Porgy and Bess* company continued its foreign tour, Breen developed another musical show he called *Blues Opera,* planning to alternate it with the Gershwin opera, using the same cast members. Cab Calloway, who had bowed out after the London run, signified his willingness to continue his dramatic and singing career in the new show. As Breen kept explaining to an unconvinced Blevins Davis, having a second production would not only advance the goal of a permanent Negro repertory company but would have great practical value.

"You see," he told Davis, "with *Porgy and Bess* alone we finish up in a given city on a Saturday night; the company and the scenery then move at the same time, thereby using up several good days in transportation. However, with a second production we will work in this way: if we are playing, for instance, in Berlin, during the last week there we would play the second show. While the second show was playing, the scenery for *Porgy and Bess* would be moved ahead to Munich and be ready when the show arrives."

It was the travel and the "no performance" days that bogged Breen down in a continual financial mire. Davis, usually from afar, was constantly urging him not only to economize but to pay him back in weekly increments for his earlier contributions. Herman Sartorius, while generous in saving the situation in critical times, nevertheless made it clear that he, too, expected to recoup what he had advanced. The financial status was bad enough that the nonprofit status of Everyman Opera would not allow him any earnings.

While newspaper items gave glowing reports about sellout houses in city after city, the accountants presented Breen and Davis with a different story. It was true enough that during the American tour the show had often sold out. But any lackluster week would eat up the profits from the good weeks. And there was the transportation of scenery and seventy-three people from city to city and the salaries to be paid whether they were onstage or not. In Canada they ran into a theatre season in the doldrums. Even in New York, where they were one of Broadway's important hits, the theatre was not always filled, while the expenses remained constant. Illnesses among the large cast could not be avoided, and Breen insisted on the best and most prompt medical treatment.

There were times when the payroll could not be met, and the back-pay red ink would grow. Royalty payments were sometimes delayed—that continual 10 percent to the authors and heirs—and the various agents and lawyers would descend on Breen like an angry swarm of bees.

Breen was firm in his belief that by running two shows, even three, the continual problem of the operating deficit could be solved. He found the antecedents of the new show in a 1946 musical, *St. Louis Woman,* which had had some mild success on Broadway. That show, in turn, had been based on *God Sends Sunday,* a novel of flashy Negro "sporting people" of the 1890s by Arna Bontemps, a Chicago literary figure during the 1930s and 1940s. Breen, with little in the way of funds but with great persuasive power, engaged Harold Arlen for the music and Johnny Mercer for the lyrics. He retained the St. Louis setting of the play and rewrote the piece as virtually a compendium of blues songs. Arlen was just about preeminent in that area and was known for such classics as "Stormy Weather" and "I Gotta Right to Sing the Blues."

Getting the new show on and adding it to the tours of *Porgy and Bess* became Breen's preoccupation for the next several years. But there were always obstacles. Harold Arlen could not meet the deadline set for him because he was heavily involved with *House of Flowers.* When he became free again, he fell seriously ill and was a long time in recovering.

Davis was not overly sympathetic to Breen's efforts to build a repertory company. He hadn't expected to be called on to lay out hundreds of thousands of dollars on behalf of *Porgy and Bess.* He believed in good causes, but there were limits, and, curiously, he advised Breen to adopt a less selfless attitude by pointing out to him that his prestige now was at such a high level that he could command handsome fees by working in Hollywood. Breen did not listen. Personal gain was far from his mind. He still had a good part of the world left to conquer with his *Porgy and Bess*, which, sooner or later, he was confident, would be joined by *Blues Opera*.

ON NEW YEAR'S EVE, the first of two performances of *Porgy and Bess* was given at Alexandria's Theatre Mohamed Aly. Breen was busy in New York, but he had instructed his publicity representative in Europe, Rose Tobias, to keep him fully informed, while Ella Gerber was to keep the cast on its toes. This she did by calling an afternoon rehearsal almost immediately after the arrival in Alexandria.

Tobias, a young blond New Yorker pursuing a career as a free-lance publicist in Europe, wrote Breen about the first-night response. "It being New Year's Eve, or a new idiom, or no belly dancing, we got a cool

Alexandria, Egypt. (Lawrence and Lee Theatre Research Institute, Ohio State University.)

reception." The cast celebrated, anyway, with a party at their hotel to welcome in the new year, 1955. As Tobias reported, "We had just a marvelous time. I don't know what it is, but all the Company has to do is to be together, and a good time is had by all."

The *Egyptian Gazette* explained the opening night's seeming frostiness. Alexandria, the writer said, was a cosmopolitan city that was used to receiving the world's finest opera and drama companies, the world's greatest soloists, "but never have we known anyone succeed in attracting an audience on New Year's Eve. Who is the person or persons responsible for foisting this American opera on this cosmopolitan city on New Year's Eve?" Even so, the house had been packed and hundreds were turned away. Though curiosity had attracted many, said the writer, it was evident from the matinee and evening performances the following day that the opera had wide general appeal. "The audiences much warmer and receptive," Tobias reported.

Maya Angelou, less concerned about the show's impact, was busy collecting impressions. When the group took its first evening meal, she wrote, "the large dining room was decorated with palm trees and paper ribbons swinging from slow moving ceiling fans. Alexandria's playboys were present in evening finery, sending champagne to the women and occasionally to a man who caught their fancy. They introduced themselves from table to table, kissed hands, bowed and offered their calling cards. A few women in low-cut satin dresses ogled the male singers; when they netted a man's attention, their red lips split in a smile to welcome a pharaoh."

Rose Tobias described their entry into Cairo as less pharaohlike and more Caesar-like. "If anyone thinks Caesar made an entry, they should speak to the company first," she wrote to Breen.

They had started off by bus from Alexandria at 11 a.m., and stopped along the way at the Pyramids. "As long as I live," she wrote, "I will never forget the company standing in front of the Sphinx and the Pyramids. It was almost a reverent moment, because no one really believed they were actually there." They were able to believe it, though, because a phalanx of photographers was also there to record the moment for the Egyptian press.

In Cairo, escorted by the Egyptian tourist police, they were given an official greeting by the American ambassador and his staff, served a sumptuous lunch at the Meena House Hotel, surrounded by an army of newsreel and still cameramen, and then American press people in attendance were taken outside for prearranged camel rides. "RB," she wrote to Breen, "to see Helen Thigpen in her Paris suit on a camel is like seeing the eighth wonder of the world. It's too funny, too beautiful to describe. 'Dig that crazy sight,' one of the male singers shouted."

Maya Angelou was pleased to note that in Cairo more black people held positions of authority. "The desk clerk at the Continental Hotel [where they stayed] was the color of cinnamon; the manager was beige but had tight crinkly hair. The woman who supervised the running of the house" had a "complexion that would never have allowed her to pass for white." Photographs of Egypt's new premier, Gamal Abdel Nasser, showed him to be brown-skinned. "Darker than Lena Horne, Billy Daniels and Dorothy Dandridge. Without a doubt, he was one of us." There were salvos of "bravos" at the performance at the opera house, but Angelou was displeased because the audience was largely European and therefore white. This was Africa, the land of her origins, and it still bore the traces of colonialism.

THE SHOW OF happy harmony among the cast that Rose Tobias reported to Breen was less evident to Ella Gerber. It was her responsibility — and she took it very seriously — to make sure the performers were ready to go on and to replace them with their alternates if necessary. "If somebody was not there," she said, "they would cover up for each other, whatever might have been the problem. One of our Besses simply disappeared in Montreal while we were there. We'd thought she'd been killed, or drowned. She finally showed up two days later." As it turned out, she was emotionally unstable, and eventually she had to leave the company and seek treatment.

With so large a cast there were bound to be liaisons. As Gerber remembered, "There was always something going on. There were all kinds of romantic entanglements, gay liaisons, too. One of our important players had a drug problem. He was a fabulous performer, but there were times when he was so high that I had to keep a watch on him, stay with him and all but go to the bathroom with him."

"Breen," said Gerber, "was always the good guy, and never reprimanded anyone. And Wilva always was full of compliments for everyone. That left me to be the villain.

"What was happening onstage was sometimes happening off. One of the actors got in a fight with another. He came to me and said, 'I'm going, but I'm going to take him with me.' He had a knife in his hand.

" 'Where?' I asked. 'I'm going to kill him,' he said. 'I don't think so,' I said. 'Not tonight. Wait until tomorrow.'

"Another time a woman in the cast called me in the middle of the night to ask my permission for her to kill the conductor. It was three in the morning. 'What the hell are you calling me for?' I asked. 'You want to kill him, kill him on your own time, but don't ask me!' Crazy things like that happened. I suppose she felt his orchestra drowned out her voice."

For Martha Flowers, Ella Gerber was anything but a villain: "Ella was a

Wilva Davis Breen—the morale booster, "always full of compliments for everyone." (Lawrence and Lee Theatre Research Institute, Ohio State University.)

really fine director and showed me things to help me overcome the fact that I was shorter than the other Besses. Irene Williams and Leontyne were perfect physically for the role, aside from their fine voices. But I had to be staged in a different way. The whole company was wonderfully supportive. And they all had such gloriously beautiful voices it lifted your spirits to the highest peak of performance."

By the time the troupe left for Athens, Martha Flowers was ready to make her debut as Bess.

BREEN REJOINED the company in Athens, bringing along with him Ethel Ayler, another candidate for the Bess role. At the time there was a wave of anti-Western feeling in Greece because of the British occupation of Cyprus and their attempt to put down a local uprising. But this in no way stemmed the rush for tickets at the Royal National Theatre; by the time of the first performance anyone without tickets who wanted to see the opera had to go to the black market. Breen was distressed that few students or young people were able to attend because of the high prices, and he arranged for a special student matinee. But even these tickets went on the black market; few if any students were able to get in the house.

Even so, if the tour's objective was good will, it was fulfilled in Athens. At the American ambassador's reception for the company, an overflow crowd of seven hundred showed up, including the entire diplomatic corps. Good will literally overflowed when members of the company sang spirituals and other songs, with piano accompaniment by the ambassador himself. "We're back in business again," a member of the embassy said, and Ambassador Cavendish Cannon reported back to State: "*Porgy and Bess* was worth millions of dollars to us here."

The arrival of the troupe was even bigger news in the next stop, Israel. The Gershwins, after all, were Jewish, and Lee Gershwin's arrival a few days early helped whip up interest. Newspapers in Tel Aviv ran advice on how to obtain tickets, the demand for which created near-hysteria during the eight performances given at the jammed Habima Theatre.

"People literally tackled the ushers to get into the theatre," Ella Gerber said. "Little old ladies were so hungry to see the show they fought the people in charge. On the last night, I had to leave the theatre to get something for one of the performers, and they had to open the doors for me. There must have been hundreds outside clamoring for a chance to get in. They'd been

American ambassador to Greece Cavendish Cannon entertains cast members at his reception for the Porgy and Bess *company. Left, rear, John McCurry. Left to right: Irving Barnes, Jerry Laws, Leonore Gershwin, Ambassador Cannon at piano, unidentified, Le Vern Hutcherson, Gloria Davy. (Sam Kasakoff photo, courtesy Ella Gerber.)*

standing there for hours and hours. 'Let them in,' I begged the guards. 'It's the last night.' And they did. They opened the doors, and these people filled the aisles, all the way down to the stage. It was thrilling."

Lionel Hampton's band had just finished an engagement in Tel Aviv, and the cast of *Porgy and Bess* met the band members at a party thrown by the American ambassador and the Israeli government. "The company," said Maya Angelou, "had not seen such a gathering of American Negroes in months. We fell on the musicians as though they were bowls of black-eyed peas." It was at this same reception that the Soviet ambassador to Israel remarked to Lee Gershwin: "If only we had a *Porgy and Bess.* How we would send it around!" She duly passed the word on to Robert Breen.

The cast by this time was expert in the ways of diplomacy. At receptions they were always generous about giving impromptu concerts; the spirituals they sang so movingly made the party occasions memorable. In Tel Aviv they included the Hebrew "*Eli Eli,*" which drew an enormous outburst of applause. The song, after all, dealt with the wanderings of the Jews after the great Dispersion. In turn, the Israelis entertained their guests by arranging for tours of Tel Aviv, Jerusalem, and the Galilee. Gloria Davy, who sang Bess while there, attracted such a crowd when she went shopping that the police had to be called to protect her from her admirers. One last gesture was made after the final performance: 150 trees were planted in the troupe's honor in the Herzl Forest.

BEFORE HEADING on to Barcelona and a subsequent swing through Italy, an air force plane flew the troupe nearly 3,000 miles to Casablanca, where a single concert performance was given for American personnel stationed at the Nouasseur Air Depot. By the time they reached Barcelona, the company was tired, and weary, too, of hotel rooms and restaurant food. But spurred on by Breen and Gerber—who were always on the watch for any drop in quality—they rallied for their ten days of performances, much like champions eager to hold on to their titles and laurels. More were received. "The best thing seen in Barcelona in twenty years," the newspaper *Destino* observed.

Ahead lay four Italian cities: Naples, Milan, Genoa, and Florence, but it was Milan and the Teatro alla Scala that roused the most anticipation among the cast members. For many it had been a lifetime and all-but-impossible goal to sing there. After a week in Naples at the Teatro San Carlo, they arrived in Milan the last week in February. Here, too, tickets had been sold out days in advance. Milan is a worldly, industrial city which likes to think of itself as unique in the fields of industry, fashion, the intellect, and, above all, music. Its conservative newspaper, *Il Corriere della Sera,* circulated throughout Italy, as did the somewhat smaller but more caustic Communist paper, *L'Unita.* The Milanese, made up on one side by the rich, powerful, and conservative and on the other by industrial workers and the poor, tended to view the United States, in spite of its strength, as somewhat juvenile, not to say barbarous; not the least of its sins was, in *L'Unita*'s view, its treatment of its downtrodden black underclass.

Into this atmosphere came the company of polished black singers and performers, well educated, courteous, and stylishly dressed. Even *L'Unita* was forced to revise some of its assumptions. But what had magnetized La Scala into inviting Breen's production was less the voices he had assembled than the name and fame of George Gershwin. For years, Riccardo Malipiero, a distinguished critic and composer, had prodded the managers to put on *Porgy and Bess* at La Scala. Now its managing director, Antonio Ghiringhelli, paced the venerable corridors and said to the Breens, "Tomorrow I will be acclaimed either an idiot or a genius."

It was something entirely unique: renowned white American tenors, sopranos, and baritones had sung here at the famous house, but that was a far cry from a huge cast of black singers. Backstage the silence was also unusual, almost ominous. The singers readied themselves behind locked doors. "When the five-minute call was given," Maya Angelou remembered, "we all went quietly to our places; not even a whisper floated over the dark stage. I was coiled tight like a spring and realized as the curtain rose that every other member of the cast had also wound themselves up taut for a shattering release. The moment the curtain opened the singers in concert pulled the elegant first-night audience into the harshness of Black Southern life. . . . When Robbins was killed the moans were real. The love story unfolded with such tenderness that the singers wept visible tears."

Martha Flowers remembered the night as one of the great moments of her career. "The beauty of the house, that oh so accomplished orchestra, the remarkable acoustics, made my voice just seem to float."

Richard Coe, present for the Washington *Post,* reported that silence greeted every note because custom dictated applause be reserved for the final curtain. Immediately on its descent, though, cheers rang out from the topmost of the six tiers, and when the cast appeared at its rise the audience came to its feet yelling and applauding. "We had sung gloriously," Maya Angelou said, "and though we faced the audience we bowed to compliment each other. We had performed *Porgy and Bess* as never before, and if the La Scala patrons loved us, it was only fitting because we certainly performed as if we were in love with one another."

The management's splendid opening-night party attracted the top of

Milanese society, the men displaying their ribbons of honor, the women so bedecked in the latest evening fashions and sparkling with jewels that Paulette Goddard (who was there) thought them "incredibly old-fashioned. I didn't think people *did* this anymore." There, too, were Dorothy Heyward and Lee Gershwin, but Ira, as usual, stayed home and gave the air ticket Breen had provided him to his agent, Irving Lazar. Others who thought they had the right to attend the event were nettled by this, Lazar's connection to the show being at this time remote.

Edward R. Murrow was frustrated, too. He had made plans to send two camera crews to televise portions of the opening performance for his "See It Now" program on CBS, but Actors Equity intervened with a request for a full week's pay for the sixty-five onstage members of the company. This was too heavy a bill for Murrow's budget, so the plan was dropped and an important moment of musical history remained unrecorded. Soon after,

John McCurry (Crown) arriving at another stop on the European tour.

Porgy and Bess *is announced at Teatro alla Scala in Milan, 1954.*
(Lawrence and Lee Theatre Research Institute, Ohio State University.)

however, CBS began negotiating with Breen and Davis for a two-hour telecast of the complete opera. These negotiations, too, broke down when Breen insisted that the sponsors be limited to no more than five minutes of commercials and that he have general supervision of the production to ensure its integrity. CBS couldn't accept these terms, it being unthinkable to them that sponsors would pay many hundreds of thousands of dollars for only five minutes of air time. In any case, the Milan appearance was one more triumph for the troupe and for the Gershwin-Heyward work, which the influential critic Rubens Tedeschi summed up as "a masterwork of the lyric theatre."

The singers, too, made an enormous impression. Gloria Davy alternated with Martha Flowers as Bess, Leslie Scott and Irving Barnes with Le Vern Hutcherson as Porgy, and Joseph Attles and Earl Jackson with Lorenzo Fuller as Sportin' Life. Not only did they all have the chance for their debuts at La Scala, but audiences assumed, rightly in this case, that America was overflowing with rich, finely trained black voices. Ghiringhelli had made a

Maya Angelou attracts attention at a reception in Rome.
(Lawrence and Lee Theatre Research Institute, Ohio State University.)

concession by booking a full week of performances; he hoped to make another when he asked Breen to extend the run for another week. Breen had to refuse. They were expected elsewhere.

First in Genoa at the Teatro Carlo Felice, then at the Teatro Comunale in Florence; from there to Lausanne, the Opéra Municipal in Marseilles, then Turin, and, in late April, coming to rest for a time in Rome at the Teatro Quattro Fontana. This theatre, a music hall, was not entirely to Breen's liking, but Rome's opera house had not been available. Breen also had the bold idea, until scotched by municipal authorities, of performing the opera under a tent, in the ruins of the Baths of Caracalla.

After three weeks of performing in Rome a hiatus occurred. Further engagements had been arranged for Zurich, Brussels, and Antwerp, but two empty weeks were left in the schedule, and with the company's balance sheet at its usual low ebb and no box-office income, there was no way to pay for the cast's two weeks of salary and living expenses. Breen held a meeting and put it frankly to the company members: either close down or stay on at their own expense and continue the tour. Almost all of them, vastly enjoying the springtime pleasures of Rome, opted to stay on. A few left, among them Maya Angelou, who became conscience-stricken about staying away from her son for so long. Ella Gerber, too, decided to leave after three years of giving her all. Jerry Laws, who played the young and lazy stevedore Mingo, and who had considerable directing experience, took on her job as the company's drillmaster.

B R E E N H A D other and momentous things on his mind. While in Rome he received word that the State Department would underwrite an extension of the tour to South America. This news came as he was actively pursuing the possibility of taking the troupe to Moscow. Through a Paris contact, Georges Soria, who had been instrumental in arranging a visit of the Comédie Française to Moscow and an exchange visit of the Bolshoi Ballet to Paris, he learned that the Soviet Union would look favorably on his bringing *Porgy and Bess*. But the situation had its delicate aspects. As Breen explained in a memorandum:

> The Russians do not want to be rebuffed or embarrassed by refusal of the Department of State or the USA to allow *Porgy* to go to Moscow if the Russians extend an invitation. They realize only too well the ridicule they would be subject to in the press if the USA were to turn it down. They want assurance that they will not be embarrassed by a turn-down from official USA sources.

Breen asked Richard Coe to be his emissary to some sympathetic officials in Washington and to sound out informally their attitudes about his going to Russia.

The Foreign Ministers' Conference of the Soviet Union, the United States, Britain, and France was taking place in Geneva as Breen pursued his next and most important goal. Among matters being discussed were East-West trade relations and, as it happened, exchange visits by scientists, schools, tourists, and professional groups. The haggling, which lasted several months, produced no concrete results, and American officials, when pondering Breen's request first for approval of a visit and then for the necessary funds to make it possible, were shy about committing themselves one way or the other.

The best encouragement Breen was able to get came in a letter from Theodore Streibert, the director of the United States Information Agency. "You would be warranted," he said carefully, "in assuring the French intermediary that there is no justification for any fear of rejection on our part of an invitation." Breen took this as a signal for moving full speed ahead. The company was already in Belgium and slated to begin its Latin American tour in Rio de Janeiro the first week of July, when he went to Geneva bearing letters.

While in Brussels he had been advised to have these letters translated into Russian; he addressed them to Premier Nikolai Bulganin, First Secretary Nikita Khrushchev, and Foreign Minister Vyacheslav Molotov and dropped them off at the Soviet legation. At the same time, in other letters, he detailed the extent of the situation to Secretary of State John Foster Dulles and Ambassador Llewellyn Thompson and met with the American ambassador to Russia, Charles Bohlen, who favored the project and advised him to get rolling on it. Breen, a man with hardly a dime to his name, whose evening dress for formal occasions had to be bought with company funds, was imbued with purpose and conviction and never hesitated to deal when necessary with the high and the mighty.

From Moscow, word soon came that the proposed visit was being taken with utmost seriousness at the highest levels. No opposition came from the American State Department, but it was made clear that no government funds would be provided. While the troupe was making its way through South America, Breen went to Washington, where he had an angry meeting with State Department and USIA representatives. He was told that the "President's Fund" for such purposes had to be "spread around" and that "other groups might be upset" if they couldn't make foreign trips. *Porgy and Bess,* it was pointed out, had already received $700,000 in assistance for tours of

Two Besses, one Crown. Martha Flowers, John McCurry, Ethel Ayler.
(Lawrence and Lee Theatre Research Institute, Ohio State University.)

Three Sportin' Lifes: Lorenzo Fuller, Earl Jackson, Joseph Attles.
(Lawrence and Lee Theatre Research Institute, Ohio State University.)

Europe, the Mediterranean, and Latin America. To provide $400,000 for a Moscow trip would use up almost all of the European budget.

Breen suspected political reasons for the refusal, one being a State Department fear that Soviet propaganda purposes would be served by the squalid living conditions of the opera's characters. Breen knew this to be an old assumption, counteracted in every country where the opera had played. Could anything be more important than opening up artistic and cultural exchange with the Soviet Union? Wasn't *Porgy and Bess* clearly the ideal vehicle for doing this? At almost the same moment came another significant invitation: the People's Republic of China proposed a sixteen-week tour that included Peking, Shanghai, Tientsin, Canton, Hankow, Nanking, and Chungking—China's first invitation ever issued to an American theatre company. From Catfish Row to Canton—the prospect all but took the company's breath away.

State Department regulations at the time stipulated that, except for special cases, passports were not valid for travel to Communist countries. The restriction was most severe for China, where a number of American citizens, including twelve American airmen, were being held. No passports were being granted, not even to newsmen. This stand was backed further by a Treasury Department ruling that under the terms of the Trading-with-the-Enemy Act the spending of dollars in Communist China would be illegal. Nevertheless, there were discussions at the State Department about making such a tour contingent on China's releasing American citizens. Presumably, feelers were made about the idea, but without result, and the State Department closed the door on the China initiative.

In Geneva, however, as the Foreign Ministers' Conference progressed, the atmosphere lightened in the area of cultural exchange. The Russians, for instance, allowed Emil Gilels and David Oistrakh to concertize in the United States.

Late in September, the State Department formally turned down Breen's request for funding. As though the Soviets were aware that this would happen—in fact, they knew before Breen did—their Ministry of Culture promptly issued a formal invitation to Breen to bring the troupe to Moscow and asked him to come there to discuss details.

Breen could keep several irons in his fire. He was working on a new tour of Germany; he had plans to take the company to several iron curtain countries, including Poland and Czechoslovakia. He shuffled in hurried trips to South America between working in New York with Harold Arlen on *Blues Opera,* and he was also contending for the film rights to *Porgy and Bess.* On top of all this the Moscow trip loomed.

Wilva Breen, who had remained in Brussels recuperating from a serious infection, worried that her overextended husband might be headed for a breakdown. Blevins Davis was being no help; in fact, he made things worse by negotiating for the film rights with a new potential partner, Kay Harrison, the head of British Technicolor, while ignoring the fact that Breen, using Ira Gershwin and Irving Lazar as his channels, had all but worked out a contractual arrangement that would allow Davis to produce and himself to direct the film. A crack developed in the relationship between Davis and Breen.

What nettled Breen most was that Davis was willing to have others such as Mamoulian, or Joseph Mankiewicz, take over the direction of the film, neither of whom would brook any creative interference from another source. Davis, for his part, complained to the Gershwin and Heyward agents he was dealing with that Breen was too free with the Everyman Opera Company funds and that all the praise he received had enlarged his ego; this in turn caused agents and estate trustees to demand payment of insignificant amounts of back royalties from Breen. There were loyalists on both sides, and it took some peacemaking efforts by Herman Sartorius to keep the two from fighting it out in court.

With all this to deal with, Breen had less time to give to the Latin American tour as it wended its way from Rio de Janeiro to Buenos Aires, Santiago, Lima, Bogotá, and Caracas; it was scheduled to end in Mexico City in late November. A young manager, Robert Dustin, handled many of the tour's business details, while Jerry Laws now kept the company at its peak performing level. Lee Gershwin, as a kind of unofficial hostess, was handy for social affairs, and there were many because of State Department involvement. American consuls in each of the cities the troupe played sent back glowing reports about its reception; newspapers reported its appearances as the cultural event of the year. Admittedly, pickings were slim in most of the countries they visited.

Even though many music lovers south of the border were acquainted with other Gershwin works, the opera was a revelation. In São Paolo, however, the critic for the Communist newspaper lamented that Gershwin had not lived long enough to write "a national opera based on different aspects of the North American people." But even though, he said, the U.S. government, "openly and rigidly subordinated to the interests of imperialist capital," had not advanced "these people economically and politically," the opera could be "accepted in friendly fashion" and was "worthy of unrestricted applause."

When Wilva Breen recovered from her illness, she stayed on in Brussels to help handle negotiations for another European tour, the centerpiece of which she hoped would be Moscow. This tour was being set up with the aid of a new Belgian booking agent, Maurice Huisman, whose theatrical and artistic sympathies were close to those of the idealistic Breens.

One day in late September 1955, only a few days after the State Department refusal, Breen, in New York, called his wife in Brussels and asked her to go to the Russian consulate and pick up a visa for a trip to Moscow. He had cut through the red tape by going directly to the Russian ambassador in Washington, and the ambassador's immediate response was an indication of the importance to the Soviet hierarchy of a visit by the celebrated opera production. With a portfolio of instructions from her husband, Wilva set off on her mission to Moscow.

Irene Williams as Bess, Lorenzo Fuller as Sportin' Life.
(Lawrence and Lee Theatre Research Institute, Ohio State University.)

15

WILVA BREEN WAS met at the Moscow airport by a dignitary from the Ministry of Culture, presented by him with flowers, shepherded through passport and customs controls, and installed in a pleasant room at the Metropole Hotel. Then a young woman interpreter arrived and told her she would be available to her at all hours and for all occasions. It was as though she were on a state visit. The Russians, she was now certain, were taking the impending visit of *Porgy and Bess* with complete seriousness.

Her presence in Moscow quickly attracted the attention of Welles Hangen, Moscow correspondent for *The New York Times,* and Daniel Schorr of CBS. She told them of her exemplary treatment and was surprised when they expressed some concern. The Soviets, they told her, usually billed Westerners for such courtesies. And the exchange rate of rubles for dollars penalized Americans.

She thought it advisable to check this out with the American consulate, and was told that, yes, she would undoubtedly be expected to pay for her room and board, but, if she ran short of money, she could obtain a loan from the embassy. Her interpreter arrived early the next morning and told her, almost breathlessly, that all her expenses were to be taken care of by the state. Wilva gained new respect for the efficiency of the Soviet intelligence apparatus.

Several friendly and productive meetings that seemed to be the idea of some important personage who was referred to but never seen took place at the Ministry of Culture. Clearly, higher levels of the Soviet bureaucracy were involved. Wilva's main contact in the negotiations was the Ministry's chargé of foreign affairs, Vladimir Stepanov. In a dashed-off memo to her husband, she said, "He expressed great interest in our having *Porgy and Bess* here, and is eager to get the opening day set. He asked when we want to come." The best news was that the Russians were ready to commit themselves to a considerable amount of financial support. They would pay for all transportation from East Germany, all the living expenses of the company, and transportation to the next country on the tour.

Details of the contract, she told the Russians, would be handled by their European representative, Anatole Heller. Could they also come to Leningrad? Stepanov asked. "He extended a definite invitation," Wilva informed Robert, who was quick to act on it. The company would play Leningrad first, then go on to Moscow. Left unresolved was how the company would finance its way to East Germany. In New York, Breen announced firmly that, if necessary, he would seek private funding; nothing would stop *Porgy and Bess* from becoming the first American theatrical venture to play in the Soviet Union since its revolution.

H E E X P R E S S E D his feelings about what would be accomplished by the company's Russian visit to Ira Gershwin. "The whole business of getting *Porgy and Bess* to Russia," he wrote, "is a bit of Never-Never-Land, believe me. There's hardly been time to think about it, much less to tell anyone about it. I can hardly believe it myself."

He had estimated the extent of the losses that would be taken and felt he had to be frank about it: "After we finish this next tour, we will go down in a blaze of glory—but with a debt of about $130,000, in addition to the $109,000 we owe Blevins. I used to worry about it, but I refuse to let myself be concerned about it anymore. *Porgy and Bess* has been a historic milestone in the history of the American theatre and culture and has done what no other production has ever done and perhaps will ever do for another 20 or 25 years. Mainly because there might not be anyone around as crazy as we are to plunge ahead into the almost impossible.

"Honestly, I just can't believe it, and when sometime ago someone mentioned about something I was doing not being 'business-like,' I immediately replied, 'Of course not! If I were a *real business man,* we would have closed *Porgy and Bess* a long time ago!' Well, it just suffices to say that when we do close, we will close loaded with debt—but who cares! We've done something no one else in the world has and it has brought glory not only to everyone concerned, but to the United States itself and we are to be very proud of it."

Wilva later said she thought her husband's frankness about incurring debt had another side to it. The Russians insisted on limiting royalty payments to $1,000 for each week of performance, far below the 12 percent of box office the estates usually demanded for overseas performing rights to the opera. Breen needed Ira's help on this. And Ira was apparently so stirred by the letter that he decided to forsake the comforts of Beverly Hills, and the pleasures of the Santa Anita racetrack, and make the trip to Moscow.

THE CONTRACT between Everyman Opera, Inc., and the Ministry of Culture of the U.S.S.R. was signed on December 3, 1955, and provided for payment of $16,000 (half in rubles at the official rate) for each week the company was in the Soviet Union. The ministry would also take "complete charge of all expenses connected with the preparation, the rehearsals and the performances of the company." Sixty-five musicians from Moscow's Stanislavsky Theatre would be provided for the Leningrad performances, and in Moscow the full Stanislavsky orchestra of eighty members would play. The Russians would also provide a grand piano in the orchestra pit, another piano for the stage, and a "domesticated she goat." The total cost of all this was estimated at $150,000.

The Russians were apparently better bargainers than Anatole Heller, for Everyman Opera stood to lose from $4,000 to $5,000 a week while in Russia. And the Russians would have a large profit—or so it appeared—on the sale of tickets. Actually, the Russians would have to pay the salaries of all the personnel, about a thousand people, of the Stanislavsky Theatre while *Porgy and Bess* was in residence there.

While Breen labored on the details in New York, Blevins Davis in London was still seeking screen rights to the opera. When he did get around to applying for his Russian visa, he bungled the instructions Breen sent him, never did get clearance, and missed the whole Russian adventure. Breen, once the news was out, was besieged by volunteers for the expedition, some with important names, such as William Paley of CBS and General David Sarnoff of RCA. He attempted to put together a group for a press plane that Air France was willing to supply, but the Russians balked at handing out so many visas. He was told by the embassy in Washington that he was limited to a total of eighty-five. The company's size being what it was, little room was left for junketeers.

Another problem was that most members of the press wanted free room and board as well as transportation. This meant that Everyman Opera would have to assume their expenses. Breen finally decided to take along Leonard Lyons, who had a nationally syndicated daily column, and the highly publicized young writer Truman Capote. Both Arnold Weissberger, Breen's lawyer, and Harold Arlen, the composer for *House of Flowers,* thought that he would be an ideal chronicler of the trip. Breen would later regret that he had taken their advice.

Another reporter, Ira Wolfert, was allowed to come, provided that his magazine, *Reader's Digest,* absorbed his expenses. Horace Sutton of *The Saturday Review* had his own means of getting to Russia, but Richard Coe was turned down, much to his dismay; he felt entitled to the trip, since he, more than anyone else, had loyally supported Breen's expeditions.

Breen, however, was willing to strain the company's resources by assuming the expenses of Ira and Lee Gershwin, Dorothy Heyward, and, as a reward for monetary service rendered, Herman Sartorius. When Ella Gerber, who had been studying Shakespeare at Stratford-on-Avon after leaving the company, clamored to go, Breen helped her with her visa, but it came too late for her to get to Leningrad in time.

Breen, far behind the lines in New York, was like a general laying out a campaign. Closer to the front lines in Brussels were Wilva and company manager Robert Dustin. The aide-de-camp in New York was Breen's assistant, Warner Watson. The date of departure from East Berlin was finally set for December 19, a Monday. Some two and a half days would be spent on the train trip to Leningrad.

Nagging difficulties remained. Ira Gershwin wasn't sure of how and when he wanted to go. Eventually, he decided to fly the polar route to Helsinki and take an Aeroflot plane from there. Harold Arlen, at the last moment, opted to go with him, but had no visa. Breen arranged to have him pick it up on his arrival in Helsinki. Dorothy Heyward, always frail, was too ill to go and asked that her daughter, Jenifer, be allowed in her place. Breen thought it only right and proper that a Heyward be present for so significant an event.

He wasn't happy, though, about having on the trip the wife of Alexander Smallens, his conductor. A large woman, and pleasant much of the time, she often drank too much on social occasions, to the point of embarrassment for Breen when so many of the occasions were of a quasi-official nature. He was well aware of the amount of vodka served on all occasions in Russia. To the always kindly Wilva he wrote a memo saying, "We just cannot have her there, if she is going to be floundering around all the time. Alec [Smallens] said he just had to take her along, and if she couldn't go, he didn't think he would go either." He thought of delaying Mrs. Smallens's visa, then relented and allowed her to make the trip.

Herman Sartorius was not feeling kindly toward Blevins Davis at this moment and made what Breen termed *"a vital request . . . that he is not required to share space on the train nor a hotel room with him. If at the last minute placed in that situation he would have to walk out of it."*

Leonard Lyons had his own vital request when on the train to Leningrad. "Mr. Lyons," the Breen memo read, "needs a private compartment on the train, inasmuch as he would be writing much of the time. *Please make a special note of this.*"

The *Porgy and Bess* company, after ending its Latin American tour in Mexico City, returned to New York in early November 1955 for a week's vacation before departing for Europe again. Anatole Heller booked a tour to Antwerp, Düsseldorf, Munich, and West Berlin to take place prior to the Russian venture; without State Department help, the bookings would have to pay for themselves and, it was hoped, get the company as far as East Berlin, where it would entrain for the Soviet Union.

After three years of touring, a celebration in Brussels, 1955. The cake is being presented to Earl Jackson, Helen Thigpen, Walter Riemer, Lorenzo Fuller, and Ella Gerber. (Sam Kasakoff photo, courtesy Ella Gerber.)

But Breen had trouble finding money to get the company off American soil. Dorothy Heyward, ill in St. Luke's Hospital in New York, was kept abreast of the situation by her play representative, John Rumsey. "Breen was in a bit of a panic last week," he wrote her, "because of the trouble he has had in raising the money to go to Moscow. It appears he is making this trip on a shoestring. The company got off on one plane. A little later an attachment for $7,000 was placed on the scenery and Bob and his attorney, Aaron Frosch [the partner of Arnold Weissberger], had a terrible time getting the matter straightened out, for Bob did not have the money to pay this debt. Just how this was taken care of I do not know. The next thing that happened was that a third plane to take the excess baggage at a cost of $3,000 was not allowed to go by the company until this was paid. Bob didn't have the money to take care of it. He called Mr. Frosch every few minutes over a period of two hours appealing for help in getting the Company and the production over to Antwerp. . . . Never in Bob's life did he need Blevins Davis more than yesterday."

Davis had not totally lost interest in the company, but his more important objective was to contract for a film production at terms that would allow him to recoup what he had put into Everyman Opera. Breen and Davis wrangled for several years over the amount of this sum. Breen said it was $109,000. Davis claimed he had advanced far more than that. Breen reminded him that money had been paid back to him from receipts, often on a weekly basis, and mentioned Davis's habit of writing out Everyman Opera checks whenever Davis needed a spare $5,000 in cash. Davis was laggard in paying bills, and his complaints about the handling of finances hurt Breen's reputation.

"Blevins was indeed a generous man," Wilva Breen explained, "full of promises of support to deserving groups and causes. But his promises were always six months ahead of his income and, rich as he was, he was often short of ready cash. Just the same, the fact that he was wealthy and carried himself as a secure gentleman of means impressed people he dealt with. John Rumsey was all for giving him screen rights against Dorothy Heyward's objections. If Davis blamed Breen for this or that, Rumsey assumed Robert was the culprit. But I still don't know how Robert got the money to send the company overseas. I suppose he put off paying some bills while clearing up the most necessary ones. State Department money to help pay for the Latin American tour was slow in coming through, and he probably was counting on that. People always assumed we were solidly supported, but the truth was we usually got along on that old shoestring."

Breen stayed behind in New York to handle money matters, while Warner

Watson took the company to Antwerp. By the time Breen was back with his performers, the company was in West Berlin, after tumultuous receptions in Düsseldorf and Munich.

From Düsseldorf M. S. Handler went beyond bare reporting in his dispatch to *The New York Times:* "The opening night was attended by 2811 persons, who packed the Apollo Theatre. The acclaim was deafening, and the production enjoyed a huge critical success. The common humanity of suffering made the Americans intelligible to the Germans in a way that has been impossible to communicate through the media of a heavily swollen bureaucracy, high-toned lectures, and white-tie artists. *Porgy and Bess* was not the America of Hollywood or the official America, with its ponderous pronouncements. *Porgy and Bess* is regarded here as one of the most effective instruments for meeting the Russians on their favored terrain—that of waging the East-West struggle on the cultural front. Its appeal to the minds and hearts of men is almost irresistible."

In Berlin, the Titania Palast Theatre sold out every night of the show's one-week reappearance. Then, on Monday, December 19, after a briefing by American Embassy officials on what to expect and how to behave in Russia, the entire complement, now grown to ninety-four persons, was bused from hotels and pensions in West Berlin through the Brandenburg Gate to the Ostbahnof in East Berlin. The Breens would be flying on ahead for advance arrangements, but the train passengers faced two days and two nights of travel to Moscow and almost another full day from there to Leningrad.

One of Breen's advance arrangements failed to materialize. He had been promised a dining car, even though the Blue Express, only recently opened to non-Communist passengers, normally had no dining facilities until it reached the border city of Brest Litovsk, some twenty hours away. The Blue Express, its cars green, not blue, was one of Europe's most famous trains, but its name belied its speed. It made twenty stops during the 1,400 miles to Moscow, and these alone consumed eleven hours. At Brest Litovsk, a four-hour stop was required to convert to the Russian wide-gauge track. Breen managed to delay the train, frantically ordered a thousand sandwiches from the Kempinski Hotel, rounded up fruits and cases of wine, and beer, and, just as the whistle of imminent departure was sounding, appeared with Wilva on the platform, followed by a porter trundling a wagon that contained the food and refreshments. The Breens, before leaving for the airport, watched with relieved parental smiles as the train left the station and disappeared into the night darkness.

The American passengers knew little about the train, or why it was famous, and probably this was just as well. Until it was opened up to Western

Stops on the way to Leningrad,
December 1955. (Sam Kasakoff
photos, courtesy Ella Gerber.)

passengers, it had mostly carried Communist diplomats and officials, Soviet military, and Red agents en route to missions outside the Eastern bloc. Vigilance was required on its way through Poland, at least so the stories went that were now and then carried in West German newspapers.

Headlines read POLISH DYNAMITE BLUE EXPRESS, RUSSIAN OFFICERS MURDERED ON BLUE EXPRESS, BLUE EXPRESS DERAILED. These incidents were supposed to be the work of an anti-Communist Polish underground. Whether the stories were true, exaggerated, or false, no one could say for sure, but for those aware of them the train's name carried a tingly aura of menace.

The contingent aboard the train included fifty-eight performers, several wives and children, seven members of the technical crew, a small office staff,

Lee Gershwin, Herman Sartorius, and three journalists—Lyons, Capote, and Wolfert, who had brought along his wife. With a long journey through the plains of Poland and Russia ahead, Capote had a made-to-order opportunity for gathering material. When his articles appeared in *The New Yorker* months later, the train sequence was not unlike a modern-day version of Chekhov's *The Steppe,* which also told of a lengthy Russian train ride.

Capote's prose did not suffer in comparison. A sample: "Coldness woke me. Snow was blowing through the window's minute opening. There were hints of sunrise on the rim of the sky, yet it was still dark, and the traces of morning color were like goldfish swimming in ink. We were on the outskirts of a city. . . ."

Capote was disturbed by the apportionment of the accommodations. Leonard Lyons was given a compartment all to himself, while he was forced to share one with the flashily dressed Earl Jackson and his fiancée, Helen Thigpen. Assigned to the same compartment was a new publicity woman, Nancy Ryan. Breen had not wanted to bring her, but Capote convinced him that she would be helpful to him and Lyons in their reporting. In Capote's eyes, she had the requisite qualities for the job. She had recently graduated from Radcliffe, was tall and attractive, and, most important, was the daughter of the beautiful and rich socialite Mrs. William Rhinelander Stewart. She figured prominently in what he wrote, and her comments and doings seemed of much more interest to him than the cast members and the history-making nature of the enterprise.

His two other compartment mates, Jackson and Thigpen, also received a good deal of his attention. Capote observed them with a certain amount of astonishment, for Jackson, especially, was a "character" in the best and worst senses of the word. He was cocky, well suited to the role of Sportin' Life—in which he alternated with Lorenzo Fuller—was given to jive talk and the wearing of flashy jewelry (while in Milan he found a pair of gloves with holes that allowed his many rings to show), and he had a plan for making history of his own. He had asked Breen to arrange for him to marry his fiancée while in Moscow. He had with him a brown-tailed wedding suit with lapels of champagne-colored satin. As the first two Negro Americans married in Moscow, he said, they were bound to make the front pages there and at home.

Capote, from the beginning, had no intention of writing a straightforward account of the event he was covering. The assignment given him by *The New Yorker* was nonspecific. From the editorial point of view, placing a sensitive writer such as Capote together with a Negro theatre company in Communist Russia boded well. During his early years in New York, Capote had worked at *The New Yorker* as an office assistant. He knew the magazine well and was aware of its special brand of journalism. Reporters such as Joseph Mitchell, Lillian Ross, A. J. Liebling, and Philip Hamburger were extending the scope and quality of nonfiction by embodying near-fictional techniques. Time sequence was not always strictly observed. "How far can we go before fact becomes fiction?" Liebling once asked a staff member. The authors, many of them supported by the magazine, took their time, sometimes requiring a year and more to polish an article to a state-of-the-art smoothness and brilliance. Editors added an additional sheen. When the methods worked, the results were immensely readable, entertaining, and sometimes devastating to unwary subjects who were "profiled."

Capote said afterward that he imagined his chronicle as "a brief, comic novel. I wanted it to be very Russian . . . a Fabergé contrivance, one of his music boxes, say, that trembled with some glittering precise, mischievous melody." Breen, of course, had no notion of this. He thought that with a gifted writer like Capote, he would have the elegantly literary reporting that he felt his venture deserved. If the idea of "a brief, comic novel" had been mentioned to him, Capote's invitation and traveling expenses would have been hastily withdrawn.

In March of 1989, *The New Yorker* published a lengthy two-part article about the ethics of journalists who "seduced" subjects into relationships that allowed them to take advantage of confidences which might not otherwise have been given. Capote was credited as one of the originators of the method. After gaining entrée, becoming a sort of participant in the story being sought, the writer could later fashion it to suit his own purposes. Capote, obviously, had not the slightest intention of doing straight and objective reportage about the Russian expedition. Nor would writing with style and flair be enough. Like other *New Yorker* writers before him, he was out to mold actuality to create a hoped-for work of art. Ironically, his was the very kind of reporting decried as unethical years later in *The New Yorker*.

Wilva Breen sensed early that her husband may have made a mistake. Before the trip, Capote said to her, "It's so chic to be going to Russia." But later on he asked her why, for so innovative an occasion, they were bringing such dreary stuff, replete with such lowly characters.

"What would you prefer?" she asked him. "*Lady Windermere's Fan?*"

"Why, yes," he replied. After all, hadn't the British recently sent over a *Hamlet* and the French their Comédie Française?

The members of the company began to sense that he regarded them as "Uncle Toms" for playing in a work about distressed slum Negroes. Among themselves they referred to him as "Little Eva." This also may have been due to his high, childish voice, his small stature, and the huge yellow cashmere scarf he wore over his head and bundled around his neck whenever he poked his head outdoors. He allowed the scarf to trail behind him when the weather permitted. If his appearance caused titters, many in the cast regarded him with the respect due his work and reputation. "I admired his writing," Martha Flowers said, "but I did find him sort of weird."

Capote's account was largely in the first person, with himself as a major character, one sensitively aware of all that was going on around him and of the experience in which he was participating. Nancy Ryan was treated as a somewhat dippy but otherwise knowledgeable, sympathetic, and comradely participant. Leonard Lyons came out as a fatuous caricature of a newspaperman and Leonore Gershwin as a cliché of a Beverly Hills matron, given to constant "dears" and "darlings," forever flaunting a display of diamonds. "She bristled with mink," Capote wrote of her, "was frosted with diamonds, and her curls peeked charmingly from under a rich, soft sable hat."

Nor did the Breens escape his delicately poisoned shafts. Wilva, one of whose major responsibilities during the tours was as a morale builder, was portrayed not unlike the too-sweet characters once played by Billie Burke in the movies. For Breen, Capote chose the traits of pomposity and self-importance.

From Breen's point of view, though, Capote needed explaining to the Russians. "He was their idea of a caricature of the decadent 'Western' artist," he said later. "They called him 'Popov' because he reminded them of one of their famous clowns. One day at the Astoria in Leningrad the lobby was full of fur-hatted Russians buzzing away. Capote came down the stairway and headed for the door. Dead silence as they swiveled their heads watching him. After he swished through the revolving door — another spell of silence, and then a booming bass-baritone voice sounded off in English: 'VE HAVE DEM LIKE DAT IN DE SOVIET TOO, BUT VE HIDE DEM.'"

Capote apparently heard the remark, although he gave no indication of it — at first. The door continued to revolve and he reappeared in the lobby, kicked up a heel in the direction of the Russians, and disappeared. Writing well, however, was his best revenge. He stayed with the company long into the Moscow run, but ended his reportage with the opening night in Leningrad. He did not cover the company's main goal, Moscow, at all. In fact, there, he took little interest in *Porgy and Bess* and was concerned more about his own entertainment. His drinking became noticeably heavier, and Leonard Lyons protectively watched over him and tried to keep him out of serious trouble, particularly if he made a pass at a native while pub-crawling.

Gerald Clarke, his biographer, mentions that while in Moscow Capote spoke to the Soviet Writers Union, an occasion arranged by Breen, and was taken up by a youthful crowd. One of its members, a young man called Victor, Capote referred to as his "Moscow beau." Clarke also reveals that he made composites of the "characters" of his "comic novel." During the stop at Brest Litovsk to change the train's wheels for Russia's wide tracks, Capote "reported" at length an encounter and conversation with a Russian. Clarke says he invented the entire scene. It would have been beyond the powers even of *The New Yorker*'s famed checking department to have authenticated a conversation that was said to have taken place in a station restaurant in Brest Litovsk. He got his days wrong, too, losing a couple along the way.

In Leningrad there was great excitement over the visit of the troupe, enough for a crowd estimated at a thousand or more to converge at the station as the train pulled in. "Long lines of black-cloaked figures materialized out of the snowy streets," Horace Sutton, *The Saturday Review*'s travel writer, reported. By the time the cast was ready to detrain there was

*Curious Russians watch the arrival in Leningrad. About to leave the station are
Leonard Lyons, Nancy Ryan, and Truman Capote.
(Sam Kasakoff photo, courtesy Ella Gerber.)*

only a narrow aisle through the mob and the players ran the gauntlet, "pummeled with flowers and applause all the way." A good many in the crowd were people of the theatre and leading figures in the arts. The crowd, as it milled about in front of the depot, stalled the company's buses and finally had to be rerouted. Tickets for all fourteen performances were already sold out; the demand was so heavy, in fact, that the venue had to be changed from the Maly Theatre to the larger Palace of Cultural and Industrial Cooperatives (its seldom used full name) with its 2,300 seats. Many buyers waited all night in the snow for tickets that cost as much as sixty rubles—fifteen dollars in the American equivalent.

Five days of rehearsal preceded the opening performance, and Breen used them to whip the company to its peak. First, though, they were installed in the Astoria Hotel, considered the best in Leningrad, a city not yet fully recovered from the devastating siege by the Nazis less than a dozen years before. Capote described the faded elegance of his room as "a miasma of romantic marble statuary, weak-bulbed lamps with tulle shades like ballerina skirts, tables covered with oriental carpeting, plush settees, flower-papered walls kaleidoscopic with gilt-framed paintings of fruit and country idylls. . . ."

Their Russian hosts provided plentiful opportunity for sightseeing (the Hermitage and other Russian museums, the new subway, and principal monuments and buildings) and entertainment, too, with the emphasis on ballet and opera. Translators and guides were with them at all times, and security people maintained an unobtrusive watch to keep them out of any trouble they might encounter. Police were stationed outside the hotel to hold back curious onlookers. When members of the troupe attended a ballet performance at the Kirov Theatre they were mobbed out front, and backstage the ballerinas were astonished to see supposedly oppressed black American women in stylish fur coats and wearing silks and jewelry.

The Astoria boasted a supper room that featured a small local jazz band; the mood of the place was dignified, if not somnolent. There was a space for dancing, but none of the patrons danced; instead, they simply sat at their tables and stared at each other, in part because the management seated people indiscriminately, and thus few knew anyone else. Returning from the ballet, several from the troupe discovered the room and decided the atmosphere was far too somber. Earl Jackson brought in a bongo drum, another brought a trumpet. Jerry Laws, the recently installed stage manager, took over the band's drums and Lorenzo Fuller the piano. To the delight of the suddenly vitalized patrons, the visitors jazzed up Gershwin's "Somebody Loves Me," and from then on it was a riotous and historic jam session which

Living it up in Leningrad—Leonard Lyons and Helen Thigpen.
(Lawrence and Lee Theatre Research Institute, Ohio State University.)

ended with Laws leading most everyone in the place around the floor singing "When the Saints Go Marchin' In." When he sat down the grateful Russians covered his face with kisses. The next night the place was packed, but the company was celebrating elsewhere on Christmas Eve. The patrons went back to staring at each other.

The Russians, on the day before Christmas, thoughtfully set up a decorated fir tree in the middle of the hotel dining room. After another trip to the Kirov—this time for a performance of Moussorgsky's opera *Khovanshchina*—the company gathered around the tree for a party. Several remembered that the previous year their party took place on the ship that bore them from Alexandria to Athens. Carol singing broke out, and at 3:15 a.m., the radio was turned on for a broadcast of carols and Christmas messages they had recorded the day before. Floating through the Soviet ether came "Joy to the World," "Silent Night," and "Gloria in Excelsis Deo." Russians who stayed awake and tuned in may have wondered if another revolution was in progress.

On Christmas Day a good many went to church, some to the Catholic Cathedral where a Polish priest intoned the mass, and others to the Evangelical Baptist Church. At the church they were asked to sing. One of the

Americans said a few words about being away from home on Christmas, and his eyes welled up with tears as he began singing. The other voices rose up behind him. The congregation was not allowed to applaud in church, so, as Sutton wrote, "they waved handkerchiefs instead, cried in them, and finally, feeling the need for some gesture, threw them at the emissaries from Catfish Row."

Breen was busy on his own solidifying Russo-American cultural relations. He was interviewed by the Soviet literary journals *Literaturnaya Gazeta* and *Neva,* and agreed to write a ten-page article for the latter; he taped a New Year's message for Moscow Radio, met with Ambassador Charles Bohlen and his wife, who arrived for the Leningrad opening, and lunched with the directors of the Pushkin Theatre, the Theatre of Comedy, and the Deputy minister of culture of the U.S.S.R. And though he continued to drill and look after the welfare of the company, he still made time to compose a speech for delivery at the premiere. He was concerned, as were others, that the Russians might assume that the opera presented a contemporary view of American Negro life. In order to forestall misinterpretation, he prepared the line, "*Porgy and Bess* is set in the past. It no more reflects the present than if it were about life in Czarist Russia." He asked for it to be included in the programs.

The morning of the premiere, a crisis faced him. He was notified that the programs — which contained a synopsis of the opera's libretto — were still at the printers and would be unavailable by performance time. A solution was devised whereby one of the company's interpreters, a young man everyone knew as Sascha, would take the stage just before the curtain of each act and outline the plot. The Ministry of Culture officials promised a microphone and sound system so that everyone in the huge hall would be able to hear.

Breen hoped for the best. It was going to be a big night. The press was here in force: Daniel Schorr from CBS, Charles Thayer from *The Saturday Evening Post,* Cyrus Sulzberger from *The New York Times,* a photographer from *Life,* newsreel and television cameramen, and members of the local and foreign press, not to mention Leonard Lyons, Truman Capote, and Ira Wolfert, poised to provide Americans at home their views of the breaking of the ice along the cultural frontier. Capote already had his title in mind. During the ride on the train, a Ministry of Culture representative had made a little speech, in which he gave his own translation of an old Latin proverb: "When the cannons are heard, the muses are silent; when the cannons are silent, the muses are heard."

Capote's piece, then, would be titled *The Muses Are Heard.* It would have a hollow ring in Breen's ear for many years after.

Porgy and Bess billboard outside Stanislavsky-Danchenko Theatre.
(Sam Kasakoff photo, courtesy Ella Gerber.)

16

AMERICAN FLAGS were scarce in Leningrad. The one that was found to grace the auditorium of the Palace of Culture for the premiere had only forty-five stars. Three more were sewn on after it was pointed out that the American union was composed of forty-eight states. When the 2,400 members of the audience took their seats they saw above the proscenium an unlikely sight—the American flag crossed with the hammer and sickle of the U.S.S.R. The gala atmosphere was heightened further by baskets of yellow and white flowers on both sides of the stage.

The curtain was scheduled to go up at eight, but first there was ceremony. The United States was well represented by its ambassador; with no Russian of equivalent rank in the house, Bohlen declined the opportunity to make a speech. The anthems of both nations were played, however, with the American taking precedence after a kind of Alphonse and Gaston routine won by the Russians. Then came a battery of photographers clicking away as a Russian ballet master made a welcoming speech in which he stressed comradeship in the arts, after which Breen answered more or less in kind and introduced to the audience the ambassador and his wife; Mrs. Gershwin, Alexander Smallens, and Ethel Ayler and Lorenzo Fuller of the cast. The latter drew a roar of applause when he pronounced the words *"Dobro poshlavat druzya,"* by way of saying, "Welcome, my friends." All this took close to an hour, and the audience became understandably impatient. Breen, as though sensing this, drew everyone off the stage. An expectant quiet descended on the auditorium.

But the curtain still did not rise. Instead, the young translator, Sascha, holding a typewritten copy of the libretto, came onstage and began reading—to the incomprehension of everyone except those in the first few rows of the huge hall. No one had thought to provide him with a microphone. This was too much for the audience to tolerate and with more than an hour gone by and still no sign of an opera, whistling, clapping, and stamping of feet broke out, further drowning Sascha's voice. Smallens finally ended the young man's agony with a lift of his baton to the orchestra.

In the view of Charles Bohlen, that opening night was "a near-disaster. The theatre was too big and the acoustics bad," he wrote in his memoirs. "They were mystified. Then, the vividly acted scene on the island shocked the Russians, who are quite prudish about sex onstage." Yet "Of the cultural, educational, and scientific exchanges that followed the relaxations of tension after Geneva, the one that stands out most vividly in my memory is *Porgy and Bess*."

During the intermission, the Americans in the lobby, the journalists among them, were concerned. Mrs. Bohlen later confided to Capote that she thought, "We laid an egg." Their mood brightened, though, during the second act. Sascha was provided with a microphone, and the audience paid attention to his explanation of what they would see. Numbers which had always been sure-fire, such as "Bess, You Is My Woman Now" (sung by Leslie Scott as Porgy to Martha Flowers as Bess), were received here just as enthusiastically. But a freeze became noticeable during the scene in which Crown appears and seduces Bess. Capote, too, was startled by Breen's bold direction of the scene. "She [Bess] rips off his shirt," he reported, "wraps her arms around him and writhes, sizzles, like bacon in a skillet."

Sascha failed to make clear the nature of the strange packets of "happy dust" dispensed so fiendishly by Sportin' Life, and theories about them developed. One was that they contained condoms. And knowing nothing of the superstitious nature of the inhabitants of Catfish Row, the Russians couldn't understand the Negroes' concern about the buzzard that hovered over Porgy's abode.

The reaction was something akin to culture shock among Russians more accustomed to the officially sanctioned "Soviet realism" and the orthodox presentation of opera. Here, for them, was something startlingly new—an opera distinct from the classic mold, throbbing with violent and realistic life and sexual passion, the whole enriched by sometimes plaintive, sometimes soaring arias and explosive cries and high-spirited rhythms. As Welles

Hangen reported to *The New York Times,* "The pleasure at the departure from neopuritanism of Soviet Society seems to have far surpassed any genuine embarrassment over the show's uninhibited eroticism. Theatregoers here were fascinated by the Americans' ingenuity in making stage action appear to be the organic outgrowth of the music."

Those onstage were aware from the beginning that they were not getting across as usual when the opening lullaby, "Summertime," was greeted with silence instead of the usual applause. But they had broken through in similar situations, and by the time the curtain fell the long evening had clearly been rescued.

For the remainder of their Leningrad performances the opera played to full and enthusiastic audiences, some thirty thousand attendees in all. The programs arrived and helped understanding noticeably. From critics the Russians learned that the Gershwin opera was "a work stamped with brilliant talent and unusual mastery," that the composer drew heavily "from the ethnic genius of the Negro people," that it belonged "in the realm of social drama." The Soviet drama critics also stressed that the engagement would help the Russians better understand the contemporary American artistic forms, although a few felt it necessary to cluck over the uninhibited behavior of Bess and Crown on Kitiwah Island, and one critic pointed out that the opera pictured "the decomposing influence of the capitalistic system on the consciousness, psyche, and moral outlook of a downtrodden people."

Most of the reviews, however, were so favorable that they belied the Bohlens' assessments of the opening-night reaction. What they had regarded as chilliness in the audience was actually an effort to understand this strange and jazzy blend of music and lively movement from America. Leonard Lyons was not far off the mark when he noted: "For fifteen years the Russians have been parched for contact with the Western world, and *Porgy and Bess* is helping to ease the drought." But how to explain the production's success in Russia and around the world, *Newsweek* wondered. The magic, it decided, "came from its direct emotional impact, which transcends any obstacles of language."

And success it turned out to be. By the time the company left for Moscow on January 7, 1956, it had made a deep impression in Leningrad. And not only on the stage. On the streets, and wherever they went, the singers made warm contact with the inhabitants. Their lack of inhibitions may not have made them the best of ambassadors from the official point of view, for they behaved as they might have anywhere else and didn't take too well to being herded around by their Russian hosts. As Bohlen stiffly recalled it, "The cast created a problem for the Russians. The freewheeling actors rebelled at being guided everywhere they went. They wandered out alone and refused to go on the tours. They always attracted large numbers of curious Russians, who, after decades of propaganda, found it difficult to believe there were well-dressed, well-educated black Americans. Soviet authorities complained to the Embassy that the cast should be more disciplined." Breen talked with individual cast members and managed to get more cooperation from them.

The evening of January 6, 1956, the entire company, having finished the Leningrad run the day before, attended its last ballet performance, *The Sleeping Beauty,* at the Kirov Theatre, returned to the hotel for a late supper, and, just before two in the morning of the next day, departed on a special train for Moscow.

It was also on January 6 that a small group of Americans gathered at the airport in Helsinki for a flight to Moscow. Ira Gershwin and Harold Arlen had flown to Stockholm over the polar route, and there they ran into Ella Gerber and Jenifer Heyward, whose visas had come through in time for them to make the Moscow opening and who had flown from New York. From Stockholm the four flew to Helsinki to pick up the Russian plane that would fly them to Moscow by way of Leningrad. But Arlen ran into a problem. Too late to arrange for his visa in California, he had been told it would be awaiting his arrival in Helsinki. Unfortunately, it had not come through, and he was about to be stranded.

Ira Gershwin was vastly upset. After all, it was Arlen who had urged him to make the Russian trip. Until the last possible moment he stayed with Arlen in the airport, making calls to Leningrad and Moscow, but was forced to leave him behind. Ella Gerber and Jenifer Heyward were already seated in the plane, its propellers whirring, while Ira was still arguing with and imploring officials. Then he made a mad dash to the plane, only to be blown back by the rush of the propellers. It took two ground attendants to lift him up the steps to the plane.

Jenifer Heyward, twenty-five, had taken her mother's place when it became clear that Dorothy was too ill to make the trip and had then joined up with Ella Gerber. It was only by chance that they ran into Ira Gershwin and Harold Arlen at the Stockholm airport. Ella would be having a reunion with her husband, who was one of the two white members of the cast, as well as the company's photographer; her visa also would allow her to fulfill another goal, that of learning about contemporary Russian theatre and acting methods. She was a confirmed devotee herself of the Stanislavsky Method.

Jenifer, however, was at loose ends. Trained as a ballet dancer, she had toured many months with the Ballet Russe, traveled to over one hundred cities, suffered through one-night stands, and had decided that a ballet

Jenifer Heyward. (Courtesy Ella Gerber.)

dancer's life involved too much drudgery and sacrifice. A trip to Moscow, she felt, was just what she needed to develop a new outlook on life.

After the stop in Leningrad, a small delegation was waiting to greet Ira upon arrival at the Moscow airport. Coming into the airport lounge from the crunchy hard-packed snow and subzero weather, the group was met by Lee Gershwin, Leonard Lyons, a bored-looking Truman Capote, Warner Watson, and a Russian woman translator. Immediately, the new arrivals were besieged by the other Americans for information about what was going on at home. They gave the impression they had been marooned in an alien land for a good part of their lifetimes. They learned that while *Porgy and Bess* was warming up the exchange between East and West on the cultural level, Nikita Khrushchev, the Soviet premier, was icing up the cold war again on the political front. "We will bury you," was his most oft-quoted remark.

At the Metropole Hotel Ella Gerber was reunited with her husband, Sam Kasakoff, who had been unable to meet her at the airport because the company was rehearsing for the next day's gala opening, and she had another reunion with the cast members she had worked with for so long. She had brought with her something of intense interest to them: a six-page *Life*

*A stroll in Moscow—Ira Gershwin, with cast member Joseph Eubanks
and his wife; between the Eubankses, Leonore Gershwin.
(Sam Kasakoff photo, courtesy Ella Gerber.)*

magazine photo spread about their stay in Leningrad. The headline read:
RUSSIANS LIONIZE "PORGY" CAST. Among the events recorded were what the
text called the "Epic Jam Session" at the Astoria Hotel and the services at
the Baptist Church. Earl Jackson was quoted as saying: "It's crazy here, but
the people are warm." Seeing himself pictured at the microphone in the
Astoria Lounge, he said, "Famous at last."

Harold Arlen's visa problem was solved in time for him to make the
opening at the Stanislavsky Theatre. He had had to spend only one night in
Helsinki. A bonus for him on the flight was meeting David Oistrakh, on his
way home from his American tour.

The 1,450-seat Stanislavsky Theatre provided a warmer, more gracious
atmosphere than Leningrad's Palace of Culture and Science. Stars of theatre,
music, and ballet were in attendance. So were members of the diplomatic
corps, and several high government officials, although the topmost rung was
missing. There was also a more proletarian contingent of factory workers
who had been awarded tickets as a bonus for excellence and productivity in
their work.

Outside, police had to hold back thousands milling around the theatre. Among these were several Negroes who had emigrated to Russia just prior to World War II; they had thought to find a better land with more opportunity, free from racial prejudice. As it was, they had jobs, mostly as laborers and delivery men, but they clearly missed their American homeland. They hung around the theatre, performance after performance, hoping for the chance to talk to people in the cast. None of them was able to see the show; they couldn't afford the price of the tickets. One expatriate, an actor who had despaired of getting work in New York, complained that even when there were black parts in plays, the roles were given to whites, who played them blackface. He wanted to come home, but as a Soviet citizen he could not.

Inside the theatre, speeches were kept brief, and Breen, after a short speech in which he took up the theme of the silent cannons, introduced Ira Gershwin to the audience, most of which knew his brother's music and accorded him his full measure of applause. If there was a failure of understanding of the opera, it wasn't apparent. *Izvestia* commented, "Our American guests have shown that original art is understandable for people of all countries."

"Some spectators wept at the end," Welles Hangen reported to *The New*

Alexander Smallens and Harold Arlen in Moscow, January 1956.
(Sam Kasakoff photo, courtesy Ella Gerber.)

York Times, "others shouted and stamped their feet, but many were still almost hypnotized by the melodies." Ira Gershwin had to be almost literally dragged to the stage after an eight-minute ovation for the cast. Afterward, the entire American contingent was invited to the ambassador's residence, Spasso House. It was quite a party, one of the best in a long history of parties on behalf of *Porgy and Bess.* The company members mingled with ambassadors, journalists, Soviet officials (Andrei Gromyko, the highest-ranking among them), and such "People's Artists" as the singer Larisa Avdeyeva and the composer Aram Khachaturian. Most welcome of all was the food, genuine American food—ham and turkey, fresh fruit. And also Coca-Cola and a plentiful supply of bourbon, Scotch, vodka, and champagne.

John McCurry was both amused and dismayed by the sight of the important Russians stuffing their pockets with oranges, apples, and bananas. "It was as though it was more fruit than they had seen in their lives," he remembered. "Back home any market would have been filled with it, but here all they had were little apples that went for about a dollar apiece."

"Mrs. Bohlen," said his wife, Dorothy, "saw the fruit disappearing, so she took a basket of it and hid it in her bedroom so the kids with us could have it the next day."

A group of eight from the company volunteered to entertain. "They sang and improvised dances," Ambassador Bohlen recalled, "and finally persuaded a young Russian basso named Petrov to sing. The scene of Petrov singing 'Old Man River' in Russian with the cast of *Porgy and Bess* sitting on the floor humming the accompaniment as in the original version of *Show Boat* was a moving one." The party didn't break up until six in the morning.

The next evening, quite to the amazement of Ministry of Culture officials, the highest hierarchy of the Soviet Union attended the performance, none less than Khrushchev, Bulganin, and Molotov. Accompanied by a sixteen-member entourage, they occupied the government box at stage left. It was a rare occurrence; when the leaders came at all it was to the final performance. Breen that evening was at the Bolshoi Theatre, where the famed ballerina Maya Plisetskaya was appearing in *Swan Lake.* Informed while there of the prestigious visitors at the Stanislavsky, he hurried back, hoping to greet them, but was too late. They had left, but not before staying through three curtain calls and joining in the applause.

Breen asked the minister of culture about Khrushchev's sudden appearance. "He's maybe afraid he couldn't get tickets if he waited," the minister replied dryly. This was not all that far from the truth. The twelve thousand tickets had disappeared before the troupe arrived. What minimal supply existed was only on the black market.

Earl Jackson and Helen Thigpen, with the active help of the Breens, made

U.S. Ambassador to Russia Charles Bohlen, here with Andrei Gromyko and Leonard Lyons, at his reception for the Porgy and Bess company. (Sam Kasakoff photo, courtesy Ella Gerber.)

Robert Breen and Ambassador Bohlen share a toast with Russian guests at the party. (Sam Kasakoff photo, courtesy Ella Gerber.)

good their promise to wed in Moscow. The Moscow Baptist Church was crammed with company members, photographers, movie cameramen, and curious Muscovites. Many more stood outside. The Bohlens attended, as did Lyons, Arlen, and Gershwin. Truman Capote was missing, having had too much of the Russian winter and headed back home. How much and just how the ceremony contributed to international amity is not known, but the Russians took it with some seriousness, including it in their newsreels and memorializing it in a half-hour film they made of highlights of the troupe's visit.

Breen kept a log, and the following is a sampling of what he recorded: a guided tour of the city, including the Kremlin, a formal discussion with members of the Soviet Society for Cultural Exchange, a round-table discussion with students of the Stanislavsky Theatre, a concert by the Red Army Ensemble at Tchaikovsky Hall, a visit to the Moscow subway, and, as a kind of finale, a viewing by the entire company of the tombs of Lenin and Stalin, complete with searchlights, newsmen, and photographers. One could almost sense the Soviets compiling propaganda brownie points. But the Americans weren't doing badly either. The black artists of the company were

Robert Breen meets Foreign Minister Gromyko.
(Sam Kasakoff photo, courtesy Ella Gerber.)

*Nancy Ryan, presswoman for the tour, shares a warm
moment with Leslie Scott, alternate for Porgy.
(Sam Kasakoff photo, courtesy Ella Gerber.)*

opening Russian eyes, as noted by Ambassador Bohlen when he attended the Ministry of Culture's farewell party—held in the huge restaurant of the Metropole Hotel, taken over and decorated for the occasion.

A sumptuous supper was served, and a highlight of the evening was a concert given by artists from the Bolshoi and other theatres. "The *Porgy and Bess* cast again surprised the Russians," Bohlen wrote, "by singing difficult classical arias in five languages, including Russian. The Russians had no idea that the black artists had been so solidly grounded in classical music."

It was a festive evening. With Gromyko and other important officials present, and all of them toasting peace and friendship, it might have been supposed that the cold war was perceptibly thawing. Ira Gershwin made a gracious thank-you speech, singling out the Ministry of Culture for its "efficiency, thoughtfulness, and kindness." He had only one complaint—his visit was too short. Breen made the final toast. He enlarged on the theme of the vital place of artistic and cultural exchange between nations and its effect in wider areas. His words were by no means empty; his call for "a two-way conveyor belt" of such exchanges was already being heeded. For him, this visit, this warm evening, with its display of talent from both countries, was the culmination of what he had dreamed for the production.

Their last day in Moscow was a hectic one for the cast, and for Breen, too. An invitation to perform in Bulgaria had come, and it could not be accepted without State Department approval. The decision, by cable and telephone, was that the cold war had indeed not thawed to that degree, and permission was denied. There would be three more stops behind the curtain: Warsaw and Stalinograd in Poland, and Prague, Czechoslovakia.

Ira Gershwin, with Harold Arlen, flew back to Beverly Hills, while his wife, Leonore, decided to remain with the company and go on to Warsaw, as did Ella Gerber and Jenifer Heyward. The cast members had the problem of what to do with the rubles paid to them as part of their salaries and more picked up by stints for Moscow radio. They could not be exchanged for dollars, and they could not be taken out of the country. So, the visitors went shopping.

The state-owned shops, however, in no way resembled Macy's or Bloomingdale's, and all had much the same wares and at the same prices. Members of the troupe bought stocks of fur hats, traveling bags, stamp albums, pieces of jewelry which might be resold back home, vodka and caviar for the train ride to Warsaw. "Except," one lady said, mournfully, "I hate to eat a thousand dollars' worth of it all in one day."

The complete sellouts in Russia resulted in a surplus of rubles for Everyman Opera. There was nothing for Breen to do with the useless money but leave it behind in a bank on Sverdlovsk Square in Moscow.

17

THE INTERNATIONAL success of *Porgy and Bess,* capped by the company's ground-breaking appearances in Leningrad and Moscow, quickened Hollywood's interest in producing a film version. Although movies with black themes performed with black casts were seldom profitable, Gershwin's opera was regarded as an exceptional case. It had long demonstrated its universal appeal and would undoubtedly bring in the foreign revenues Hollywood so badly needed in this time of competition from television.

Breen was insistent on directing the film, and certain of the bidders weren't willing to go along with an untried film director. Blevins Davis complicated matters by vacillating in his loyalty to Breen. There was a period when if they had stood together they might well have controlled the rights, and it was usually Davis who managed to muddle things up by demanding payment for the money he had invested in the stage production.

But both Breen and Davis might have been pushed out of the negotiations if it weren't for the option Dorothy Heyward had given them on *her* rights a few years before. Davis had paid her $5,000 for their control of her ownership of 30 percent of a screen sale. What it amounted to for Breen and Davis was a veto power over any offer anyone else made. Unfortunately, they more often used it against each other.

There were periods of frostiness and anger between them and other periods when they would agree to work together in the same manner in which they had originally created their production. One of these rapprochements was in December 1955, when Breen stopped off in London on his way to Russia. Davis, with partners, had been negotiating to get the rights in his own name and was convinced that Breen had been doing the same for himself. Breen assured him that his main concern was to direct the film, but he was also anxious to get back the money Davis had put into the production and to make him a handsome profit besides.

New bidders kept popping up, and the sums offered increased. Joseph L. Mankiewicz angled for "the property." So did Hal Wallis, Jerry Wald, Otto Preminger, Louis B. Mayer, Harry Cohn, and the director–producer team of George Seaton and William Perlberg. If George Gershwin and DuBose Heyward had been able to look down from their heavens they could only have been astonished by the scramble they had initiated.

As for the rights holders, there were various camps. One was made up of Gershwin family members—beneficiaries of Rose Gershwin's estate and thus copyright owners. Dorothy Heyward was also a copyright owner, and she, with her agent, John Rumsey, and her late husband's agents, Audrey Wood and William Liebling, formed another camp. A third camp was from the Theatre Guild—Lawrence Langner and the Guild's lawyers. On the West Coast, Ira and Leonore Gershwin were banded with agent Irving Lazar.

Dorothy Heyward's agents thought her interests resided with Davis rather than Breen, while the Gershwins and Lazar were more sympathetic to Breen. Actually, Lazar and Ira would have been happier to have both out of the way, so they could handle any negotiations with producers or studios unencumbered.

Breen, on his side, had his lawyers, Aaron Frosch and Arnold Weissberger, while Davis, on his, had his partners, Kay Harrison, head of British Technicolor, and a lawyer, David Stillman.

It was Ira Gershwin, though, who, with the tacit consent of East Coast family members, quietly dominated the situation, even though his share of proceeds would come to only $6^2/_3$ percent of the total. His vital concern (and Leonore's, too) was the artistic protection of his brother's work. But he was tempted strongly by the million-dollar offer made by Columbia Pictures. By then he had fended off, so he later said, some ninety offers for the film rights to the opera. The option Dorothy Heyward had given Breen stood in the way of dealing with Columbia. It would not run out until 1958. Ira queried Dorothy if she would be willing to forgo her loyalty to Breen as the director. In spite of her agent's advice, she held firm. Ira and Leonore also felt some loyalty to Breen—they appreciated all he had done to bring international prestige to the opera—but they were doubtful about his ability to handle the complex task of directing a film. About Davis Ira was much more certain; he thought him far too muddle-headed to be a screen producer.

Ira's way of resolving the situation was to tell Breen to hold off all film negotiations until the touring was completed. This stand made Lawrence Langner particularly unhappy. The Theatre Guild, after all, had lost its entire investment doing the original production of the opera, and had not made a penny on it since, while the copyright holders were reaping a harvest of fees and royalties. He regarded it as arrogant that Ira, with his minuscule $6^2/3$ percentage, could thwart a sale. He favored Davis as the producer. He regarded him as a fine gentleman, but he saw Breen in a less favorable light. He believed the gossip that Breen was a profligate spender of other people's money, that he had loaded Davis and himself with debt. And he had never directed a film.

John Rumsey was angry, too, not only at Ira, but at his agent, Lazar, who, he surmised, had his own Machiavellian interests. Rumsey told Dorothy Heyward that in his opinion Lazar was hoping to collect commissions from Ira, Breen, and whoever finally purchased the rights. As it turned out, Lazar was then having talks with Samuel Goldwyn, who had decided at age seventy-seven that *Porgy and Bess* would be the masterwork of his long and prestigious career. Goldwyn's productions were already part of Hollywood legend: *Dodsworth, Dead End, Wuthering Heights, The Best Years of Our Lives, The Little Foxes,* and, most recently, *Guys and Dolls.* He was also noted for some of the most striking bons mots in the English language, such as "Gentlemen, kindly include me out" and "An oral agreement is not worth the paper it is written on." Whether or not he actually said these things didn't matter. They were attributed to him anyway and were known as "Goldwynisms." But he was not a man to be taken lightly.

THROUGH THE late winter and the spring of 1956, Breen's troupe continued its performances behind the iron curtain. Long before the company arrived in Warsaw on January 24, the twelve thousand tickets available for the week of performances at the National Opera House were sold out, as were those for an additional week at the Wyspianski Theatre in Stalinograd.

Ambassador Joseph Jacobs sent word to the State Department that "people came in on carts from various parts of Poland. They stood around the streets for nights, even though they knew it was sold out, hoping against hope that they might get in or that a little music might filter out."

It was in Warsaw, during the midst of the enthusiasm they created, that a sorry incident cast a pall over the company. Earl Jackson, alternating as Sportin' Life, created a serious disturbance when officials of the Ministry of Culture refused a car to take him to a hospital where Warner Watson, Breen's assistant, was undergoing an operation. It should have been a minor matter. No car was available. And, in any case, Watson was not being allowed visitors.

Jackson became violent, striking and all but knocking out one of the ministry officials. He remained in this state for some time; his tearful wife, Helen Thigpen, and other company members were unable to help. Jackson at this time had been unable to sleep for four nights. Shortly afterward, he left on his own, saying he was going to see a doctor in Rome.

Helen Thigpen remained with the company throughout the rest of the tour. As Wilva Breen said, "The role of Serena and the opportunities it provided her career meant too much to her to give up. And although they had been married for only two weeks, they had been together for well over a year. They were reunited when the tour ended, and Jackson did overcome his troubles, going on to a career in nightclubs."

In Poland, and in Czechoslovakia, too, *Porgy and Bess* came, from all reports, as an eye-opening advance in the staging of opera. Ira Wolfert traveled to Prague with the company and had a talk with a composer whose own new opera was about to go into rehearsal: "He had just seen *Porgy and Bess* and was so excited, ideas were coming to him so rapidly he could hardly speak coherently. He was stopping rehearsals at once to plan a whole new production and he was so full of thoughts about it that he couldn't take time to finish expressing one of them before starting on another."

Maurice Huisman, the former director of the Belgian National Theatre, took over the booking of the tour when the company arrived back in Germany. He was more sympathetically attuned to Breen's purposes and style than had been his predecessor, Anatole Heller. Performances were given in Munich, Stuttgart, Düsseldorf, and Hamburg; in Hamburg more diamonds were worn on opening night than at any time since the city was smashed and burned into near-oblivion during World War II.

From there, it was on to The Hague and Rotterdam in the Netherlands, to Oslo, Norway, Aarhus in Denmark, and to Amsterdam again, where the tour ended on June 3, 1956.

Huisman, a man of cultural refinement, with a love for theatre in all its forms, regarded Breen as an innovator whose influence directly affected European opera long after he left.

"Our opera directors," he said in 1988, "had not come from the stage, from straight theatre, so to speak. No production of the quality Breen gave

Porgy and Bess had been done in the opera field. It was a great surprise for our audiences. He was the first important theatre director to see the staging possibilities in opera. Since Breen's time it has changed, for the better, and it came, partly at least, from his example." His association with Breen did not end with *Porgy and Bess,* for Breen was still preparing to put on his *Blues Opera* (renamed *Free and Easy*) and to tour it in Europe under Huisman's management.

The tour might have continued on if there had been enough theatres large enough to play it. As it was, they had all but exhausted the available large houses, and smaller houses could not sustain the expense of the large cast. Breen, however, was still making plans for more touring, this time to a continent left so far unexplored by him—Australia. Once more he came to the Gershwin trustees, asking for a reduction in the burdensome royalty rate. He was hoping, too, that State Department help would make a tour of the Orient possible. Meanwhile, the scenery was left behind under Huisman's care in Brussels to forestall its attachment by the creditors of Everyman Opera.

W H I L E *Porgy and Bess* was running its final course in Europe, Truman Capote was the guest of Peggy Guggenheim in her Venetian palazzo, writing his account of the long train ride and the troupe's sojourn in Leningrad. Breen had returned to New York in early May, and, as he wrote Ira, "Capote arrived in New York this morning [May 9] and called me this afternoon. I told him I heard he was going to 'murder us' and that he didn't like us or Russia or anything. He claims that he feels we'll be very amused by the piece, and when he finishes it soon, he wants to bring it in and read it to me. He wanted to get permission to quote from one of my letters to Ambassador Bohlen. I readily gave him an okay."

Breen tended to have too trusting a nature, as he realized when he read the first of two long pieces called *The Muses Are Heard* that appeared in *The New Yorker* in October of the same year. He was appalled, as was just about everyone else who had been part of the tour, by the overall satiric tone of Capote's 52,000 words. To make matters worse, the pieces were brought out as a book two months later by Random House to a wide sale around the country.

The effect of it was, for Breen, to make his endeavor seem like a self-aggrandizing venture, its cultural and ambassadorial values a sham. Many of the favorable reviews of the book sustained this notion.

The reviewer for *Time* was delighted with the book, calling it "a wise and witty report on Russia," and regarded as shrewd Capote's guess that Soviet permission for the tour came from "the opera's message about people being happy because they have 'plenty of nothin'.'"

Meyer Levin, writing in the Newark *Star-Ledger*, confessed to reading the book with "sadistic enjoyment. Mr. Capote has long, sharp fingernails. Anyone who wants to learn how to be a cultural snob in one lesson need only read this report and follow the Capote line of attack." Capote, he went on, managed to make "everyone but himself look vulgar and sound stupid. Virtually every remark he quotes is inane. And the reader's pleasure comes, of course, in feeling that like Capote, he, too, is smarter than all those supposedly bright and clever people here impaled."

The chief victims, he went on, were Leonard Lyons and "the hapless Mrs. Ira Gershwin, whose love for wearing diamonds makes her oh so vulnerable. The producers of the show, Mr. and Mrs. Breen, are sitting ducks for Capote's acid-tipped arrows."

What was grand fun to Levin was not nearly so amusing to Horace Sutton, who, after all, had been there. "One unfamiliar with the facts," he wrote in *The Saturday Review*, "might easily come away with the notion that a second rate company was taken to Russia as the personal publicity stunt of Robert Breen and that the result did little but perplex the Russians.

"Anyone who fought through all but impenetrable crowds in front of the theatre in Moscow, who witnessed the warm personal exchanges between the Russian people and the American company, who watched the rapt attention and the emotion created by the performances could scarcely have doubted the success of *Porgy* in Russia."

Sutton found Capote's reportorial capabilities questionable, especially when "the author wonders why he is being stared at and followed. After all, in his black pumps, his striped shirts with white cuffs, his bangs, and his long, flaming red scarf frequently worn babushka style he might well have been an awesome sight in New York." Then Sutton ended with a little scratching of his own: "At spotting a human foible in his fellow travelers Capote is quick as a cat. And when he turns his pen on them the mewlings are heard."

And indeed they were. Quite poignant were those of Catherine Van Buren, who had been a member of the troupe and who reviewed the book for the Berkshire *Eagle*. She countered his "reportage" with some of her own adventures, the cultural value of the trip for her, some touching encounters with Soviet citizens. "But Mr. Capote," she wrote, "was not interested in things like these or in our other efforts. He made no attempt to circulate with the cast as a whole. How can one report on something one doesn't know about? For me, the overall tinge of his book is a tattle-tale gray highlighting the comical and the ridiculous."

In later times, such an account as that of Capote's might have resulted in a suit for slander, for enough testimony could have been gathered to show the considerable rearrangements and distortions of fact, as well as some outright invention. And, in fact, when Breen heard that Reader's Digest Books was preparing a concise version of it he did threaten suit, thus keeping it from a much larger readership. A similar threat might well have deterred *The New Yorker,* or at least caused a more severe checking of fact. He had an offer to do his own book on the trip, but never got around to it.

Understandably, in view of their provenance in *The New Yorker,* the articles were accepted as completely factual. Those of an anti-Soviet persuasion found in them fuel for their convictions. Some reviewers focused, with apparent satisfaction, on the bleak picture presented of life in the Communist society.

For Capote, it was a new vein to pursue, and he followed it with a crushing portrait of Marlon Brando, after which he spent years writing what he called a "nonfiction novel," *In Cold Blood.* When Gerald Clarke's biography of Capote came along in 1988 and he heralded *The Muses Are Heard* as the important precursor of the form, *The New Yorker* was deluged with requests for copies of the pieces.

The Muses Are Heard is still resented by the many survivors of the Russian expedition. Breen and Blevins Davis kept rueing the day they ever staked Capote to the trip, and Leonard Lyons carried a grudge for years. Yet Lyons did have a revenge of sorts. When *In Cold Blood* came out, he mocked Capote's claim, given to interviewers, of his faculty for total recall, thus having no need to take notes. Capote, in each interview he gave, kept changing the percentage his memory retained of events. It would range, as Lyons pointed out, between 90 and 97 percent. He also warned Capote that because he had misquoted him he was going to make Gore Vidal, his rival, the most popular, attractive young writer in America. No reaction came from Capote, until Lyons mentioned in a column that Vidal's sixteenth book was coming out "and he's not yet thirty." This time Capote phoned him immediately. "He's thirty-two!" he shrieked. Lyons printed the response.

On May 8, 1957, Samuel Goldwyn announced at a press conference that he had acquired the screen rights to *Porgy and Bess,* and that the purchase price would be $650,000, a sum which he described as only a down payment against 10 percent of the film's gross earnings. The announcement included the information that Robert Breen would be associate producer of the production.

Breen also had something to tell the reporters. The owners of the opera, he said, had considered other offers of a million dollars, but Goldwyn's offer was accepted because the owners had confidence that the producer would "preserve the integrity of *Porgy and Bess*." He added, "We are lucky to have a man of such passionate zeal."

Much maneuvering had preceded Goldwyn's declaration, and much of it was by Irving Lazar, who was in an anomalous position: He was Ira's agent, but he was also helping Goldwyn obtain the rights he wanted. He wouldn't be allowed to collect commissions from both, although everyone at the New York end assumed that was his aim. Eventually, he and Goldwyn were driving through Beverly Hills one day, and Goldwyn asked him what he could do for him. Lazar pointed to a Rolls-Royce they happened to be passing, and said, "That's what I want." Goldwyn bought it for him—a bargain, for at that time a 10 percent commission would have cost him much more.

Breen had proved a stubborn obstacle to any sale, unless he would be significantly involved in the production, and he had further strengthened his position by acquiring sole possession of the Dorothy Heyward option from Blevins Davis.

It was Herman Sartorius who brought the two former partners together in harmony once more. Breen was able to convince Davis that it would be better if he acted alone on their behalf. In return for Davis's share of the option he agreed to assume Everyman Opera's debts and to repay Davis his earlier investments. He also paid Davis back the $5,000 given to Dorothy Heyward earlier. Breen, penniless as always, managed this by first borrowing $5,000 from Harold Arlen and then borrowing $5,000 from Sartorius to repay Arlen. The enormous debt he took on, amounting to nearly $300,000, he would be able to repay, he assumed optimistically, from the earnings that would come from the film.

Just about everyone who would benefit from a film sale was growing weary of Breen's veto of every offer that came along. Only Dorothy Heyward held firm, although she, too, was having doubts about the wisdom of entrusting her interest to Breen. Goldwyn and Lazar saw the way to solve the impasse: if Breen wanted to be part of the picture process, make him part of it. Goldwyn was a very canny man who knew the value of oral agreements. Lazar talked to Breen and told him that Goldwyn would agree to make him a partner in the proposed production and that it was likely he would want him to direct it, too. These talks occurred in April 1957.

Early in May, Breen, accompanied by Wilva, flew to California and had some meetings with Goldwyn. What he apparently did not know was that

Goldwyn, in making his offer, had already informed the owners of the rights that the Breen option would not be an obstacle and that Lazar would not claim his usual 10 percent commission for arranging the sale. Lazar, in other words, was now the agent for Goldwyn.

Breen found Goldwyn engaging, liked him immediately, and soon felt they were in agreement about a general approach to the film. And, in any case, said Goldwyn, if Breen joined him as associate producer they would jointly decide everything, including the matter of Breen's directing. There would be no discussions with other directors meanwhile.

"What happens if we disagree on a certain sequence?" Breen asked. "Then," said Goldwyn, "we'll shoot it both ways." There was one other thing—that option Breen held. Now, if Breen would sign that over to Goldwyn they could come to a most mutually satisfactory agreement. This he defined as first and prime consideration as the director, an expense allowance during the making of the film, and 5 percent of the film's profits, which he rosily estimated, as Breen's share, at somewhere between $800,000 and a million dollars.

Charmed by Goldwyn, swayed by Lazar, Breen at a private meeting signed away his option on the Heyward rights to Samuel Goldwyn Productions for what were described as "good and valuable considerations." Just what these were would be further defined and set down in a contract to be written. The contracts with the authors and the estates had to be worked out, too, and the signings were some months away. Anyone familiar with Hollywood wheeling and dealing would have had a faint feeling of sickness in the stomach from the naïveté with which Breen let go the only trump card he held. But Breen believed what people told him. He liked Goldwyn, and Sam, Jr., Goldwyn's son, said later that his father genuinely liked Breen and respected his abilities.

"I never should have let Robert go alone to that lunch with Goldwyn," Wilva said afterward.

Where were Breen's lawyers when this was happening? They were in New York in their offices, and Breen was out there alone, physically unrepresented except, as he assumed, by Lazar. And why should he not trust Goldwyn, with his fine track record, who had been close to the Gershwins, who was still on a friendly basis with Ira, who had already made it clear that he thought Goldwyn, a fiercely independent mogul, the best suited to do justice to the filming of the opera. Two days after Breen signed the paper, Goldwyn, the last impediment removed, made his announcement about his acquisition of the rights.

On his return to New York, Breen waited for his contract to arrive and meanwhile busied himself drafting the screenplay he expected to direct and with the preparation of *Free and Easy* for a projected European tour, not unlike the way he had first traveled with *Porgy and Bess*. He was now hoping to extend *Porgy*'s range over most of the inhabited portions of the globe, along with presenting it as an American entry in the 1958 Brussels World's Fair.

Urgent messages soon came from Hollywood requesting him to come to the West Coast to begin work with Goldwyn. Early in July, he halted his other activities and flew there with Wilva, where they were put up at the Beverly Wilshire Hotel in true Hollywood luxury style.

His contract was still "in preparation," but he reported each day to the studio anyway and had occasional talks with Goldwyn and with his assistants. In the Goldwyn Studio commissary he heard disquieting rumors that talks were being held with other directors, that in fact they had begun soon after he had signed the paper. He was told by Goldwyn associates not to make an issue of it, to "wait and play it by ear." The old man, as they called Goldwyn, not only liked him, but enjoyed working with him.

He presented his own screenplay version of the opera, in which he had made changes that allowed for more variety and visual movement; for instance, instead of opening with the singing of "Summertime," the first scene had Sportin' Life arriving on a boat at the wharf in Charleston. When Ira Gershwin read it, he complained, "What the hell are we going to do for music?" Goldwyn privately went searching for his own screenwriter.

For the cast, Breen had a barrelful of possibilities from performers he had assembled over several years, but Goldwyn saw none of them as possibilities for the leads. He believed profoundly in stars. On one personality, they were in agreement: Sammy Davis, Jr., as Sportin' Life. Breen vastly admired the entertainer and had directed him in some excerpts from the opera that were performed at a Waldorf-Astoria benefit and later at the White House. In any case, Davis was already angling and promoting himself for the role.

A month after Breen arrived at the studio came the blow. Goldwyn, during a meeting with him, remarked in a fatherly way that he knew how much he had his heart set on directing the film, but the problem was that he had never directed a film before and that this was going to be a very expensive picture, costing several million dollars. Now if it were to be, say, a million-dollar picture, then Robert could direct. As it was, he would like it if Robert would work on other pictures with him afterward and on pictures with his son, Sam, Jr.

"Do you understand what I'm thinking?" Goldwyn asked.

Breen replied: "I hear what you think, but I also know what I think."

It was finally clear to him that he should have had a lawyer at his side when he had first met with Goldwyn. In fact, Aaron Frosch, in New York, had advised him that he should not have started work without the promised contract.

In desperation, Wilva wrote Frosch from Hollywood: "Robert has taken everything on faith and trust—and really believed everything they told him. And he has become very fond of Mr. Goldwyn, whom he finds fascinating. His enthusiasm for and belief in Goldwyn, and in the integrity of his word caused Robert to go forward without (rather against) advice of counsel— and without any representation. It now becomes obvious that there is no faint idea of his directing—and that there never was!" Their only resort, she concluded, was to stop the signing of the contracts with the authors and the estates, which was imminent.

Breen flew back to New York and made the effort. But now, not even Dorothy Heyward was on his side.

Late that August, she wrote Audrey Wood to say she would sign the Goldwyn contract and would also sign "a legal-language letter telling Breen to get lost. I have been on friendly terms with Breen for many years, have accepted many favors (probably at Davis's expense) and feel that I ought at least to write and say I am sorry his whole life is disintegrating—as it obviously is, since, for some strange reason, he has made *Porgy and Bess* his life. I had been waiting for a call from Bob and wanted to urge him to face the fact that it would take a dozen years to persuade all the owners to sign with him. He apparently feels that with me in his pocket he can win the day. But he seems to me not a man who wants revenge, but one who really expects to produce the film—plus the world tour."

She was angry on another account. Breen had never notified her that he had transferred her option to Goldwyn. One of her reasons for giving it to him was that he had assured her he would want her to work on the scenario so that she could maintain some control of it. But now she had lost this opportunity. Goldwyn had shown no signs of consulting her on the screenplay, while Ira, she said, would have certain privileges regarding the music and lyrics. She was thankful for only one thing, that the hassling and haggling over a screen version of *Porgy and Bess* for more than a quarter of a century was at an end.

Breen must have had something of a Don Quixote in him to think he could tilt against a man as powerful as Goldwyn. His efforts to maintain control of what he had signed away were foolhardy, if not downright foolish. He could have stayed in Hollywood, accepted his "associate producer" status, and collected a handsome salary. As it was, he had nothing—nothing but the prospect of a long, bitter legal battle with Goldwyn.

"Breen was a very nice man," Sam Goldwyn, Jr., said recently. "The problem was that he wanted a picture close to the way he had directed the production. My father had never seen that version. What he had seen was the original opera as it had been done in nineteen thirty-five, and he retained a fond memory of it and wanted it done in that way. It was inevitable that they would disagree."

PART THREE

PORGY REDUX

Samuel Goldwyn inveigled Sidney Poitier into playing Porgy in his film production of Porgy and Bess. *(Museum of Modern Art Film Stills Archive.)*

18

SAMUEL GOLDWYN looked upon *Porgy and Bess* as the culmination of his long and successful career. Born in Warsaw as Schmuel Gelbfisz, he emigrated to the United States when he was sixteen and settled in Gloversville, New York, where he changed his name to Samuel Goldfish, and, fittingly, he became a glove salesman. Through his marriage to the sister of Jesse L. Lasky, a motion picture pioneer, he entered the movie business in 1913 and, with Lasky and Cecil B. DeMille, produced one of the earliest pictures made in Hollywood, *The Squaw Man*.

In 1922, after adding his name to Metro-Goldwyn-Mayer, he went independent as a producer and remained fiercely so ever after. For him, independence meant exercising total control over a film, from its making to its marketing. "I make my pictures to please myself," he often said. And he also said: "I am the producer. I do not shove the money under the door and go home." These attitudes of his may help explain some but not all of the flare-ups and vicissitudes that befell *Porgy and Bess* during its checkered journey to the screen.

Being independent, using his own financing, meant that Goldwyn brooked no interference from studio bosses, corporate chairmen, or bank loan officers. He owned his studio at the junction of 3rd Street and Formosa Avenue in Los Angeles and rented out space when not in production himself. Just what magic or formula he possessed that resulted in so many successful films over the years was a continuing subject of speculation. He didn't write, didn't direct, and several who had worked for him in these capacities claimed that he had little understanding of their creative problems. Ben Hecht once described his treatment of writers as comparable to an irritated man shaking a slot machine.

Conversely, he admired writers and thought their contributions the key to the success of pictures. He had enough story sense himself to buy the kind of properties which, when given hands-on treatment, would result in box-office success. Early on, he tried to get George Bernard Shaw to write for him, and they had a discussion in London over tea. Goldwyn emphasized to Shaw the quality he wanted to bring to motion pictures. From Shaw then came the often quoted remark: "The trouble is, Mr. Goldwyn, that you are only interested in art and I am only interested in money."

Goldwyn believed in star quality as a key to picture success, and the list of stars that graced his films reads like an honor roll of Hollywood's best, brightest, and most beautiful: Gary Cooper, Walter Huston, Laurence Olivier, Lana Turner, Loretta Young, Danny Kaye, Marlon Brando. Twenty-seven of his films won Academy Awards in various categories; his *The Best Years of Our Lives* received a total of seven. William Wyler was the director, as he was for several others of Goldwyn's most honored films. The caliber of the directors he chose may have helped explain his success. Wyler also directed *Dodsworth, Dead End, These Three, The Westerner, The Little Foxes,* and *Wuthering Heights,* all great Goldwyn successes—and he made sure they were known as *his* accomplishments.

He seldom moved out of the mainstream. "Motion pictures," he stated, "should never embarrass a man when he brings his wife to the theatre." And "I seriously object to seeing on the screen what belongs in the bedroom." (The mainstream has shifted radically since those statements were made.) Lindsay Anderson, the English filmmaker, once said in attempting to account for Goldwyn's success, "There are lucky ones whose great hearts, shallow and commonplace as bedpans, beat in instinctive tune with the great heart of the public. Goldwyn is blessed with that divine confidence in the rightness of his own intuition."

Anderson's assessment came from outside the traditions and scheme of things in Hollywood. Goldwyn's astuteness also lay in his choice of material, good writers, directors, and actors. It was a familiar enough formula for producing, but he worked it far better than most. Lillian Hellman's play *The Little Foxes* was a Broadway hit; combined with Wyler's direction and Bette Davis's astringent performance, it became a movie hit, too. But with the long-proven *Guys and Dolls* it would have been hard to miss. He expected nothing less from *Porgy and Bess,* a work of proven popularity as well as quality.

Within his own milieu, Goldwyn had the respect due his years of accomplishment. "Samuel Goldwyn Presents" was a trademark comparable to Cadillac in automobiles. Other moguls, such as Louis B. Mayer, were being ditched by studios in a time of drastic change in Hollywood, but Goldwyn still retained his cachet and power. His attention to detail in every aspect of the production and exploitation of a film was part of the legend of "the Goldwyn touch." William Wyler wondered just what that touch was, since he had directed the most honored of Goldwyn's films. More than coincidence, he thought.

And while his publicists claimed that Goldwyn had been trying to obtain the screen rights to the Gershwin-Heyward opera for many years, it was not until his studio manager suggested it in early 1957 as a project that he actively made his bid.

W H E N A L L T H E contracts were signed by the many parties on October 8, 1957, Ira wrote Goldwyn: "For *Porgy and Bess* to reach the screen under your guidance with your devotion to finer pictures is a matter of great importance and satisfaction to all of us."

Dorothy Heyward sent him a message, too. "Now *Porgy and Bess* has reached the high distinction of being a Samuel Goldwyn Production. I feel safe now that I know a precious possession is in your keeping."

The chances are good that both messages were written at the prodding of Goldwyn's press agent. Lawrence Stewart, an assistant to Ira at the time, recalled that Ira was never enthusiastic about having a film made from the opera, nor were other members of the Gershwin family. They feared its debasement in Hollywood hands. "Ira's wife, Leonore," Stewart said, "was particularly adamant about it. I think they both felt movies went downhill after *Sunset Boulevard.* Ira probably regarded Goldwyn as the best of a poor lot, and I think he just wanted to get the movie out of his hair, finally."

It was almost to be expected that Goldwyn, once the Robert Breen obstacle had been removed, would turn to the director who had mounted the first stage production of the opera. Rouben Mamoulian was better acquainted with the story, the complexities of staging it in musical and dramatic terms; he was also highly regarded for his fluent command of the film medium. However, the directors Goldwyn talked to first (rumors of which had reached Breen) were Elia Kazan, King Vidor, and Frank Capra.

Mamoulian, after being away from motion pictures for nearly ten years, had just finished *Silk Stockings,* an adaptation of the Cole Porter musical based on *Ninotchka.* It is likely that Ira Gershwin had his doubts about Mamoulian, owing to his reputation for being headstrong, but still he seemed the best available choice.

Goldwyn was confident that *Porgy and Bess* would be the greatest of all his films. Wasn't George Gershwin without doubt the greatest American composer? He was convinced, too, that the DuBose Heyward libretto was the greatest in all American musical theater. "I am as excited about this as if it were my first picture," he told reporters. "They couldn't afford to do in the theatre what I am doing."

AFTER BREEN'S screenplay was discarded (it was never seriously considered), Goldwyn cast about for a writer. Ketti Frings was brought in to do a treatment for $40,000 — a large sum then. She decided to go back to the Heyward novel and the play for additional material. She found in the book the cemetery scene in which the superstitious mourners rushed from the graveyard for fear the last one out would be the next one in. "She emphasized the primitive superstitious elements," Stewart said, "and when Ira read it he all but went through the roof, because he thought it was condescending and racist. Goldwyn wasn't bothered by it, but he brought in another screenwriter."

The new writer was N. Richard Nash, one of the crop of writers out of television and author of the successful play and film *The Rainmaker.* He stayed as close as possible to the libretto. While Oliver Smith developed sketches and plans for the settings, Goldwyn went about the business of casting. And here he encountered unexpected obstacles. When Harry Belafonte was mentioned for the part of Porgy, he quickly announced that he didn't want to play a part on his knees. (Whether the role was actually offered him is doubtful.)

Then an ad appeared in *The Hollywood Reporter* under the aegis of the "Council for the Improvement of Negro Theater Arts." Few had heard of the organization, but the double-page spread was impressive. It called loudly on black performers not to work in Goldwyn's production, and the tone of its condemnation had a familiar ring.

Dorothy and DuBose Heyward used the race situation in the South to write a lot of allegories in which Negroes were violent or gentle, humble or conniving, and given to erupting with all sorts of goings-on after their day's work in the white folks' kitchen or the white folks' yard was over, like sniffing happy dust, careless love, crapshooting, drinking, topping it all off with knife play.

But it never occurred to them that the Negro was not innately any of this, and that he was just like anybody else and that this was a human being's way of reacting to the dehumanizing pressure of a master race.

Goldwyn counterattacked by pledging that all his profits from *Porgy and Bess* would be devoted to charity. He also gave $1,000 to a local fund-raising drive by the NAACP, causing the council to accuse him of trying to buy his way into the good graces of the black community. Emotions were running high because of events outside Hollywood. Headline news came almost daily from Little Rock, Arkansas, where the National Guard blocked black students from entering a high school, where President Eisenhower sent in federal troops to safeguard their admission.

The West Coast chapter of the NAACP poured some oil on the troubled waters by saying that it "had complete confidence that Mr. Goldwyn's production will be done in the best of taste with the utmost regard for the dignity of the Negro people." Sammy Davis, Jr.'s desire to play Sportin' Life was not lessened. To win the part he mobilized friends such as Frank Sinatra, George Burns, and Jack Benny to use their influence with Goldwyn. One evening, Goldwyn appeared at the dressing room door of the nightclub in which Davis was appearing and said, "Mr. Davis, you are Sportin' Life. The part is yours. Now will you get all these guys off my back?"

Sidney Poitier was far less willing to play Porgy when it was announced he was Goldwyn's choice for the role. "In my judgment," he wrote later, "*Porgy and Bess* was not material complimentary to black people." In his own rising career, beginning with *No Way Out* in 1950, he had played roles that in their idealism, humanity, and courage emphasized values approved of by both whites and blacks. He was almost alone among black actors in being regarded as an important draw at the box office.

Poitier refused the role of Porgy and then learned to his consternation that one of his agents had already committed him to Goldwyn. Worse, any conflict over fulfilling the commitment would endanger another role he was anxious to play, in Stanley Kramer's *The Defiant Ones*.

Soon pressure on Poitier came from both blacks and whites, undoubtedly stimulated by Goldwyn's press agents. Leonard Lyons helpfully reported in his column that Ralph Bunche and other important black personages were prevailing on Poitier to change his mind about playing Porgy. And true enough, several did call him, pointing out that the opera was a classic, that it was not demeaning to black people, and that surely Goldwyn, of all people, would make the film with the requisite dignity. On the other hand, Harry Belafonte, buttressed by Lena Horne, urged him to hold firm in his refusal.

Poitier met with Goldwyn to explain his position. As a Goldwyn biographer wrote, "This was like a fly inviting himself up to dine with a spider." As Poitier told it, he drove with his agent "to Mr. Goldwyn's residence. It was, as I expected, a fantastically beautiful house with a croquet court on the grounds, a swimming pool, and all the rest of an American dream as fully realized as you could ever hope to find . . . within a few minutes a very solicitous, very charming Sam Goldwyn appears."

As wary as Poitier was, he was soon enough worn down. Goldwyn was always at his persuasive best in a tête-à-tête situation. He devoutly promised Poitier that the film would become a classic, that the role was the greatest to befall any actor, and that from it would come superstardom. These prophecies did not sway Poitier as much as his fear of losing the role in *The Defiant Ones* if he continued to thwart Goldwyn. He agreed, finally, telling Goldwyn he would do the role to the best of his ability. Goldwyn suggested a joint statement for the press, which, when it appeared, made Poitier realize he should be more wary about agreeing to press statements that he did not compose himself.

He was quoted as saying to Goldwyn, "I am happy to say that my reservations were washed away by Mr. Goldwyn in his plan for *Porgy and Bess*. I am very happy that I met with Mr. Goldwyn. I found him almost as sensitive as I am."

His agreement helped bring Dorothy Dandridge into the fold as Bess and Pearl Bailey as Serena. Both had had their qualms and had been subjected to pressure. Mail came to them, some with threats. A letter to Dandridge asked: "Why do you always have to play a prostitute role, when you are supposed to be holding up Negro womanhood with dignity?" The inaccurate reference was to her role in *Carmen Jones*, the film directed by Otto Preminger a few years earlier.

Pearl Bailey had less objection to the story than to the heavy dialect, which she thought detracted from the dignity of the inhabitants of Catfish Row. She was promised that she would be listened to if she requested changes. She did. The word "watermelon" distressed her greatly, and it was removed.

In March 1958, Goldwyn, his casting problems resolved, met with his production heads and told them that filming would begin in the early summer, and money was to be no object. Catfish Row would be built on Stage 8, one of the largest in Hollywood. Irene Sharaff would do the costumes, Oliver Smith the sets, and André Previn would arrange and supervise the music.

Richard Nash's screenplay, though it followed the stage version closely, had to go through several drafts before Goldwyn was satisfied with it. He was concerned about the pace and tempo of the story movement; wherever possible, he wanted cuts in the dialogue and the recitative. Some of the crowd singing he felt too "operatic" to be understood by general audiences.

Mamoulian had many suggestions, too, and they didn't always jibe with Goldwyn's. Mamoulian wanted the action to move outside Catfish Row for certain scenes, while Goldwyn preferred them confined within the set. Mamoulian thought location shooting in and around Charleston would help the atmosphere of the film. Goldwyn didn't think such a trip necessary. The Kitiwah Island backgrounds could be found closer to home.

Mamoulian also worried about the size and details of the huge Catfish Row set being built on the lot. He wanted in it some of the steamy, decayed atmosphere he had seen in Charleston when he was researching the stage play. He cautioned Smith: "While it is necessary to enlarge this set and give it greater diversity for filmic purposes, still this should be done within proper bounds, so that it is not open to the usual reproach that Hollywood automatically magnifies and glamorizes everything it touches. While stylized, the set should still carry the illusion of reality and the flavor of authenticity—it should convincingly belong to the Charleston of 1912."

BY THE TIME the monumental set was completed and decorated at a cost of more than $2,000,000, its dimensions had not been notably diminished; filming would be done in the curvilinear and spacious Todd-AO process, with its six-track stereophonic sound system. To build the interiors and exteriors of Catfish Row required three months' work, as noted by Goldwyn's publicist, "from forty carpenters, ten laborers, eight plasterers, ten grips, eight property men, ten special effects men and ten painters."

Irene Sharaff designed two sets of clothes for the cast—everyday working clothes and "finery" for the picnic scenes. For the former a good deal of time and work went into dyeing, wrinkling, pulling, and even sandpapering to make the clothes appear used and worn; for the latter, the award-winning designer expressed her color sense by giving the men purple, pink, yellow, and orchid shirts, and on the women she put varicolored plumed hats.

THE FIRST DRESS rehearsal on the set was called for 9 a.m. on July 3, 1958. A telephone call came to the Goldwyn house at six that same morning. Sam was not yet awake, so his wife, Frances, answered. She waited until she heard her husband stirring in his bedroom and then told him the news. A huge fire had consumed the sound stage that held the Catfish Row set and all the costumes.

Goldwyn took the news with surprising calm. "Was anybody hurt?" he asked, and went about eating his breakfast.

By the time he arrived at the studio, the sound stage and everything on it was a smoking ruin. Fire trucks and hoses were everywhere in the company street. Employees stood in a purposeless huddle; Irene Sharaff was in a state of near hysteria. Goldwyn went to his office to handle the crisis and found messages of condolence and support already there. One came from Cecil B. DeMille. "The phoenix arose from the ashes of a great fire," it read, "and so will you with your great strength."

Later the same day, Goldwyn called an emergency meeting in his office. Among those there were Mamoulian, the principal members of the cast, and the heads of Goldwyn's production department. He soon lifted their morale. Although production would have to be postponed, the film would still be made, he told them. A new set would be built, new costumes made, and the result would be an even greater picture. "And God's will be done," Pearl Bailey said.

The official cause given for the fire was faulty wiring, but suspicions grew from the fact that it had started so early in the morning, when the studio was empty. The Los Angeles fire chief said he would investigate arson as a possible cause, and there was a theory that the fire had been set to sabotage the project. Goldwyn took issue with this, as did the local chapter of the NAACP, which issued a statement saying such "implications were ridiculous."

With time on their hands while the new set was being built, Goldwyn and Mamoulian discussed possible changes in their plans. Mamoulian still wanted to make use of some Charleston backgrounds; he thought the new set being built was losing the flavor and reality of Catfish Row. He spoke with the authority of his work on the stage versions of the play and opera and from his travels to Charleston. More important from Goldwyn's point of view, as knowledgeable Hollywood watchers said, Mamoulian was turning it into *his* rather than a Goldwyn picture. He had even gone so far as to hire Russell Birdwell as his personal press agent.

On a Sunday morning late in July, Goldwyn, after notifying Mamoulian's agent, the same Irving Lazar who had assisted his purchase of the rights, issued a press statement: "I have the greatest respect for Rouben Mamoulian, but he and I could not see eye to eye on various matters. Rather than go on with basic differences of opinion between us I have relieved him and engaged Otto Preminger to direct *Porgy and Bess*."

Mamoulian, understandably, reacted with outrage. He had worked on the project for eight months, he said, and there had not been an iota of dissension between them. He admitted that they had disagreed on a matter relating to his "personal and private life." This involved Goldwyn's dictate that in all publicity he would be identified as the "sole creator" of the film, and Mamoulian was not to give any press interviews on his own about the film. Lazar had urged him to capitulate to Goldwyn on this issue and take a more anonymous role as the director, but Mamoulian refused. He would not allow his rights as an individual and a director to be trampled upon. And he had also refused to work without pay during the layoff period caused by the fire.

Goldwyn countered by paying him his entire director's fee of $75,000, but Mamoulian was hardly mollified when he learned that Otto Preminger would be getting twice that amount. He still bore a wound from being fired while directing *Laura* several years before and being replaced by the same Preminger. While Birdwell battled Goldwyn in the press, Mamoulian took his complaints to the Screen Directors Guild, which quickly supported him. Goldwyn was "condemned" for dismissing a director for "frivolous, spiteful, or dictatorial reasons."

Although this might have meant picketing and refusal to work by several on the picture, Goldwyn maintained a dignified silence and refused to meet with the Directors Guild board to explain his actions. He had time on his side, and he waited for matters to simmer down.

But another uproar came when Birdwell held a press conference at which he produced Leigh Whipper, a veteran black actor. Whipper described himself as the president of the Negro Actors Guild of America and announced he was withdrawing from the role of the Crab Man in *Porgy and Bess*.

"In unknowing or unsympathetic hands," he went on, the opera could be made into a slur upon his people. But as directed by Mamoulian in the past the play and the opera "achieved the heights of human dignity and spiritual content." Other versions, he claimed, "trampled the Negro in degradation." Now the film version was in hands, he believed, "unsympathetic to my people. I have first-hand information concerning the new director which brands him, to me, as a man who has no respect for my people."

Birdwell, as it turned out, had made a strategic error, and Goldwyn's publicists were quick to take advantage. They marshaled Pearl Bailey, Sammy Davis, Jr., and Brock Peters (cast as Crown) in rebuttal. "As far as Mr. Preminger being anti-anything," Bailey said, "I think that is an awful statement. I think Mr. Preminger is going to do a wonderful job."

"He is a very sensitive man," Davis said of Preminger. "*Porgy and Bess* would be as great even if it were done with Polish actors. I think someone along the line is starting up a lot of unrest."

Whipper, during the press conference, said that his contract with Goldwyn, which he would no longer honor, was for fifteen weeks' work as an actor and as a counselor on the script. Goldwyn's people were able to show that Whipper's "letter of agreement" called for two days of work for a salary of $300 and that was all. Then it turned out that the Negro Actors Guild was not a labor group, but a benevolent organization.

The upshot of the furor was that support turned against Mamoulian, who was rumored to have instigated the Whipper charges (he claimed he had not), in favor of Goldwyn. Sidney Poitier, who was away from Hollywood at the time, said that Whipper's statement was ridiculous. The Screen Actors Guild black members deplored the injection of racial issues into the production.

"When we—the estate, and Mrs. DuBose Heyward and myself," said Ira Gershwin, "granted the picture rights to Mr. Goldwyn we did not seek to impose any restrictions upon him as to who should direct the picture because of our complete confidence in his taste and judgment."

A Screen Directors Guild board meeting was held which Goldwyn finally agreed to attend. "I am exhausted from not saying anything," he explained. Preminger was there, too, ready to sue Mamoulian and defend himself. "I'm Jewish," he declared. "I ran away from Hitler. How can they say I'm anti-Negro?"

Peace soon broke out. Preminger was cleared of any taint of racial bias. Mamoulian retreated after renouncing Birdwell and firing Lazar as his agent. Goldwyn mollified the board. And, as the new set rose like a phoenix from the ashes of the old, Otto Preminger took over the direction.

Mamoulian's battle with Goldwyn all but marked the effective end of his career as a film director. Why this became so is hard to determine. He had reached the age of sixty, but he had a long thirty years of life ahead of him. There were those who said he was too self-willed, always convinced of the rightness of his approaches, and that these traits hampered his relationships with producers and the financial powers that controlled the industry.

He was an elegant man, whose leanings were as much those of an artist as a craftsman. He had one last chance when a few years later he was hired to direct *Cleopatra,* a project that had as its main asset Elizabeth Taylor, who was persuaded to star in it for a salary of a million dollars—larger than any yet offered to anyone. The filming in England was plagued by cost-cutting due to the financial troubles of 20th Century-Fox, and then the near-fatal illness of Taylor. Shooting was halted after ten minutes had been put on film. By the time it began again, locations were switched to Italy, the film was being rewritten, Mamoulian resigned, and Joseph L. Mankiewicz took over the direction.

Some of the ten minutes shot by Mamoulian are said to be in the bloated three-and-a-half-hour finished film. His successful career began with his direction of *Porgy,* and it would have been fitting if it had ended with *Porgy.* The circle, unfortunately, did not close.

Mamoulian continued, however, to be sought out by scholars, students, and admirers of his fluency and style, "his unerring sense," as one critic summed him up, "of rhythm in exploring the sensuous pleasures of movement."

Bess tries to resist the lure of Sportin' Life's "happy dust." Sammy Davis, Jr., sang; Dandridge was dubbed. (Museum of Modern Art Film Stills Archive.)

19

OTTO PREMINGER was not known for a light touch as a film director nor for a gentle way with actors. When he began work on *Porgy and Bess* his reputation as a tyrant and monster on the set had preceded him, and cast members were already wondering who would be the first to encounter his rage. He also was known to be a battler against censorship, and he had fought the good fight by defying the Production Code Administration in refusing to excise the word "virgin" from his film *The Moon Is Blue*. His *The Man With the Golden Arm* was a graphic (for the times) and powerful depiction of drug addiction.

Goldwyn's choice of Preminger, however, was largely due to his film version of *Carmen Jones,* which he had produced and directed in 1954. Taken from the Oscar Hammerstein II musical (a modernization of the Bizet opera with a black cast), Preminger assembled as remarkable a group of black performers yet to appear in a single Hollywood production. The delicately beautiful Dorothy Dandridge played the title role, a worker in a Southern parachute factory; Harry Belafonte, in his second film, was her ill-fated lover, Joe. Also in the cast were Pearl Bailey and the youthful Diahann Carroll. Since none had truly operatic voices, Preminger dubbed Marilyn Horne for Carmen and Le Vern Hutcherson for Joe. The film was a popular and critical success.

When Sidney Poitier reported for rehearsals in mid-September, the new set was built, the costumes re-created, and the music prerecorded. He looked for signs, as he said, "to confirm the presence of furies lying dormant somewhere in the strong, muscular, bald-headed director." He found none. Preminger had a warm, kind, and generous side. He told stories, liked to joke and laugh. Poitier decided that the tales of temper had been exaggerated.

Poitier wasn't present or needed during the location scenes, which were filmed first near Stockton, California, 350 miles from the studio. As Porgy, he was confined to the Catfish Row set. He spent the intervening days in a San Francisco hotel room working on synchronizing his lip movements to the prerecorded songs, "ghosted" by the baritone Robert McFerrin.

By then, he had spent a good deal of time with McFerrin, who had never sung Porgy before but had sung *Rigoletto* at the Metropolitan Opera. While McFerrin sang, Poitier would study every move he made, and, in turn, Poitier would read the lines and act them out to help McFerrin get in the right dramatic mood. In San Francisco he had with him three long-playing recordings of the score. He sang the songs while listening to the records, staring into a mirror to make sure his lips and tongue were coinciding with McFerrin's singing.

A ghost was hired for Dorothy Dandridge, too, but she was soon dismissed because it was decided she didn't sound the way the actress looked. Her place was taken by the Bach specialist Adele Addison, whose phrasing and crystal-clear voice were regarded as a suitable match for Dandridge. Although Poitier and Dandridge clutched each other and sang together often in the film, McFerrin and Addison never sang together. The process involved recording the orchestral accompaniment first, then dubbing in McFerrin and Addison separately.

"There I was," Addison recalled, "singing some glorious love duets, and my lover wasn't even in the building. Just the conductor and I, each listening on earphones to an orchestra that had been disbanded months before."

Diahann Carroll's voice was not regarded as suitable either. As Clara, she had the plum song, "Summertime." Goldwyn was insistent on having black singers for all off-screen voices, but, strangely, none could be found with the quality André Previn demanded. A French-English white girl, Loulie Jean Norman, was chosen to be Carroll's singing voice. Her major experience was in choral groups that sang background music for movies and popular records.

Stranger still was the fact that after the film's release, Diahann Carroll recorded an album in which she sang (very well) not only "Summertime," but virtually all the songs of the show. The conductor for the record was the same André Previn.

Pearl Bailey and Sammy Davis, Jr., did their own singing in the film, but

Davis was missing from the soundtrack album. He was contracted to sing only for Decca Records, and the film album was put out by Columbia. Thus, on that album, Cab Calloway sings Sportin' Life.

But this sort of thing is to be expected from Hollywood, just as one would expect to find the wharves of Charleston re-created on Venice Island in the San Joaquin River, a 5,500-acre chunk of peat that rose and fell with the tide. The pier and wharves were built not only for the trip to Kitiwah Island, but for an opening scene in which the fishermen return home to the strains of "Summertime," as sung by Clara, as sung by Loulie Jean Norman. Kitiwah Island was discovered on the other side of the river, an expanse of sand and brush. In this characterless landscape Sammy Davis, Jr., sang and danced the show-stopper "It Ain't Necessarily So" and Dandridge was dragged off into the brush by Brock Peters who (as Crown) sang for himself.

When the cast was reassembled on Catfish Row at the studio, Poitier got

Dorothy Dandridge bares a bit of leg as Bess in the Goldwyn film.
(Museum of Modern Art Film Stills Archive.)

his first glimpse of the Preminger of legend. Dorothy Dandridge was his first victim. "What's the matter with you, Dorothy?" he snarled at her over something he thought not quite right. "You're supposed to be an actress. Now what kind of actress are you that you can't do such a simple thing?"

The scene was tried again, with Dandridge attempting to control her shattered nerves, but she hadn't gotten far before there was another explosion.

"No, no, no!" Preminger shrieked. "What's the matter with you? That's stupid what you're doing. You don't have any intelligence at all. You don't even know who Bess is. You call yourself an actress. You get paid to perform, not to do stupid things."

The others watched the tableau, frozen, unable to react. Poitier saw what to him was Dandridge's pathetic attempt to maintain her dignity. "On that day," he wrote, "I learned that the serene look she wore only served to mask the fears, frustrations, and insecurities that were tumbling around inside her all the time." To Sammy Davis, Jr., "She was simply out on another plane

Otto Preminger, the irascible director of the film.
(Museum of Modern Art Film Stills Archive.)

somewhere, and none of us knew where she was heading. Sometimes it seemed as if she weren't there."

In her own account, she told of her doubts about the project. She had thought she might be able to bring some dignity into playing the role of Bess, in that way countering some of the pressure, and even threats, against her. Before the fire that had destroyed the set, she had had the guidance of Mamoulian, who had given her ideas on how to play the role. She admired Mamoulian and agreed with his position that they should utilize Charleston backgrounds. When the new set was built it struck her that "a cleanup" was under way, "an actual attempt to make life on Catfish Row look not so bad. Everyone connected with the movie embarked on a program to take the terror, fright and oppression out of ghetto living."

With Preminger she had felt safe at the beginning. It was his direction of her in *Carmen Jones* that had brought her to stardom. And at the time he had taken a romantic interest in her. Her shock was all the greater when the first onslaught came and he made her the butt of his anger. "The old romance was now as cold as iced cucumbers," she wrote.

Then it was Poitier's turn to feel the fury. It happened in the midst of his "singing" "Bess, You Is My Woman Now," as he hobbled around on the shin shoes attached to his knees. From up high, where Preminger was sitting on a crane, came a shriek: "What's the matter with you?" The entire crew, more than a hundred, grew alert, and Poitier was aware of their attention. "Don't you know how to sing the song?" Preminger went on. "Didn't you study the lip sync? You've got to feel it and make the audience feel it."

"Yes, I understand that," Poitier said, determined to remain professional.

"Then why are you doing this stupid thing?"

Poitier remained silent, and the tension eased. But hardly a half minute into the next take, Preminger yelled, "Cut, cut! Mr. Poitier, you call yourself an actor. What kind of actor are you? Don't talk. I am the director here. I'll tell you what you are—an actor who doesn't know what he is doing."

Through the ranting, Poitier quietly removed the shin shoes and stood up. "I'm going home," he told Preminger. "To my hotel. When you have the time, and come and apologize in person, I will consider coming back."

The telephone rang in his hotel room soon after. "Sidney, Sidney, can't you take a little joke?" Preminger wheedled. Poitier made clear to him the way he expected to be treated from then on, and there were no more tirades directed at him during the making of the film, though Preminger did not mend his ways with others in the cast. "It was the way he was," Poitier said, and he shared the feeling of many others that Preminger was better suited to producing than directing.

For Sammy Davis, Jr., working with Preminger could not have been, as he said, "more pleasurable." They not only got along well together, but they socialized off the set. "We'd hit the nightclubs most nights," Davis remembered. "All he ever wanted to talk about was broads. As I could always muster up half a dozen good-looking ladies with a couple of phone calls, I soon found I couldn't get rid of Otto even if I'd wanted to."

It was inevitable that Preminger and Goldwyn would clash. Preminger had his own power as a producer and could be just as tough and hard-headed. He had been warned early on by the director Billy Wilder, "Look out for yourself. We all know this is going to be Goldwyn's last picture. Don't make it yours, too." But Preminger knew how to protect himself. He could not only shout back, he had his own way of keeping others from meddling with his work, and this was to "cut the film in his head" as he went along—instead of shooting scenes from a variety of angles, from which choices would be made later in the editing room, he filmed little more than he expected to use.

The net result was that there was less leeway for Goldwyn to reedit the film after Preminger made the first or "director's" cut. Goldwyn was infuriated when he discovered what Preminger was up to. "He was shooting nothing but boom shots," a Goldwyn employee said—in other words, seldom coming in for the close-ups that would give more intimacy to a scene. During one lengthy love duet between Poitier and Dandridge the camera remained head-on and unmoving throughout the entire song. He may have thought this treatment to be more operatic, but the overall effect was to slow the pace of the film to a crawl. The 70mm Todd-AO scope worked to better advantage where scenes had more sweep and spectacle.

Goldwyn's complaints did him no good. Preminger threatened to abandon the film if the producer did not stay out of his way. From then on, Goldwyn was seldom seen on the set. The thought of firing Preminger undoubtedly occurred to him, but his budget was soaring to a high $7,000,000 level as it was, and it would hardly be seemly for him to fire another director.

Preminger, on his side, had little respect for Goldwyn's understanding of the technical areas of filmmaking; he claimed that the producer was unaware the 70mm negative could be reduced in the laboratory to standard 35mm size, and wanted Preminger to shoot in both. He said afterward that Goldwyn failed to "contribute one useful thought, or word of advice throughout the entire production. He had a very good business brain. He tried to get the most out of his money and he tested people to see if they really knew their business, even when they had proved themselves. He only knew always to buy the best."

Goldwyn had a revenge of sorts on Preminger. In addition to his fee,

Crown (Brock Peters) locked in a death struggle with Porgy (Sidney Poitier) in the film. (Museum of Modern Art Film Stills Archive.)

Goldwyn had offered him a 10 percent profit percentage. Preminger's agent objected that this was far below his usual share, and Preminger ended the impasse by saying grandly, "When the picture is finished, we will leave it to you to determine the profit percentage." He may not have been aware of Goldwyn's feeling about the worth of verbal agreements.

When Preminger finished his directing stint, his agent went to see Goldwyn and asked him to decide the profit percentage that would be owed his client. "You remember that we left it up to you," he reminded him.

"You left the participation to me?" said Goldwyn. "So, there is no participation."

Once Preminger was gone, Goldwyn settled into his routine of fine-tuning the film. He ran the film over and over again, checking the color balance, insisting that in the rerecording of voices, music, and sound effects every word of the dialogue and lyrics be absolutely understandable. Because of the stereophonic soundtrack, voices and sounds had to be keyed to the positions from where they emanated from the screen. Six different soundtracks were needed to accomplish this; sound volume had to be adjusted, too, over the screen's wide expanse. Otherwise, someone fifty yards from Porgy would be heard by the audience at his same sound level. That process took months.

Goldwyn was finally ready to show the completed film to the executives of Columbia Pictures, which would handle its distribution. They praised it for the most part, but one of them wondered if the story wasn't too downbeat. Perhaps, he suggested, in the last scene Porgy could get up and walk.

Ira Gershwin declared himself satisfied. "It is everything we hoped for," he said. Dorothy Heyward said, "The film exceeds our highest expectations." Bennett Cerf, at Random House, which published a million souvenir books for the film, lauded it in advance in *This Week* magazine. The critic for *The Hollywood Reporter* was so overawed at a preview that his raving about it could only have been equaled by a dedicated team of Goldwyn press agents. The other film trade paper, *Variety,* found no fault either, but wondered about the box-office prospects of an operatic movie with an all-black cast.

Following the ballyhoo, during which the Goldwyn name predominated (a ten-page section in *Life* seemed to assume that the producer had pretty much done the whole thing himself), the film opened in four cities in June 1959, playing on a two-performance-a-day basis. Goldwyn could not have asked for a better review than the one he read when he opened the *New York Times*.

"The mills of the gods have ground slowly," critic Bosley Crowther wrote, "but they have ground exceedingly well in delivering at last a fine film version of the famous folk opera." He went on to praise it as a "stunning, exciting and moving film, packed with human emotions and cheerful and mournful melodies. It bids fair to be as much a classic on the screen as it is on the stage."

But other reviews were not as roseate. Some, like that in *Time,* blamed the "colossal Todd-AO process" for making Catfish Row look "almost as big as a football field, and the action often feels about as intimate as line play seen from the second tier." The *New Yorker* critic judged the set about the size of Levittown on Long Island.

The stereophonic sound system came in for blame. The voices blaring from a dozen loudspeakers made the spectator "feel trapped in the middle of a cheering section." *The New Yorker* advised sitting as far back as possible in the theatre. Worse, though, was "the cinematic monotony: Preminger has directed it as though it were a Bayreuth production of *Götterdämmerung*," said *Time.* "Choruses march and countermarch; actors lumber woodenly about the stage obviously counting their steps."

It was also pointed out that the opera was scrubbed clean of "its itch-and-scratch folksiness. The actors speak in precise, cultivated accents that are miles away from the Negro slums of South Carolina."

All of Mamoulian's (and Breen's) fears that a too lavish treatment would work against the film were realized. Catfish Row looked less like anything found in Charleston than a charmingly run-down but still genteel area of Greenwich Village. Arthur Knight in *The Saturday Review* struggled to be kind, but the sets bothered him: too theatrical, and they clashed with a real fishing wharf (so he thought) and a real steamer on its way to Kitiwah Island. And the costumes were far too lavish for the milieu. No one liked the French cocotte-style slit skirt worn by Dorothy Dandridge.

She was also faulted for being much too sweet, gentle, and ladylike a former prostitute. ("She emphasizes the elegance of her bones more than the sins of her flesh," said *Time*.) As for Sidney Poitier, the role of the humble

Dandridge and Poitier on a set "almost as big as a football field."
(Museum of Modern Art Film Stills Archive.)

Pearl Bailey, here with Sidney Poitier and Dorothy Dandridge, asked
Goldwyn to remove the word "watermelon," and he did.
(Museum of Modern Art Film Stills Archive.)

beggar, Porgy, did his career no good (although it was quickly lifted up by a fine performance in *The Defiant Ones*). He came across as a fine, exceedingly handsome young gentleman, physically handicapped and temporarily impoverished to be sure and only goaded to violence for love of and to protect a good woman. At the end, the audience could feel certain that he would find his Bess again in New York. Dorothy Heyward did eventually complain about this, pointing out that the ending (which she had suggested originally) was supposed to be pathetic and not uplifting.

Bosley Crowther, somewhat out on a limb with his opinion, wrote a Sunday piece for his newspaper in which he recommended seeing the movie twice, as he had done. On the second viewing he saw meaningful implications in the performance of Sammy Davis, Jr., who played Sportin' Life as the incarnation of evil. "He is a sneering, glinting spokesman for downright godlessness and a sly Pied Piper for licentiousness when he leads the people in a wild dance at the end of the song. He has added a dimension to *Porgy and Bess*."

But on this second viewing he noticed certain flaws, although he took a shot at other critics who had not reacted to the film as he had: "The entertainment does have the operatic form and by such is liberated from the aesthetic demand of realism that some critics of the film have curiously wished to impose." He now acknowledged, however, that Preminger and Goldwyn might have made the time and the milieu clearer, that Dandridge's skirt was a bit much, and that he doubted that Porgy, as played so upstandingly by Poitier, would have been attracted "by such a dame." And he rather regretted the aura of optimism at the film's end.

The attack of the killer critics may have hurt the box office, but more likely it was the nature of the film that kept people from thronging into the theatres. It was well publicized that the singing voices of most of the actors were not their own. (In addition to Brock Peters, Pearl Bailey's voice was authentic, as were those of Earl Jackson, Helen Thigpen, and Moses LaMarr of the Breen production, who were seen and heard in minor roles.) Putting an opera on the screen — realistically or unrealistically — was cumbersome enough without artful techniques to overcome the static moments, but a synthetic version had even less appeal. Star singers such as Leontyne Price and William Warfield might well have served the film better and given it a more genuine quality. But that would have required Goldwyn to abandon his Hollywood standards for judging physical star appeal.

As it turned out, Goldwyn's swan song was that of a dying swan. To make matters worse, there was now more complaint from the black community, not over the film's cinematic deficiencies but "for its stereotypes," its portrayal of Negroes "at their worst." *Ebony* magazine called it "the same old kettle of catfish."

Playwright Lorraine Hansberry was virulently outspoken: "We object to roles which consistently depict our women as wicked and our men as weak. We do not want to see six-foot Sidney Poitier on his knees crying for a slit-skirted wench. We do not want the wench to be beautiful Dorothy Dandridge who sniffs 'happy dust' and drinks liquor from a bottle at the rim of an alley crap game. We do not like to see our intelligent stars reduced to the level of Catfish Row when they have already risen to the heights of La Scala. . . ." She failed to mention that those heights had been reached by the same *Porgy and Bess*.

In the Los Angeles *Sentinel,* A. S. Young proposed that Goldwyn atone for his sin with an antidote: "If he will spend $7 million to make the story of Martin Luther King Jr. and the Montgomery walkers, and distribute this great progressive saga around the world, then I'll say, let him have *Porgy and Bess*."

The film encountered more trouble with its Southern engagements when some theatre owners refused to allow blacks to see the film in their segregated houses. As might have been expected, the theatres were picketed by black organizations. In Louisville, Kentucky, a Unitarian congregation organized a bus trip to take a mixed group of blacks and whites to a performance in Indianapolis, Indiana. In Atlanta, Georgia, the Fine Arts Theatre was prepared to show the film to a nonsegregated audience, but suddenly Goldwyn (probably more from anger and frustration rather than fear) canceled all showings in the South, declaring that he did not want to contribute to racial tensions there.

The Atlanta *Journal* chastised him for what it regarded as censorship from Hollywood. "Presenting it for a limited engagement," it said, "would be child's play compared to operating a lunch counter in the South these days." But the Charleston *News and Courier* blamed the situation on black pressure, saying that "a concerted campaign of bias, bigotry, and misplaced racial consciousness has chased this work of art out of motion picture theatres."

On its release in Europe, the film met no opposition other than a lack of enthusiasm from critics and public alike. For those who had seen the Breen-Davis touring version, it was a disappointment, in no way comparable to the liveliness and freshness of the stage version's talented cast. In Europe, the star names in the film meant little.

Just how much money the film lost, Goldwyn never mentioned. In any case, it had been funded by his charitable organization, the Goldwyn Foundation, where its profits were also destined to go. The authors' estates never saw the profit percentages they were supposed to get, although some money did come in from the sale of the soundtrack album.

The film disappeared from view, and it remains unavailable, owing to an ironic circumstance. Instead of an outright sale, Goldwyn had bought a fifteen-year lease of the rights. After that time lapse, the film could not be shown without permission of the authors or their estates and, even if permission were given, would have required an additional payment. According to law, a print of every American film made must be placed in the Library of Congress. Goldwyn's *Porgy and Bess* can be seen there, by appointment. It's not easy. The film is in nine reels, each one of which must be placed on a viewing machine in a small cubicle seating one.

Sam Goldwyn, Jr., a successful producer himself, deeply regretted being unable to rerelease the film after the lease ran out in 1972. (His father died in 1974 at age ninety-one, lingering five years after suffering a stroke in 1969.) The necessary permissions were denied by family members and estate inheritors, it has been said. In addition, the situation regarding rights became increasingly complicated when they were acquired by music publishing and recording entities.

T H E R E L E A S E of the film did have an important side effect: it spawned a host of recordings of the opera and the music from it. All that was missing, said one record reviewer, was a set of *Porgy* variations played by harpsichordist Wanda Landowska and a symphonic synthesis by Leopold Stokowski. Otherwise, there was a large menu to choose from. There was, of course, the original soundtrack recording (Columbia) from the film, the album cover featuring Poitier and Dandridge, though neither was heard on the record. Adele Addison, who actually sang Bess, received no mention, although her lovely voice added immeasurably to the quality of the album, which also demonstrated that Gershwin was reasonably well served by André Previn, the film's musical director.

RCA Victor seized the opportunity to release on its Camden label a long-playing version of the recording it made, following the premiere of the opera, with Lawrence Tibbett and Helen Jepson. One of its features was the "Buzzard Song," omitted until then, and another was its fine rendition by Tibbett of "I Got Plenty o' Nuttin'." Columbia also brought back into stock its 1951 three-record set produced by Goddard Lieberson, which was found to hold up remarkably well. Decca's 1940 album, made with Todd Duncan, Anne Brown, and Avon Long, also came back into record stores.

Jazz artists were attracted to the Gershwin score soon after the opera's debut. Nine months after the opening, Billie Holiday made a recording of "Summertime" that was anything but a lullaby in its mood; "hot and anxious" was the way one reviewer described it. The small instrumental group that accompanied her was of equal note; it included Artie Shaw, Bunny Berigan, and Joe Bushkin.

Coincident with the release of the movie version came a recording by Ella Fitzgerald and Louis Armstrong, one of the finest albums ever to treat the score in the jazz idiom. As supervised by Norman Granz, Fitzgerald sang the female parts and Armstrong the male, he also providing the trumpet solos. About Armstrong a critic reported, "Out of nowhere comes Louis' trumpet, playing 'Summertime' so as to get the scalp tingling . . . probably the only musician who ever lived who could blast out a lullaby on a trumpet, and still make it sound like a lullaby."

Sammy Davis, Jr., and Diahann Carroll recorded their own albums of *Porgy* songs, and another was made by Harry Belafonte and Lena Horne, in spite of their previous opposition to the opera. Miles Davis, Rex Stewart, and

Cootie Williams chimed in with jazz versions in their individual styles. They were followed by many others over the years—importantly by Mel Tormé and Frances Faye, together in a three-record set—all attesting to the perennial appeal and durability of the music in a popular, or "nonoperatic," vein, as well as its place in the world's musical history.

20

ROBERT BREEN'S relationship with *Porgy and Bess* did not end with his exit from the Goldwyn film production. In attempting to finance a production of Harold Arlen's *Free and Easy* he went back to his idea of pairing and alternating it with *Porgy and Bess.* This meant, though, that he would need a renewal of the stage rights from the opera's authors and trustees. As before, the negotiations were frustrating, partly due to his insistence on having exclusive worldwide rights to stage performances.

But there was already a hitch. Rights had been granted to the Debin Agency, a New York–based assembler of stock productions for summer tent theatres, for a series of road performances in 1958. Breen not only regarded this as a betrayal of what he had assumed were negotiations in good faith with agents and lawyers, but he was startled to learn another piece of news. As he wrote Ira: "A juicy bit of information received from the P & B company grapevine is that ELLA GERBER is slated to 'direct' the various stock versions. This is just about the end!"

A much more powerful obstacle to his plans was Samuel Goldwyn, then in the midst of producing the film version. He had thoughtfully inserted a clause into *his* contract that expressly blocked stage versions from playing anywhere while the film was in its release patterns. Breen fumed and fought, but for Goldwyn a contract on paper was worth its weight in gold. More gall for Breen came when one of his former company managers entered into the bidding war. Eventually the negotiations became academic due to the increasing demand for *Porgy and Bess* by opera companies in many countries that wished to add it to their repertories.

Unable to capitalize *Free and Easy* on his own, Breen enlisted a young New Yorker, Stanley Chase, who had produced off-Broadway the long-running Weill's *The Threepenny Opera* and on Broadway a revival of O'Neill's *A Moon for the Misbegotten*. Conflicts between them soon developed, mainly because each considered himself the show's producer.

Breen, though lacking finances, had already done much to develop the show from its earlier basis in the Arna Bontemps novel *God Sends Sunday* and from a stage version by the black poet Countee Cullen. Both Cab Calloway and Sammy Davis, Jr., had opted out of the starring role of a jockey, and the tap dancer Harold Nicholas was cast instead, along with Irene Williams, who had sung Bess in *Porgy and Bess*. Other *Porgy* tour veterans took roles, too, among them Martha Flowers, Moses LaMarr, and Lillian Hayman.

The frothy plot about a country-boy jockey enamored of the "Queen of the St. Louis Women" served mainly to justify a series of blues and jazz numbers and dances that ranged from the cakewalk to tap. One of the show's lasting numbers was "Blues in the Night." Breen attempted to direct in line with his ideas about total theatre—the integration of music, songs, dance, dialogue, and action. This took work and exhaustive rehearsal, and progress was too slow for the impatient Stanley Chase.

It was expected that the show would follow a path similar to the vaunted *Porgy and Bess* tour: after the tryout engagements in Europe it would open in New York and would continue on tour. Breen's hope, too, was that a new production of *Porgy and Bess* could be alternated with it. In Brussels, where the rehearsals took place, Maurice Huisman, who had arranged bookings in Amsterdam, Brussels, and Paris, wondered if Breen was having a nervous breakdown: "He would give a performer a small movement and have him do it over and over while the others stood around. It was like a needle sticking in a record groove."

A blowup came, finally. Chase put the show's musical director, Quincy Jones, in charge of the stage direction, and Breen was all but banished from the rehearsal hall. Ten weeks of performances demonstrated that the show lacked the power to captivate audiences.

After the closing, in early 1960, of *Free and Easy* in Paris, where he was relegated to the role of an onlooker, Breen spent much of the next four years pursuing a legal case against Goldwyn for fraud and breach of contract. The case was postponed again and again, and when it did come to trial, a parade

Prior to the rehearsal for Free and Easy: *Robert Breen, musical director
Quincy Jones, Irene Williams, and, standing, producer Stanley Chase.
(Courtesy Stanley Chase.)*

of famous Hollywood names took to the witness stand, where one and all proclaimed the by now eighty-one-year-old Goldwyn a man of honor, integrity, and, above all, his word. The jury was duly impressed. The case was lost.

Breen had reached the lowest point in his life and career. He was penniless. During long stretches in Hollywood while the trial took its prolonged course, he had to depend on the kindness of friends for a place to stay. Wilva, in New York, took odd jobs to pay the rent on the apartment and was able to send him only a few dollars' pocket money. When he returned to New York he was out of the stream of things. He busied himself with plans for plays, movies, a new tour of *Porgy and Bess,* but was unable to fulfill them.

Breen eventually abandoned his plan for another tour, but not before he attempted to organize one for Japan and other countries of the Orient. Dorothy Heyward and other copyright holders were in favor of the tour, but Ira withheld his approval. Dorothy, probably at Breen's urging, wrote Ira in April 1960. The film by this time was having hard going. In the exchange of letters Dorothy said, "I am distressed that Mr. Lazar is again making trouble for the proposed Oriental tour." She also charged Ira with holding up the sale of the movie rights for so many years so that it eventually fell into Goldwyn's hands.

Ira's letter in answer is interesting in the shifts of mind and intention it indicates. It was true, he said, that he had not favored most of the offers over the previous twenty years. But that was because he questioned the artistic integrity of some of the promoters, or the terms offered, or both: "Actually, when I looked most favorably upon the million-dollar offer from Columbia Pictures, it was your signed agreement with Bob whereby he could purchase your share that stymied this deal and the deal with Mr. Goldwyn almost didn't come off because of the same."

In his recent biography of Goldwyn, A. Scott Berg cites some gossip about the offer by Columbia's Harry Cohn: "Gershwin never seriously considered Harry Cohn's proposal, once he said he hoped to produce the film with a white cast in blackface—Al Jolson as Porgy, Fred Astaire as . . . Sportin' Life, and Rita Hayworth as Bess." In fact, Al Jolson had made his own offer for the rights, and it was Jerry Wald who hoped to produce the film for Columbia with a black cast and an outstanding director. Ira had earlier attempted to persuade Breen to go along with the Columbia offer. Such anecdotes about producers abound in Hollywood.

Ira went on to say to Dorothy, "Incidentally, I must tell you that I received no pay whatsoever for all the time I spent on the movie—there must have been at least fifty conferences—and I do think Mr. Goldwyn did a splendid job. You, too, are on record as saying you were pleased with the film."

After denying that Lazar had anything to do with spiking Breen's Oriental tour, Ira carefully said he was in favor of it but didn't think it cricket to have a company play a foreign city before the film finished its run overseas. Thus he threw his support to Goldwyn, and it would seem, too, that this was a nice way of saying he was washing his hands of Breen, especially at a time when he was suing his agent and producer. While Ira never publicly disavowed Goldwyn's film, in later years, in private, he professed to dislike it intensely.

Breen's supporters began to fade away, some literally. The first to go was his faithful friend Herman Sartorius, who died of a stroke in May 1960. Dorothy Heyward went into a New York hospital in November 1961 for an appendectomy. Always frail, she had had a long series of illnesses, but even so, the operation was regarded as routine. She did not survive it.

Ella Gerber, during the trip to Eastern Europe, had formed a close friendship with Jenifer Heyward. Disconsolate after learning of her mother's death, Jenifer went to Ella's apartment, and it was Ella who telephoned Breen the evening of Sunday, November 19, with the sad news. Breen relayed it to Blevins Davis: "Am rushing this note to you. Dorothy Heyward died Sunday night. The operation was very successful (they also removed gallstones) and Dorothy was cheery and very fine indeed. Jenifer visited her at 5:pm. By the time she got back to her apartment, the hospital phoned and said Dorothy had gone into a coma. They had no idea what caused her to go at the time. Jenifer is leaving this afternoon with Dorothy's body for Charleston and there will be no service of any kind here—only in Charleston."

The service for Dorothy Heyward was held in Saint Philip's Protestant Episcopal Church, and she was buried in the church's cemetery next to where her husband lay. Only a few blocks away was Cabbage Row, prettified now and a mecca for tourists and, in a sense, a monument to the two of them.

Breen and Davis had by this time repaired most of their differences. "What a shock and a blow!" he wrote Davis about Dorothy's death. They seldom met, but they kept up a correspondence which revealed their ruefulness and regret at the way things had turned out for them. *Porgy and Bess* had catapulted them literally onto the world's stages, but it also caused them great bitterness.

"You and I," Davis wrote Breen in 1961 from Kansas City, "could have been the two most important forces in the American theatre, but with two or three exceptions that despicable entourage, and the Fifth Columnists who surrounded you, succeeded in writing the verdict. Perhaps the time is not too late. The door is wide open and always has been . . . I think it is a burning shame that the written record of *Porgy* which also appeared in *The New Yorker* stands today as the reference book in the libraries about our joint effort."

Davis castigated the Goldwyn film: "No verve or life. Sammy Davis is absolutely revolting and Dandridge so refined it was laughable. Preminger's direction has the aura of *Mourning Becomes Electra*. They are doing no business whatsoever in Kansas City. It's too bad that the whole thing went on the rocks, because it could have been a classic. I think we both deserve just what we got out of the deal, however, because trusting those Gershwins and the rest of the pack only made come true what I told you the first day of rehearsal in Dallas. You and I could have done some great things in the theatre and maybe before it is too late we can do something again worthwhile."

Breen was not inclined to blame the Gershwins for the loss of the screen rights and gently reproached Davis for his own blunders, but he agreed with him that theirs was the only good and true approach to *Porgy and Bess*. When the City Center Opera Company in New York gave it sixteen performances during the spring of 1961, he wrote Davis, "*Opera* they have made it. They proved that P and B can be dull, just as Goldwyn did. Hell, we could have made a better movie with a Polaroid camera and a stapler."

In the same letter, detailing the work he had to do in supplying documents to his lawyer for the trial, he complained, "I almost wish I had never heard of *Porgy and Bess*—much less had anything to do with it!" From then on, he said, he would abandon theatre and concentrate on films.

That arena proved difficult for him, too. He developed script ideas, but they never reached the production stage. Now and then he took on a role in a television drama, but times were generally hard for him, and he and Wilva were often behind in the rent for the apartment they shared above the Hudson Theatre. It was Wilva who would go out and work at anything from typing to typesetting to keep them afloat. Breen was profoundly gratified by a signal event of March 1965: On March 11 President Lyndon Johnson presented to Congress a bill for a National Endowment for the Arts. "I was so damned happy, I nearly cried," he wrote Davis.

They discussed writing a book about their association with *Porgy and Bess*. "The amusing thing about Capote's book," Breen wrote him in 1966, "we all think it is dreadful and horrible. But people in general think it is great, and are envious of our being the subjects of it. There's a new paperback edition of it and I notice at the local bookstore that it sells like proverbial hotcakes. The public thinks we are most proud of it!"

The life of Blevins Davis had by this time taken an odd turn. To most of his friends he had mysteriously disappeared, and certainly from his usual circuit of Kansas City, New York, Washington, and London. Much of the fortune left him by his wife was gone, owing partly to his generosity and partly to bad investments. One of these investments was a mine in the Peruvian Andes thought to have a rich lode of molybdenum. He went to Lima to live and to further explore his claim, certain that one day he would strike it rich. A local priest became his friend and live-in companion.

In 1970 Davis was dickering with a group of Swiss and German bankers for $10,000,000 he was hoping they would invest in his mine. He wrote Breen that soon he expected to have his fortune back. It was only a matter of time. "Before long," he added, "we will pick up where we left off."

In May 1971, Breen reminded Davis that he had never wanted to hear of P & B again, but there was a new development. "You'll remember I wrote you some time ago that Goldwyn had only leased the film rights. His time runs out a year and a half from now. Hugo Pollack—one of the attorneys for the Gershwin Estate—called me several weeks ago and bemoaned the fact that I hadn't directed the film, and what a big mistake they had all made, and so on. I told him we were interested in making another film when Goldwyn's rights run out. He was ecstatic—and said when we were ready he was sure they could negotiate a release from Goldwyn before the final date of his expiration.

"But—this project is not one we would jump into. The stage and film version would have to be prepared at the same time. We would open the stage production in Europe—then go to Prague and shoot the film. . . ." As Maurice Huisman, who remained Breen's good friend, said of him, "He always looked forward, always recovered from blows or failures, always was ready to try again."

Two months later, Davis was in London, combining a business and pleasure trip. He was in an apartment building elevator, on his way to visit an old friend, when he collapsed and died of a heart attack. He was sixty-eight. His mine had still not produced molybdenum, but, as he had earlier phoned Breen, he "was bubbling over with hope for it." The obituaries noted his achievements in the field of the performing arts, notably those projects which sent representatives of the performing arts, including *Porgy and Bess,* to other nations. "His wife," one said, "the widow of James Norman Hill, the railroad magnate, left him roughly $9 million, which paid the bills for what subsequently became national policy."

For Breen, there was no more talk of *Porgy and Bess.* And soon there was no more talk of anything. Slowly, over the years, his memory loss became increasingly apparent. Eventually, he was diagnosed as a victim of Alzheimer's disease. Wilva took over his care, and kept him, an invalid, with her in the same apartment that had seen many years of his involvements with ANTA and *Porgy and Bess.* Finally, he had to be institutionalized, a gentle man, without a memory. He died on March 31, 1990.

When the men of the Debin Agency came to Ella Gerber to ask her to direct the road show they were planning, she was busy directing local stock companies in theatres in various cities. She was surprised they had not gone to Robert Breen, but agreed to take on the show, provided they not cause interference with the way she would do it. She had the Breen model to rely on and some ideas of her own.

Gerber, then a dynamic woman in her early forties, never had the slightest doubt about her abilities and could take charge of a production as efficiently as anyone else. The sets built for the traveling show had to serve for both proscenium and in-the-round theatres. Although not based on Wolfgang Roth's settings for the Breen-Davis production, in his eyes they were close

In New Zealand, 1965, Ella Gerber directed a production of Porgy and Bess *with Martha Flowers and the renowned Maori baritone Inia Te Wiata as the leads. (Courtesy Ella Gerber. Credit: The Auckland Star.)*

enough to warrant threatening a lawsuit. Gerber persuaded John Bubbles to reprise the role of Sportin' Life and brought back two of her favorites as Porgy and Bess, Le Vern Hutcherson and Martha Flowers.

The seventeen-week tour was a large success and demonstrated that *Porgy and Bess* could fill summer theatres seating audiences of as many as three thousand. From then on, Ella Gerber was in constant demand as a director of the opera. During the next two decades she was the director for no fewer than twenty-one different productions.

The most unusual of these was done in New Zealand in 1965, when she was invited by the New Zealand Opera Company to direct it with a Maori cast, except for a few principals brought from the States. Amateurs, with the exception of Inia Te Wiata, who sang Porgy, the Maoris required eight weeks of training rather than the more usual five. During the performances around the country, Gerber flew back to New York to stage the opera at City Center, then returned to the Maori company for an Australian tour.

That same year *Porgy and Bess* was brought into the Vienna Volksoper's permanent repertory, with William Warfield imported to sing Porgy. Other major European opera houses soon followed: in 1967, Sweden's Göteborg Opera and the Oslo Opera in Norway. In France, between 1967 and 1969, seven city opera houses, from Rouen to Nice, gave performances. During that period the opera also played in West Germany, Hungary, Czechoslovakia, Bulgaria, and Turkey. In 1970, East Berliners saw it for the first time at their innovative Komische Oper. A young director, Götz Friedrich, gave it a vigorous staging according to a correspondent for *Opera News,* in a "superbly designed" set by Reinhardt Zimmerman. Seventeen years later, Friedrich came to the United States to audition singers for a new production he was mounting in West Berlin.

Ella Gerber was called on again in 1970 to stage the opera for the first time in Charleston, South Carolina, on the occasion of the three-hundredth anniversary of the city's founding. Local amateurs made up the cast, and so many flocked to Gerber's casting call that she decided to fill the stage with more than a hundred men, women, and children. "They worked so hard and enthusiastically," she said, "that for me it was the best performance ever given." Times had changed. The theatre was desegregated, and at the sumptuous party thrown afterward, blacks and whites socialized freely.

By the seventies, *Porgy and Bess* had securely established its place as one of America's most important musical works. But there were clouds over it still, and, all its success to the contrary, they would not dissipate. In his passionate book *The Crisis of the Negro Intellectual,* Harold Cruze called the work "the most contradictory cultural symbol ever created in the Western World."

He went so far as to demand that it be "forever banned by all Negro performers."

Some critics continued to question its credentials as an opera, while others thought Breen's vividly dramatic staging, followed in her own fashion by Ella Gerber, had veered it from Gershwin's original intentions. Gerber's 1975 staging of a Los Angeles Light Opera production drew criticism from the local critics for liberties taken with the score. The audience turnout was poorer than expected.

The ever rising esteem for Gershwin brought increasing musicological examination of the work. To what degree had he conceived it as an opera and as a theatre piece? For a time the compass needle appeared to be swinging toward opera. In 1961 Jean Dalrymple of the New York City Center Light Opera Company had announced her production, with William Warfield as Porgy, as "new and different." She said she was returning to the opera concept of Gershwin and Heyward, "staged, designed, and rebuilt from scratch." The recitatives were reinstalled, but not the entire score, and, oddly, there was no goat.

Warfield's Porgy was admired, as was his alternate, Robert McFerrin, who had sung the role, unseen, in the film. Leesa Foster played Bess as a wild, childlike creature. "Best of all," Raymond Ericson reported in *The New York Times*, "was the sound of the entire ensemble, principals and chorus. This was magnificent."

He still wondered, though, if it was a musical show, musical play, folk opera, light opera, or just plain opera. Perhaps, he said, it depended on who was presenting it, which in this case made it light opera.

FOR LORIN MAAZEL, conductor of the Cleveland Orchestra, Gershwin's intention was clear enough, even though the work he had completed late in August 1935 had never been performed in its entirety. During the rehearsals, throughout the tryout in Boston, and to the opening night in New York, nearly a fourth of the original score had been excised. That score survived in two forms: a published piano-vocal score and an orchestral score deposited in the Library of Congress.

Maazel, in 1975, led his orchestra, soloists, and chorus in a concert performance of the "full score." Early the following year London Records released that version, billing it as "The World Premiere Complete Performance." Maazel, in notes for what turned out to be the best-selling album, enthused: "How glorious it is to hear the entire opera, without dozens of cuts that have mutilated form, flow, and dramatic function."

A good many critics agreed with him. Finally, said Peter G. Davis in *The New York Times,* there was the chance to assess the work on an operatic basis. What made *Porgy* an opera was its "technical and expressive scope: as in the operas of Mozart and Verdi, nearly every element fuses to produce a fully realized, balanced, musical-dramatic entity." The Maazel recording thus was "an indispensable document and an often moving account of an operatic masterpiece."

So, at long last, *Porgy* was an opera, and a masterpiece at that. The battle seemed over and won. Well, not just yet.

Bess is Porgy's woman now: Donnie Ray Albert, Clamma Dale.
(Sherwin M. Goldman.)

21

As THE BICENTENNIAL year approached, plans were discussed at the Metropolitan Opera about mounting a production of America's preeminent operatic work, *Porgy and Bess,* but no action was taken. The Met, at this moment, was not fiscally strong; there would be the expense of hiring more than fifty black singers beyond those of the standing company and then keeping them on salary for two seasons of repertory. Yet there was mounting opinion that the Gershwin-Heyward work belonged at the Met and, after some forty years, that it was high time. One thirty-five-year-old admirer of the opera, Sherwin M. Goldman, active in New York cultural affairs, also thought it high time that the opera be performed in its entirety. He went so far as to explore a coproducing arrangement with the Met, but without success.

Goldman was not exactly an impresario, certainly not then. A native of Fort Worth, Texas, he graduated summa cum laude from Yale with a liberal arts degree, went to Oxford for a year's study of politics and economics, and returned to Yale to get a degree in law. He worked in government, practiced law in New York, and participated actively in affairs of the New York Civil Liberties Union and the New York Urban Coalition. None of this, obviously, had much to do with *Porgy.*

But he was a fan of the opera, ever since, he said, "as a kid, when I encountered a recording of the music with Mel Tormé. It was a profound experience. Then during my senior year at Yale there was another encounter with it through Robert Kimball, who had become enamored of Gershwin's music and the lyrics. From listening to his recordings I became aware of it as an opera, and, from Bob, that it had never been performed completely."

Kimball, now a well-known specialist in the history of the American musical theatre, had become Yale's curator of its American musical theatre collection, then had a spell as the New York *Post*'s music critic, and, with Alfred Simon, published in 1973 a lavishly illustrated volume, *The Gershwins*. Goldman, he said, "always took a large interest in the arts and theatre, was musically inclined himself, and had excellent standards of taste. His background in law and finance made him a natural choice to head the American Ballet Theatre, which at the time was having its problems."

Goldman was president of ABT from 1969 to 1974 and was credited with its revitalization. After he left the organization he made some fortunate investments in real estate and oil and gas exploration. "When Goldman forms an attachment for a project it becomes a deep involvement," Kimball said. "In this case it was *Porgy and Bess*. I remember him coming to me to talk about doing a full version, and the problems he was having getting people interested—at this time Maazel hadn't done his concert version—and I said to him something like, 'Why not do it yourself?'"

"I told Bob I didn't know much of anything about voices," Goldman said, "and he reminded me that I didn't know much about dancers either when I took on Ballet Theatre. However, the first step was getting the rights. In mid-1975 Bob accompanied me to call on Louis Aborn, head of the Tams-Witmark Music Library, who was now the agent for the copyright owners. I told him I wanted to put on a complete performance of the opera, and he was most encouraging, and said it was certainly time someone tried that. He said he would help me with the families."

The "families" now included Ira and Leonore Gershwin, Frances Godowsky and her three daughters and son, Arthur Gershwin and his son, and the sole surviving Heyward, Jenifer. All were participants in the estate and required consulting about rights. But it was Ira, with Lee, who was still the protective bulldog of his brother's work and who would most need convincing. Goldman and Aborn flew to the West Coast and met with Ira and Lee.

"Why tamper with it?" Ira asked him. "It's a great success as it is." Leonore suggested a small, experimental production in some out-of-the-way place. "What's the harm of trying, so long as no one sees it?"

"I told her," said Goldman, "it would cost a great deal of money, and since I would have to get the money back I couldn't do it under a bushel basket. The end result was that they agreed to consider a proposal."

Sherwin M. Goldman, who produced the "full" version of Porgy and Bess *in 1976. (Sherwin M. Goldman.)*

During that stage, Aborn was helpful. He obtained the "family" permissions and Jenifer Heyward's. Kimball put Goldman in touch with Kay Swift. She, after all, had been there through most of the phases of Gershwin's composing, and there was never any doubt in her mind that Gershwin had meant to compose an *opera*.

Goldman, seeking a sponsoring organization, made the rounds of opera companies. He contacted the San Francisco Opera Society and those of Boston, Washington, and Dallas. There was no real interest.

Goldman went to see Broadway theatre owners and producers, and in that area, too, couldn't awaken interest. "Most people," Goldman said, "thought they knew what *Porgy* was. They'd all seen one version or another, and most of them were quite willing to tell me it wasn't an opera. During this period I heard that Lorin Maazel was planning a concert version and a recording of the full opera, and I tried to talk him into doing it for the opera house, but he wasn't interested."

When an investment in a natural gas stock went from thirty cents to a dollar and ten cents a share, Goldman took it as a sign and decided to assemble his own production. He had the advantage of knowing a great many people in the theatre, music, and dance fields through his ABT involvement. For so large an undertaking—one that made the management of the Met quail—the control of costs was essential. "I found a designer, lighting director, and costumer who were willing to work very inexpensively. Someone associated with Ballet Theatre said he'd arrange to get me lighting equipment on the q.t. If we got going we'd pay for it; if not, send it back.

"I was auditioning singers all around the country, I guess thirty cities in all, from theatre groups to church choirs, but was having a hard time finding directors. I talked to several, some of whom were encouraging. But the black directors among them were much less so. Some were very specific about their regarding the opera as Uncle Tom. I don't think there was a single black person, of those who had never been associated with *Porgy*, who didn't seriously bad-mouth it. I had worked with Duke Ellington and Alvin Ailey when they made a ballet for Ballet Theatre. I told them it was not in the material as written. 'It will come out when it's done,' they said."

Goldman met what seemed a stone wall when he discovered that the rules of Actors Equity were unsuited to the performance of an opera. "Those rules were directed at musical shows in which singers sang eight performances a week," he said. "No one doing a full-length *Porgy* could sing eight shows a week. There was no accommodation for those who sang three a week; they would have to be paid for the full week, and the same rules applied to their alternates.

"Then there were the tax laws, which were very much to the disadvantage of a show which clearly could not be commercial. All of this argued for a nonprofit organization; if I could manage that, I could save a third of the cost. I discovered that if I made an arrangement with the Guild of Musical Artists I would be able to cut costs down another third. The pieces were beginning to fit together, so out I went on the road again to try to find an organization willing to act as the employer in a nonprofit venture."

Diana Clark, the general manager of the Dallas Opera, told Goldman that the best possibility for an opera company's participation was the Houston Opera, now run by the enterprising David Gockley, who had done much to popularize opera by presenting performances in both English and the original language with alternating casts. During 1975 he sent a production of Scott Joplin's *Treemonisha* on a national tour that reached Broadway. Clark introduced Goldman and Gockley, who said at once that he was very much interested and soon after agreed to sponsor the work.

"This gave us an employer of record," Goldman said, "and we were able to use AGMA for our contracts with the singers. We'd already done a lot of casting, but the Houston company provided us with our biggest asset, their musical director, John DeMain, a young man with an impressive record around the country as an assistant and guest conductor with major orchestras and opera companies. He had just the right feel for the music and its voice needs. We completed auditions, but still had no director, and, in fact, had none until four days before the start of rehearsals." These were to be held in New York.

John DeMain happened to remember a young director he had worked with on an experimental piece at Juilliard. He was thirty-seven-year-old Jack O'Brien, who had begun his career with Ellis Raab's APA repertory theatre company and worked his way around the country directing for regional theatre and opera companies. He called himself "a repertory baby" and was one of a generation of dynamic young theatre people who didn't regard Broadway as the be and end all of theatrical success. In fact, all those now associated in this *Porgy* project were of a new generation of music and theatre artists and entrepreneurs; they were all in their thirties; they believed in expanding the music and theatre experiences of audiences everywhere. They, in a sense, embodied the long-ago purposes of ANTA and the WPA Theatre Project, both of which, coincidentally, were born during the year that Gershwin and Heyward premiered their opera.

O'Brien and DeMain, with no time to spare, put their heads together over the score. Goldman wanted a full-length *Porgy,* but it also had to be held to no more than a three-hour length because of union costs if it ran over. O'Brien said, "First we included every single note Gershwin wrote, and then we began to look for viable cuts, a reprise here, something very small there— nothing anybody would notice. We fought for every note, and wound up with two minutes to spare." All told, twenty-three pages were eliminated from a full score that ran 450 pages.

"Actually it was in Gershwin's own notations," Goldman said. "There were lots of them in the orchestral score. He would say use only as much of this as you need to get the scenery changed."

O'Brien met his singers on an early June Monday, two days after his appointment. "I walked into that rehearsal hall," he related, "and felt very white indeed. I was nervous—I'd never done anything with a black cast before—even though I believed that *Porgy* was not a put-down of blacks, written by whites, but a moving story about people who happen to be black. I was determined to tell the truth about the show as I felt it, in terms of how it dealt with love, jealousy, death and adversity. What a revelation! The company went with me all the way."

The cast that had been recruited had exceptional voices, and their backgrounds were impressive. Donnie Ray Albert, who would sing Porgy, was the winner of the 1975 Metropolitan Opera's Southwest regional auditions; he had a master of music degree from Southern Methodist University and had appeared with the Houston Grand Opera. Clamma Dale, as Bess, was a

Donnie Ray Albert (Porgy) and the fiery Clamma Dale (Bess).
(Sherwin M. Goldman.)

member of the New York City Opera, a Naumburg Foundation Award winner, and had already sung Bess in the Los Angeles Light Opera production. Larry Marshall, as Sportin' Life, had been a soloist with the New York Philharmonic in its "Tribute to Gershwin" and had appeared on Broadway, at the Metropolitan, and Kennedy Center. So it went down the line — Juilliard graduates, award winners, those with long lists of operatic appearances here and abroad, professors of music at institutions around the country — a distant cry from the days when Gershwin had searched in Harlem nightclubs and vaudeville houses for his performers.

Robert Breen's earlier example was followed by refashioning the three acts into two, and there was help from another quarter. In order to save the cost of building Catfish Row, Goldman rented the set done by Robert Randolph for the 1973–1974 Los Angeles Light Opera production, which had been directed by Ella Gerber. That set had a reversal unit, not unlike Wolfgang

Roth's for the Breen production; it swiveled to provide the interiors for Robbins's wake and the hurricane episode. Everything could then play in a single, continuous sequence, with the "Buzzard Song" brought into its proper place, before the intermission. Some refurbishing and redesign was done, and a new and more realistic set was built for the Kitiwah Island sequence.

Goldman and Gockley, when they consulted with Kay Swift, felt themselves on the right track. The cuts that had been made in the first production were anathema to Gershwin, she told them, and she felt he may have been too conciliatory, a little too easily manipulated. She exacted a promise from Goldman — that, if this new production were ever to play in Boston it would be in the Colonial Theatre, where the opera had first seen light, and that she would be invited to the premiere. He promised, but without knowing if they would ever reach Boston.

After four weeks of rehearsal, the production opened on July 1, 1976, in Jones Hall, the home facility of the Houston Grand Opera. A grant from the city of Houston provided the house, the advertising, and the local orchestra. The total outlay from Goldman came to $280,000, about a third, he said, of what it would have cost "if I had done it as a commercial venture. Without Houston's name on it we couldn't have done it at all. On the other hand, it was a good arrangement for them. They got a show for free."

Leonore Gershwin came to see it and, "to her amazement, liked it a lot, after which Ira gave us his blessings. Fortunately so, because we had already made arrangements to play other cities, and advance payments had been made."

The next stop was Philadelphia, and now the adventures of this *Porgy and Bess* took on an ominous note. The principals and staff were put up at the Bellevue Stratford, exactly at the moment of the outbreak of Legionnaire's disease in the hotel. The Academy of Music, where the show played, was just around the corner, and not many people wanted to go out in that vicinity.

Philadelphia's Bicentennial Commission had dissolved two weeks before. The money had been dissipated, "including," Goldman said, "our guarantee. When I arrived in town the theatre demanded to be paid in cash, the orchestra and stagehands, too. It was a terrible time in which I had to come up with cash twice a week. The house during our weeks there was seldom more than half full, and here I was with this huge cast, an elaborate set and the stagehands needed to work it. I nearly went under. I sold everything I owned, including my house. I got some people down from New York to see the show, and they divided in their opinions about its viability on Broadway. Half of them didn't like it, the other half thought the New York audiences wouldn't like it. What everyone thought was that it would never make it commercially."

Philadelphia was the rock-bottom point. Once out of there, matters improved. The engagements at Wolf Trap (the open-air theatre outside Washington), in Ottawa, and in Toronto were splendidly profitable. The show moved on to Boston. Goldman, remembering Kay Swift's request, insisted on playing at the Colonial Theatre, even though the orchestra would not fit in the pit. Since that week in 1935 the theatre where *Porgy and Bess* was unveiled had been remodeled, and box seats had replaced much of the orchestra pit. The theatre was redone and the pit enlarged by removing some of the rows of seats.

"Kay," said Goldman, "told me what seats she wanted on opening night.

Maria (Carol Brice) wants Sportin' Life (Larry Marshall) out of
Catfish Row. (Sherwin M. Goldman.)

She wasn't quite sure exactly which ones, so I blocked off several. They were toward the back of the house. When we came to the theatre she remembered the seats and we sat together. 'Now you've given me my gift,' she said."

She explained to him: "So many years ago I sat with George in these seats. I was in tears because of all the cuts that were being made in his work. 'George,' I said, 'they're not going to hear and see what you wrote.' He told me, 'Someday, Kay, you'll sit in that same seat and you'll hear what I wrote. I promise you.'"

By the end of the Boston run the ticket sales were such that Goldman was able to pay off his debts and consider moving on to New York. The Uris Theatre—its pit large enough to accommodate the forty-three-piece orchestra—was rented for a four-week run. What Goldman had not expected, even in his more optimistic moments, was for the show to become a major Broadway hit.

After the opening on September 26, 1976, Douglas Watt, the critic for the New York *Daily News,* hailed it as "the most musical, moving, and profoundly beautiful production playing in New York." In *The New York Times,* Clive Barnes described the voices of the singers as floating up "in the style of Verdi, yet their acting was pure Negro Ensemble Company." The opera needed, he went on, "this kind of a re-evaluation of what Gershwin really meant."

Walter Kerr followed with a second and even more rhapsodic opinion in his Sunday *Times* column. He had showered with praise the 1953 production at the Ziegfeld Theatre. Now he had new ammunition. "The current venture is just plain thrilling, in part because it is so brilliantly sung (above all by the tall, willowy, musically and dramatically astonishing Clamma Dale) and in part because we can see now that Gershwin made no bones about the rhythmic flesh he was putting bones on. It's all there in the overture, when, after massive chords . . . the jazz piano takes over boldly. . . ." (The audience saw this as well as heard it, as Jasbo Brown at a honky-tonk piano materialized behind a scrim.) Gershwin, Kerr said, "is declaring himself, insisting upon his origins . . . scrawling a signature in sound . . . daring to put a date on it as well." And in this version Kerr saw the characters taking on a stature—"a size and splendor we have never seen before."

Of those characters, the Bess of Clamma Dale emerged most strikingly. In *Newsweek,* critic Jack Kroll described her as "a tall beauty with an animal elegance and a voice like molten gold." Dale, twenty-eight, the daughter of a jazz musician, was something of a child prodigy on piano and clarinet in Chester, Pennsylvania, before turning to voice. Singing Bess in 1974 in Los

Andrew Smith as the hulking Crown, reclaiming his woman, Bess (Clamma Dale)
on Kitiwah Island in the Sherwin Goldman–Houston Grand Opera production.
(Sherwin M. Goldman.)

Angeles, she wasn't happy with what she called the production's "musical comedy" aspect. (Ella Gerber, it might be mentioned, was not happy with Dale's attitude, either.) Goldman came across her at Ballet Theatre when she sang in a Jerome Robbins ballet, Stravinsky's *Les Noces,* which used four pianos, percussionists, and four singers. He auditioned her for *Porgy* when he saw her in the New York City Opera's *Tales of Hoffmann.* "We took to fighting right away," he said. "We argued endlessly."

Not only was she a woman of strong opinion and high intelligence, she had ideas and theories about her role. "The era of fist-shaking honky-calling is over," she told a reporter. "Militancy is only valid if it's a creative action. Otherwise, it's not worth a dime." She saw the action of the opera pivoting around Bess. "Which," she said, "is the way I think Gershwin wanted it. She's the only new element in the life of Catfish Row. She's extremely vulnerable, but has somehow, as most black women have always had, an ability to survive. My silent script for her is that she had to leave home, she had to survive, had to hustle, not just as a prostitute, but hustle the way I do as an artist—doing church jobs, temple jobs, children's jobs—to keep herself together. She's looking for someone to protect her."

Crown, she thought, was "the type of person who, when slavery was in effect, everybody wanted to buy. That kind of strength is important to see how black people have been valued—somebody that big and strong can take in a whole lot of cotton." Porgy, however, was an epitome of strength in the Catfish Row community. "You don't see a crybaby; you see a whole human being." It was Bess, though, who she thought was the one character who speaks to the black community. But not the people of Catfish Row. "She represents a threat to that society. They hate her because she can turn their men on." Nor did she think it surprising that she leaves Porgy. "It's as though she's saying, 'I'm going to go on and do what I like.'"

Perhaps because of the very longevity and popularity of the opera, its story was getting more analysis, some of which may have surprised Heyward and Gershwin. Michael Feingold, in *The Village Voice,* saw it as two interwoven stories—one, the more sentimental, that of Porgy; the other, that of Bess, more naturalistic and sordid: "The misanthropic cripple is redeemed by love, although in the novel he doesn't follow after Bess when she, the agent of his redemption, runs away."

Bess becomes Porgy's grail, he said; he is transfigured by the happiness of his quest. If they lived happily ever after, it would not suit the ending of the "Bess" play.

He agreed in essence with Clamma Dale that Bess was a woman who would not have stayed long with any man. He saw her as escaping to New

Another Crown (George Merritt); another Bess (Wilhelmenia Fernandez) in the Goldman–Houston Grand Opera version. (Sherwin M. Goldman.)

York and becoming "perhaps a hooker, a high fashion model, a Harlem nightclub star, an ordinary ghetto mother—none of them suitable objects for a holy love pursuit."

Thus it was the disparity between the two stories that had its effect on the music: "The sweet aura around Porgy makes for great tunes instead of great arias, and keeps turning the work back into operetta or musical comedy." The makings of grand opera were in the other characters, with their faults, the good mixed with bad. "Bess and Crown might have made a grand opera." Nevertheless, he concluded, *Porgy and Bess* was a masterpiece, because Gershwin did his work brilliantly on both opera and light-opera levels.

Not so according to Harold C. Schonberg, chief music critic of *The New York Times*. His scathing review a few weeks after the opening ran directly counter to those of the paper's two drama critics and another of its music critics. He called his piece "A Minority Report" and admitted he felt like a snake in the Garden of Eden and Scrooge at Christmastime in view of the otherwise unanimous praise for the production. But all he could experience at the Uris Theatre, he said, "were some pretty songs, connected up by a libretto full of stereotypes, with a phony and sentimental ending that makes a cheap assault on the emotions, and by music that has no connective tissue at all."

Schonberg poured it on, his disdain becoming a diatribe — "three hours of aimless meandering . . . white man's music, not the real thing . . . largely, at basis, commercial, slick and sentimental." For good measure, he tossed in

Serena (Dolores Ivory) mourns. Seen here as Bess is Naomi Moody.
(Sherwin M. Goldman.)

an aside about Gershwin's *Rhapsody in Blue* and *An American in Paris,* which he termed "junk music."

The outcry against the review was immediate, and the *Times* printed several letters that took Schonberg to task. One writer reminded Schonberg and readers that DuBose Heyward had fashioned his novel (and play) on characters and an atmosphere that he knew, that Gershwin had absorbed much of his material from what he heard in Gullah churches and prayer meetings, and advised a reading of the tightly constructed score "with a distinguishing musical motive for each character."

Edward Jablonski, a noted Gershwin authority, found fault with several of Schonberg's "facts," pointing out that the Theatre Guild in its original production had not dropped the recitatives, as Schonberg had claimed, and rebutting the charge that the opera was designed to be "slick and commercial."

Clearly, Schonberg had not done his research well; the article seemed to have been turned out quickly and in a fit of pique. He attacked the new version for its lavish "half million dollar" budget in contrast to the "fifty thousand" spent by the Theatre Guild. The actual figures were $280,000 and $70,000. In any case, a $50,000 Broadway musical in 1935 would have easily been the equivalent of a half-million-dollar musical in 1976. The Metropolitan Opera had shown "good sense," he said, when it wisely abandoned its production. If he had checked a report in his own paper he would have seen that the main reason was financial.

Oddly, Schonberg echoed many of the charges made against the opera by black critics during the 1950s and 1960s. But times had changed. During the early seventies a new kind of racial consciousness came to television in the form of situation comedies such as "The Jeffersons," "Sanford and Son," and "Good Times." The roles carried their own stereotypes—as, of course, did white sitcoms—but there was now a note of racial pride, and the language didn't hesitate to stress differences in social and economic backgrounds. Black heroes and black villains in television dramas and movies took their places alongside their white partners. *Porgy and Bess* took on more and more the aura of a period piece, one that, if anything, emphasized how far black Americans had traveled in terms of growth of opportunity, education, and the erosion of racial barriers.

Black opposition to the opera had all but died away, as evidenced in Didier Delauney's review in *The Black American,* a weekly paper. He had nothing but praise for the new production, calling it the best he had seen. Nowhere in the review could be found any mention of black stereotypes or of white music pretending to be black. For Delauney it was an opera sung by superb operatic voices in a setting that he called "exquisitely accurate."

Criticism of a quite different and surprising kind came some years later from musicologist Charles Hamm. His case in *Journal of the American Musicological Society* was that these "complete" versions were not true to Gershwin's intentions, which he thought were embodied in the 1935 performances at the Alvin Theatre. Nor were the scores used in the Maazel and Houston performances those used during the 1935 rehearsals.

To back up his argument, Hamm contrasted the full vocal and orchestral scores with three others in collections at Harvard, Yale, and the Library of Congress. Each score, he said, represented different stages in the production history of the opera. He pointed out that Gershwin had initiated many of the changes himself, as well as being fully involved in further cuts. So it was the

The same Porgy (Donnie Ray Albert) but another fine Bess—
Gail Nelson, in the successful Goldman–Houston Grand Opera production.
(Sherwin M. Goldman.)

Theatre Guild version, through editing and shaping, that represented Gershwin's vision of the work as an entity. Subsequently, the living tradition of the opera was lost. "We should consider the option," said Hamm, "of doing it that way today."

The problem remains, though, of just what Gershwin would have included and what he would have cut if he were alive to supervise an "authentic" performance of his opera. We do know that he cut the "Buzzard Song" to save Todd Duncan, who had no alternate, from strain through eight performances a week.

Other arguments can be made against Hamm's case. The "Six Prayers" which came to Gershwin in a burst of inspiration while working on the opera with Heyward were drastically truncated out of time considerations. The "Jasbo Brown" piano sequence, excised in the original production, was an idea of Heyward's that Gershwin liked and accepted and that he seemed to leave out just as cheerfully. Yet we have the testimony of Kay Swift, who was with him constantly through the scoring, that he considered himself to be working on a "grand" opera which, though presented on Broadway, was by no means meant as a Broadway musical. The Metropolitan Opera may very well have done it then, if it had the many black singers it required on its roster. If so, would Gershwin have cut what he was pressured to cut by the exigencies of Broadway standards?

There are, however, those on Hamm's side who say that the longer and more traditionally operatic the work becomes the more it loses its flavor and vitality. Hamm offers a way of testing this by ear—through the Goddard Lieberson recording made for Columbia in 1951, which featured a few members of the original cast and thus retained some of the "living tradition." It is not a good test—the recording is dated in comparison to more recent ones.

Coincidental with the opening of *Porgy and Bess* there was an innovative radio program called "The RCA Magic Key" broadcast on Sunday afternoons. It featured segments "live" from various locations. During the first week of the run, RCA engineers went to the Alvin Theatre and sent out over the airwaves selections sung by members of the cast. Thus, all over America, listeners heard Abby Mitchell singing "Summertime," Todd Duncan "I Got Plenty o' Nuttin'," and Duncan and Anne Brown together with "Bess, You Is My Woman Now"—the "living tradition," if there ever was one.

Many years later, Miles Kreuger, now the president of the Institute of American Musical Theatre, was working at NBC and happened to come across an air-check recording of the broadcast. He taped it and eventually added it to his institute's collection. In it Mitchell sings "Summertime" with just the right nuance of sweet, warm laziness. Duncan gives his solo number rich and enormous gusto, and his duet with Anne Brown is alive with passion and tenderness. All three of the singers give the words the quality of dialect appropriate to the characters. Somehow one senses the presence of that "good, old-fashioned Gershwin" in the renditions, as though this is the way he wants his music sung. And something more: the overall effect (perhaps of "selling" the songs to an audience) is more akin to Broadway than that of the opera house. Purists on either side can make of this what they will.

Charles Williams, Sportin' Life in the Metropolitan Opera production, 1985.
(Winnie Klotz, photographer, Metropolitan Opera Association, Inc.,
Lincoln Center, New York, NY 10023.)

22

PROBABLY NO worse nightmare exists for a Broadway producer than to have an important hit on his hands and no theatre to play it in. Sherwin Goldman was confined to a four-week lease on the Uris Theatre, and the only way to keep *Porgy and Bess* going was to buy out the following engagements. These were mostly of a special nature and for two or three weeks each. Goldman already had a high break-even point of $150,000 a week—almost twice that for most musicals. With the additional rental costs he would virtually have to fill the house at every performance.

The show's attractiveness, however, stood out even more when compared with what was currently playing on Broadway: aside from the long-running *A Chorus Line,* there was little competition from Stephen Sondheim's lackluster *Pacific Overtures* and the lively but slight *Bubbling Brown Sugar.* The season for straight plays was not exciting either beyond Neil Simon's *California Suite* and a revival of O'Neill's *Long Day's Journey into Night.* Goldman first bought off a Dutch ballet company, then a troupe of Chinese acrobats. Bing Crosby was next in line for a two-week engagement and, after him, pop singer Barry Manilow.

Crosby had chosen the Uris because it was the only theatre that allowed his limousine to be driven into an elevator and lifted up, so that he could step from it directly onto the stage. "He might have been persuaded to postpone," Goldman said, "but Manilow refused to budge."

James Nederlander, the owner of the Uris, came up with what he thought was a solution by taking a lease on the large Mark Hellinger Theatre and moving *Porgy* there. Its orchestra pit wasn't large enough for the oversize (for Broadway) orchestra, so the first few rows of seats were removed. No sooner was it ensconced there than box-office business fell off, as often happens when a show moves to a new house. Even though audiences increased, too much ground had to be made up, and the show closed after 128 New York performances. Goldman might have been able to carry on by reducing the size of the orchestra and the cast. He called a meeting of the cast to discuss the possibility, and almost all agreed with him that Gershwin's intentions would be subverted by those economies.

Meanwhile, the work of the performers achieved some permanence through a recording that was made during the run of the show. Goldman had resistance even here. The Maazel–Cleveland Orchestra recording was not only selling well, it won a Grammy Award. Could a new recording compete? Goldman convinced RCA Records to do it, but had to come up with some of the funding himself. Then came another obstacle, from the Musicians' Union—the same old one of whether to classify *Porgy* as an opera or a musical, the pay scales being lower for the former. At first the union refused an operatic classification, but when RCA threatened to record in Europe, it changed its collective mind. Houston's full-score recording is valuable both as a replica of the stage-performance run and as a display of the virtuosity of the singers.

When the first pressing came out in 1977, Goldman took a copy to the West Coast and gave it to Ira Gershwin. "He played it," Goldman said, "and was very emotional that day hearing the full range of his brother's work. He told me that it wasn't until now that he fully appreciated *Porgy and Bess*."

Goldman, in 1977, was rewarded with a Tony Award for "The Most Innovative Revival of a Musical Work" and that same year took a reconstituted production, with several cast changes, on a national tour and then to Europe for several engagements. Inquiries came from La Scala, but scheduling problems interfered with a visit there. In any case, the tour was foreshortened, Goldman said, "when the set—which by this time we had paid for— finally collapsed in Palermo. The Italian stagehands tore it apart. We had several other offers to do it over the next few years, but we had no set. Then one day in March of 1982 a call came from the Radio City Music Hall."

The caller was Bernard Gersten, a former Broadway producer who had just been appointed executive director of Radio City Music Hall Productions. The Music Hall had been refurbished after a New York City commission had designated the fifty-year-old monster of a theatre a "National Landmark."

"He was just two days on the job," Goldman said. "And what he was calling about was that he wanted me to do a production for the Hall of *Porgy and Bess.*"

Goldman regarded the immensity of the theatre with its 5,882 seats (more than the Uris and the Metropolitan in Lincoln Center combined) as antithetical to the opera, and its cavernous acoustics as another detriment. A set to fill its maw of a stage would have to be as large or larger than any hitherto built for a musical production. "I said, 'no' and 'no' again," said Goldman.

Gersten was persistent. It was Goldman's understanding that David Rockefeller, thwarted by the landmark ruling in his aim of converting the property to another use, had then decreed the theatre be used for larger and more innovative events rather than its usual fare, a film presentation and a

The set for Sherwin M. Goldman's production was used in the United States and abroad, until stagehands in Italy ruined it. (Sherwin M. Goldman.)

stage show. The Music Hall staff came up with such extravaganzas as "The Night of a Hundred Stars" and a showing of Abel Gance's giant-screen film *Napoleon,* but no one could think of a legitimate stage production until *Porgy and Bess* came to mind. "I felt," Gersten said, "that this production would redefine the Hall. Its very size suggests grander productions."

His offer to Goldman included bankrolling as grand a production as he might be able to envisage, no matter how extravagant the settings, the size of the cast, the number of musicians in the orchestra. Goldman by then had something else in mind. At the Metropolitan there were already plans afoot to present the opera during its 1985 season, coincident with the fiftieth anniversary of its first presentation. Goldman was interested in aligning himself with the Met. "They told me," he said, "if you do it at the Music Hall you can't do it here."

Gersten assured Goldman that the acoustical problems could be solved with advanced electronic wizardry. Still undecided, Goldman flew with Gersten to the West Coast to talk it over with the Gershwins. Ira was not well, and it was Lee they talked to. "She reacted enthusiastically to the idea. She felt that done at the Music Hall, and at ticket prices lower than charged for traditional opera, *Porgy* would attract a new and large audience, including blacks." Both she and Goldman had been disturbed by the sparse attendance of blacks at a show that was, after all, about black people and performed by fine black musical artists. She doubted that it had much to do with the old charge of stereotyping. "It's because of the word 'opera,' that's the reason," she said. At Radio City, she thought, they would come and see it.

"As it turned out," Goldman said, "she was right."

He recruited many of the people who had worked with him earlier: Jack O'Brien again to direct, Nancy Potts for the costumes, Heleine Head as the assistant director and production supervisor. The cast was almost entirely new, one of the few exceptions being Larry Marshall, the Sportin' Life of Goldman's earlier production. Four Besses, four Porgys, and two Crowns were recruited.

To satisfy the mammoth dimensions of the Music Hall, the cast was increased to ninety singers and actors and twelve dancers and the Radio City orchestra was expanded to fifty-six by adding on certain instruments, mainly trumpets and violins. Douglas W. Schmidt created the huge six-house set: it measured nearly a hundred feet wide, thirty feet high, and was forty feet deep. The center house revolved to reveal the interior of Serena's room. Another set was built for the picnic scene on Kitiwah Island.

"This hall used to be a movie house," director Jack O'Brien said of his intentions, "and we want to compose the stage as if for a camera. The effects will be spectacular. The hurricane scene will have howling winds, rain, thunder and lightning and will be fantastic!"

The worry, though, was the sound. There was no way to make the hall smaller for far-off viewers, but acoustics expert Christopher Jaffe attempted to do so for their ears. He came up with a complex system of microphones, speakers, and other technical equipment that would delay and rearrange the spatial effect of sound waves. The idea was to create a "lower" electronic ceiling and "shrink" the space between the walls. A problem arose from the hall's landmark status; little could be done—in fact, it would be illegal—in the way of physical alterations. The number of people in the hall would affect the quality of sound, too, because of both reflection and absorption. Jaffe confidently assured Goldman and O'Brien that the problems could be solved.

All told, 416 people were involved with producing the show, which was to run for six weeks. Could George Gershwin or DuBose Heyward ever have imagined their collaboration would mushroom into so giant an undertaking? Harold Schonberg, who had worried about the cost of the show at the Uris, might have worried more this time: the bill ran to four million. Yet the ticket prices were considerably lower than for an opera at the Metropolitan, running, as they did, from fifteen to thirty dollars. There was no worry about getting the money back. The advance sale alone came to $2,500,000.

As Clive Barnes said in his opening-night review in the New York *Post*, the "monumental production makes history on various levels, but then *Porgy and Bess* has never been shy of making history."

Walter Kerr of *The New York Times* was now a bona-fide expert: this was the fourth version he had seen, and he noted that it was being "raptly attended by more people per performance than could have been packed into any auditorium since that all-embracing arena at Epidaurus shut up shop a few thousand years ago."

He felt it was necessary to talk about the show in terms of the size of the hall it was housed in, that "the great wave of gently banked seats that sweeps from the orchestra pit back toward Sixth Avenue" was a pronounced aspect "of one's current experience of 'Porgy.'" He didn't see how the show could have worked in this home of the giant screen, the giant organ, and the giant everything else, "but in some unpredictable and possibly undecipherable way it does."

There were the "lively panoramas. On a hot summer night along Catfish Row a dice game is interrupted by a very mean knife fight. The simple enough sight of a chair being flung, in tumbling orbit, clear across the hall's city-block proscenium is enough to pin your ears back." He admired the hurricane, with dozens of shutters clattering, and lightning bolts creating blazing terror among the inhabitants of the row, and also the picnic, with a setting sun casting a red glow over the parasols and sashes. At the same time, there was more to *hear* than ever before, with the full score played by a full orchestra. But the trouble was with the amplified sound. He said it didn't really work well for all the areas of the house. It was better in certain locations, worse in others. "I saw it but didn't hear it," one patron commented.

"Yes, it was really sad," Goldman said. "Chris Jaffe was sure he could solve it. It worked better for some performances than for others."

But for Clive Barnes, "The full grandeur of Gershwin's original concept is here completed. It has always been regarded—quite wrongly—as simply a Broadway musical. It was always something much more, and indeed a pointer to the future of both the Broadway musical and opera itself."

Serena's house, part of the huge stage set for the Radio City Music Hall production, 1983. (Sherwin M. Goldman.)

Barnes went on to suggest that the living future of opera, or, if that word was bothersome, of serious musical theatre, belonged more in the hands of men like Kurt Weill, Leonard Bernstein, and Stephen Sondheim. He heretically claimed (shades of Robert Breen) that the opera of the classically oriented composers was "deader than a dead dodo . . . a superb fossilized art, the preserve of interpreters rather than creators." Gershwin had sensed the future and it worked. "*Porgy* emerges as grand opera and grand popular entertainment."

After the successful and profitable Radio City run, Goldman took the show out on the road again, presenting it in some of the nation's largest theatres, including Boston's Wang Center and the Kennedy Center in Washington, D.C. The massive set built for the Music Hall stage was taken along "because," Goldman said, "it was like an accordion. It was never out of scale. There was just a lot more of it. We cut it down to size, and dropped forty of the hundred or so people we'd had on stage. Most of these came from the chorus, which we had doubled from thirty-two to sixty-four."

One of the originators of the opera, Ira Gershwin, never saw this grand-scale revival. Now eighty-six, he had suffered a stroke that affected his left side and he had mostly taken to his bed. His mind remained unaffected, and he continued to work on a project dear to him: a large folio of his brother's songs and instrumentals, including reproductions of the manuscripts. In Edward Jablonski's words, "He was the keeper of the Gershwin keys," and so regarded himself. To the very end, he retained his loyalty to his brother and his work. His own achievements notwithstanding, for him, Jablonski said, "The spotlight belonged to the dashing George."

On August 15, 1983, sitting in bed, Ira was eating the chocolates he relished when his heart failed and he died.

ONLY A YEAR and a half later, fifty years after its premiere, his brother's work was virtually canonized by being brought into the repertory of the Metropolitan Opera. The Met became fiscally strong in the 1980s; in its company now were dozens of black singers. James Levine, music director and conductor of its orchestra, had long wanted to do *Porgy* and, in fact, declared categorically that it was not only an opera, but a great one. "It has everything great opera has," he said, "great music, great drama, and a psychological and social milieu that is as involving as the milieu of *Don Giovanni* or *Boris Godunov*."

The production and direction of the opera was put in the hands of a Met veteran, Nathaniel Merrill, and settings and costumes were designed by

Kitiwah Island on the stage of the Radio City Music Hall, 1983.
(Sherwin M. Goldman.)

another Met regular, Robert O'Hearn. The cost—$800,000—was high by Met standards, and the extra funding needed came from several well-heeled patrons from as far afield as Houston.

One reason for the cost—the Met board had used this as an excuse for not performing the work earlier—was the requirement of the Gershwin estate that blacks be used for the principal roles and the chorus. The requirement was not enforced abroad; otherwise few foreign productions would have been possible. The Met had a plentiful supply of principal black singers, but only three black members in its chorus, and these were already engaged in rehearsals for *Die Meistersinger.* Going entirely outside its own roster to make up the chorus, the Met placed ads in *Variety* and *Back Stage* for "only legitimate opera voices." Additionally, Arthur Mitchell, the director of the Dance Theatre of Harlem, brought in his young workshop ensemble for dances and also coached the singers in their movements.

No sooner was *Porgy* announced for its 1985 season than, as the Met's press officer reported, "the phones began ringing off the hook." There had been some worry that the recent Music Hall version might have exhausted New York City's interest, but it was needless. The nearly sixty thousand seats for the sixteen scheduled performances were sold out well in advance of the premiere. An astonished spokesman said, "We had no way of predicting this overwhelming response."

The media just as quickly seized on the presentation as a history-making event, and not only because 1985 marked the fiftieth anniversary of the opera's first presentation. Samuel G. Freedman in *The New York Times* heralded it as "the ultimate establishment embrace of a work that continues to stir controversy with both its musical daring and its depiction of black life by three white men. . . ."

James Levine regarded the production as historic because "it is probably the first time this opera is played in an opera house with opera singers, without cuts and without microphones, as close to the original operatic conception as possible." Upon reading this statement, Sherwin Goldman bridled. His production, he said, had played several opera houses and not in all cases with amplification. But it was true that the Met production included just about every last note that could be found in the Gershwin scores.

For the title roles, two decidedly mature stars, Simon Estes and Grace Bumbry, were chosen, although prima donna Bumbry had to be coaxed to play Bess. "I resisted the role at first," she said, "possibly because I didn't really know the score, and I think because of the racial aspect. I thought it was beneath me, I felt we had worked far too hard, that we had come far too far to have to retrogress to 1935. My way of dealing with it was to see that it was really a piece of Americana, of American history, whether we like it or not. Whether I sang it or not, it was still going to be there."

Bumbry had indeed gone far from her beginnings in St. Louis as the daughter of a railroad freight handler. When she was seventeen she won a radio talent contest. At Northwestern University she studied under Lotte Lehmann and she was only twenty-three when she stunned the Bayreuth Festival as Venus in *Tannhäuser*. She went on to triumphs in *Carmen* and *Salome,* and at Covent Garden she evoked some astonishment as well as keen binocular interest by her relatively unveiled dance of the seven veils. She admitted having to slim down for the role of Bess.

Simon Estes needed no persuasion. His operatic career had embraced ninety-two roles, and he had already sung Porgy seven years earlier in Zurich. He saw himself as an heir to previous great black singers—Todd Duncan, Paul Robeson, William Warfield. "I feel a sense of connection," he said. "Those people, they were men with operatic voices who should've been singing not only in the Met but at all the great opera houses. I would hope

Slightly overage at the Met. Simon Estes (Porgy), Grace Bumbry (Bess).
(Theatre Collection, Museum of the City of New York.)

those men could somehow see this production and say, 'What we went through was not superfluous.'"

The eighty-six-year-old Rouben Mamoulian was contacted for his comments, and he obliged. "Critics at the time," he said, "complained it wasn't an opera and it wasn't a musical. You give someone something delicious to eat and they complain because they have no name for it."

In the welter of newspaperese and hullabaloo about this "coming of age" production, the impression was given that the Gershwin–Heyward collaboration had been badly maltreated over the years, that it had been subjected to continual change and dismemberment, and that it had been sung by inferior voices. Also, that the genius inherent in the music had gone generally unrecognized and that charges of racial stereotyping had dogged its every performance. So, now, the expectation was that the work would at last reach its full flower on the broad stage and in the rich interior of the Metropolitan.

True enough, differences had marked previous productions. The most radical operation was performed in Cheryl Crawford's 1942 revival. Mostly, this had to do with the substitution of dialogue for recitative, but the cast was still a notable one, and no one ever performed a livelier, better sung, or better acted Porgy than Todd Duncan. It was this production that caused Virgil Thomson to change his mind about the merits of the music.

In each production a search was made for the best possible voices, and important discoveries came about, notably that of Leontyne Price. John Bubbles and Avon Long established the standards for Sportin' Life, and Cab Calloway added his own individual and delightful interpretation to the characterization. A reading of the work script of the libretto followed by Robert Breen shows a good deal of restoration of elements dropped from the 1935 original and much use of recitative. Some ad-libbed remarks for atmosphere and realism were injected during that production's long history and, as carefully noted down by Ella Gerber, became literally part of the script she employed. Since little or no musical notation was involved, it is doubtful that Gershwin was much harmed. By all accounts, the direction by both Mamoulian and Breen was brilliant, and the musicality of the musical direction by Alexander Smallens was never in question. The fact was that the work always had loving care, even though interpretations varied, and the only lingering question about it was just how to categorize it. When Breen's version played La Scala, however, no one had any doubt that it was anything but an opera. Perhaps if from the very beginning it had been labeled a music drama or a dramatic musical, critics would have protested that it was really an opera and that Gershwin and the Theatre Guild were attempting to disguise the fact. Even then, though, when *Porgy and Bess* was labeled a "folk opera," it was mostly — excepting a sour few — hailed as a serious and splendid work.

The matter of black protestation was overblown, too. What is more surprising is how little attention was paid to the work by the black populace from its beginnings as a novel. One reason for this was that white fiction about blacks was all but ignored or scorned by the black populace, which was more concerned about its social and economic conditions. *Porgy* as a play attracted a mainly white audience, as did the opera for most of its years. When protest came along, it was generally from a strident few on grounds more applicable to a larger or a current cause than to the work itself. Their objective was achieved when the press took notice, as it invariably did. Almost always, however, other black voices rose quickly to the defense, and no one in the audiences was persuaded that the life portrayed on Catfish Row represented the common condition of America's black population.

Almost forgotten at the time of the Metropolitan premiere was the important history made by the opera when it breached the iron curtain and revealed the immensity of talent that came from the diverse American strains, black and white.

So, now at the Metropolitan, *Porgy and Bess* would have its fullest and most faithful rendition, albeit with a larger chorus and orchestra than Gershwin had envisioned, with a dance company not called for by the libretto, and with an added and previously unspecified setting.

There would, of course, have to be an opening-night party—these days known as a gala—for so great an occasion. It would benefit that important charity, the Metropolitan Opera Guild. Tickets were already pricy: $30 for the farthest reaches of the balcony, $150 for the orchestra—which would also allow the holder to purchase a place at the supper dance following the performance—and $1,600 for a parterre box seating eight. The gala for eight hundred guests, the largest ever held at the Met, occupied all three tiers. As described by Suzy in the New York *Daily News,* and syndicated widely, Philip Baloun did the decorations "in an art deco rhapsody of black satin and silver *lamé* reminiscent of the Gershwin era."

An hour before the performance two important visitors went backstage to meet with Grace Bumbry and Simon Estes. They were Todd Duncan, now eighty-two, and Anne Brown, ten years younger. He came up from Washington, she had flown in from her home in Norway. Anne Brown was there first in Bumbry's dressing room, and when Duncan entered, she said, "I think you know me."

"Oh, darling," Duncan exclaimed delightedly, and they exchanged hugs and kisses. The three then went to Estes' dressing room where the singer, as it happened, was already on crutches. He would have to play the role that way because of an accident in rehearsal the previous day that had dislocated his knee.

Outside the dressing room, Anne Brown remarked that she had been born too soon. "If I were young now, I would start my career here, but of course I could not do that then." Duncan agreed that he would have been at the Met, too. "There's no doubt in my mind that if I'd been another color, that's just where I would have been. I didn't look too badly. I didn't sing too badly. And drama was my great forte." But he had few regrets. "It's a great night for the Metropolitan," he said, "that they took this giant step."

It was four hours after the curtain rose, including the two intermissions, that the opera ended, and it was a late night for those who also went to the party. Leonore Gershwin had come in from Los Angeles for the affair, and other Gershwin family members were there too. Of those, Frances Godowsky was the last surviving member of the immediate family of George

*Fifty years after the premiere, Anne Brown and Todd Duncan meet with the leads,
Simon Estes and Grace Bumbry, in the Metropolitan Opera production, 1985.
(Winnie Klotz, photographer, Metropolitan Opera Association, Inc.,
Lincoln Center, New York, NY 10023.)*

and Ira. The crowd was hardly the equal in status and celebrity of those at the
Theatre Guild premiere in New York, but it included Harold Prince, Jule
Styne, and Harvey Fierstein from the world of theatre, Joanne Woodward of
films, William Warfield and Jessye Norman from opera, and a good many
Met regulars and benefactors.

Many of the first reviews were as celebratory as the occasion. Headlines
read: PORGY REBORN AT THE MET. BIG BRAVO FOR PORGY AND BESS. PORGY
DELUXE. Douglas Watt in the *Daily News* thought, "It may have been the
most important night in the history of the Metropolitan. Certainly it was the
most thrilling . . . a production that realized the magnificence of the work."
Almost all the reviewers remarked that the opera had generally been mis-
treated before, mainly because it had been performed as a Broadway musical. Most liked Simon Estes as Porgy. Grace Bumbry fared less well as Bess;
she was faulted for excessive maturity, shrill voice, and unsuitability to the
role. Almost everyone, while saluting the Met for including all of Gershwin's
music, thought it was a long, long pull to get to the final curtain.

There was plenty of counteropinion, too. Peter G. Davis, in *New York
Magazine,* called it "a production that lurches, staggers, and finally col-
lapses under the burden of its own respectability." With several others, he

Catfish Row on the Met's stage. Too sanitized? (Winnie Klotz, photographer,
Metropolitan Opera Association, Inc., Lincoln Center, New York, NY 10023.)

noticed the "spick and span Catfish Row tenement house and Hollywood
back lot Kitiwah Island." This "lacklustre Porgy" buried the piece's real
passion under "mounds of pointless, ponderous details."

Andrew Porter in *The New Yorker* took a somewhat similar tack, but
thought the "overblown" quality was perhaps inevitable in a Met production. He compared it unfavorably to "a buoyant, stylish, and totally enjoyable" performance he had seen given five years before by the Indiana
University Theatre. No one was harsher, though, than Barton Wimble, the
Daily News "entertainment critic," who rebutted the rave by the same
paper's Douglas Watt.

The talented black singers, he charged, had to fight for four hours "a
smothering seventy piece orchestra." *Porgy and Bess*'s desperately poor
blacks were "transformed into characters from *The Music Man*. . . . The
costumes are Alexander's basement. . . . Diva Bumbry waddles her way
through the role with complete indifference to all but her very loud
claque. . . . I have never heard a production in English that has so much
unintelligible diction. . . ."

A trace of Met-bashing could be detected in the unfavorable barrage, but
it was true that members of the audience were seen consulting their librettos

to learn what was going on. Sherwin Goldman was disappointed in the production and thought one of its faults lay in James Levine's "attempting to outdo us in authenticity and taking everything to its full conclusion. He used all this turnaround music for sets, and scene changes, entrances—filler music that Gershwin had provided in case of need." Leonore Gershwin and Frances Godowsky were disappointed, too. In public, Leonore politely complimented the Met, but to Goldman she said, "This is going to do us unlimited damage."

These reactions may have accounted for the fact that permission to broadcast a performance on public television was refused by the copyright holders. A month after the premiere there were wholesale cast changes in the production. Roberta Alexander, who had made her reputation in Europe, took on the role of Bess and received a warm welcome from the music critics, but Robert Moseley as Porgy was criticized for "barking, sputtering, and shouting in the most bewildering fashion." Audiences, nevertheless, remained loyal through the sixteen performances, and there was again a sellout when the production was brought back for sixteen more during the following fall and winter. It was not scheduled again until late in 1989, when it was re-staged by Arvin Brown.

Meanwhile, opera companies all over the country were clamoring to the copyright owners for the opportunity to present the work.

Roberta Alexander was highly praised for her Bess at the Met, 1986. Robert Moseley as Porgy was less impressive.
(Winnie Klotz, photographer, Metropolitan Opera Association, Inc., Lincoln Center, New York, NY 10023.)

23

I<small>T NOW LOOKED</small> as though immortality had been granted to *Porgy and Bess,* as new productions sprang up with increasing frequency. Charleston, South Carolina, a city that prided itself on being historical, presented it on October 10, 1985, precisely fifty years after its Broadway premiere. The lead singers and the director were recruited from elsewhere; local talent supplied the chorus, and the orchestra was the Charleston Symphony. Tickets to the ten performances were so sought after that many were stolen, and some people showed up for the same seats. The police were on hand to straighten matters out.

Sammy Smalls, the progenitor of Porgy, was once more in the limelight as searches were made to locate his place of birth and burial. There were those who claimed to remember him and the smell of his goat. Guides took tourists to Cabbage Row. One driver was under the impression that DuBose Heyward was black; he was surprised to be corrected.

The following July, Glyndebourne, England, was the site of a much admired revival. The annual festival and the opera were almost the same age, but no American opera had ever graced its stage during its fifty-odd years of existence. Glyndebourne, in the pastoral settings of Lewes, Sussex, was renowned for its carefully prepared and meticulously staged productions of classic opera. Given there, *Porgy and Bess* was virtually knighted. Its elegant audiences came in formal dress and consumed cold salmon and champagne on the green lawn of the estate, with sheep seen grazing in the distance.

This, too, was an uncut version. Performances began at four in the afternoon, and, in all, took five hours because of two intermissions, one lasting for more than an hour for alimentary purposes. The London Philharmonic Orchestra was led by the young and brilliant Simon Rattle, and the director was Trevor Nunn, who had staged *Cats* and *Nicholas Nickleby*.

Nunn's aim was not only to breathe new life into the opera, but to give it a new interpretation. *Porgy* would be less of a folk tale than a drama of a man's heroic struggle for survival. Porgy when first seen is an embittered misanthropic cripple, who through the action rises to tragic stature. Nunn dispensed with the traditional goat and cart, and instead put Porgy on crutches. The reason for this, he told Marc Gershwin, the son of Arthur Gershwin and one of the copyright owners, was that he could not see Bess falling in love with someone so pitifully lacking legs and mobility. He had to be more of a man, Nunn said. The denizens of Catfish Row were also less traditionally docile, and they jeered when the police arrived to investigate the killing of Robbins. A line change had to be made in the ending. Since there was no goat, Porgy had to sing "Bring me my coat."

Seats for the performances were all but impossible to obtain. For one thing, the theatre seated only six hundred. For another, season-ticket holders guarded their privileges the way those did who clung to their center court seats at Wimbledon.

Despite the restricted seating, the production was sumptuous, with a fittingly ramshackle clapboard setting by John Gunter, and singers of high quality. The financing was largely provided by Citicorp's European head, John Botts. The singers were recruited from the United States, one exception being Willard White, a Jamaican bass who had sung Porgy in the Maazel concert version. A recording of the Nunn-Rattle production was made by EMI (Angel in the United States) and is one of the preferred versions. (Nunn also wanted to do a film version, but the project bogged down because of the cost and the usually dismal fate of filmed operas at the box office.)

At the performances, though, the audience virtually stomped their enthusiasm, and critics were equally impressed. "SOMETHING VITAL, URGENTLY SAID" ran the headline in *The Times* of London. The Manchester *Guardian*'s critic called it "one of the great operas created in this century . . . attributed only to the electrical force of genius."

Art and entertainment became one, he said, in a tale about oppression, alienation, corruption, and the inviolability of a radical innocence of spirit. So this *Porgy and Bess* gave off darker meanings and, in a sense, was truer to the spirit of DuBose Heyward's novel.

No one else mentioned the author, though, and one critic attributed the libretto and lyrics completely to the two Gershwins. It was George who was analyzed and, oddly, compared to Porgy:

> Though Gershwin was not, like his Porgy, a physical cripple, he was a psychological cripple: an archetypical White Negro, a poor boy who made good, a Jew who knew about spiritual isolation and had opportunity enough to learn about corruption. Through these hazards he preserved, like Porgy, an innocence which shines through the radiant "Summertime" lullaby.

Maybe so, maybe not, and one can only imagine the astonishment of George and DuBose if they had had the opportunity to read this assessment. All unknowing, in this view, Heyward would have come across the Charleston beggar and his smelly goat and in some mystical way connected him with the composer of *Rhapsody in Blue*! And how soon his own fame had faded, while that of Gershwin continued to climb and climb.

M O S T   I N N O V A T I V E of all the productions of *Porgy and Bess* was that produced and directed by Götz Friedrich in West Berlin during the spring of 1988. His vision of the opera was decidedly at odds with traditional interpretations. The setting at the Theater Des Westens, by Hans Schavernoch, had next to nothing to do with the Catfish Row of DuBose Heyward but instead was a harshly "industrial-art" kind of tubular scaffolding. When audiences took their seats they saw in a box near the stage a man sitting dressed as Abraham Lincoln. Behind him were mannequins in the uniforms of Union and Confederate soldiers. Götz Friedrich apparently had something symbolic in mind that escaped those Americans present.

The Kitiwah Island set was quite different, too. Instead of a jungle re-creation, large plastic coils descended, wiggling their way to the stage floor. To Marc Gershwin and his cousin, Leopold Godowsky III, Friedrich explained that the picnickers were likely to be on drugs, and that this was the way the jungle might look to them. Gershwin family members gave the name "slinkies" to the odd-looking coils. Dress also had oddities. Cast members scoured Berlin for the Reeboks the costumer dictated. Friedrich or the set designer, or both, seemed to have little idea of distances in America. When Porgy is about to set off for New York, the skyscrapers of the city can already be seen in the distance, giving the impression that Catfish Row was in northern New Jersey.

Even so, standing-room-only Berlin audiences loved the show as much as any of the productions previously seen there, and Friedrich made plans to bring his production back the following year and organize a touring version. This did not make Sherwin Goldman happy, for one. He felt Friedrich, in casting Clamma Dale, Wilhelmenia Fernandez, Donnie Ray Albert, and other fine singers, was eating seriously into the supply available for the production he wanted to tour in Europe and those which he helped arrange in the United States.

That night of the first performance at the Metropolitan, Houston's David Gockley said to Sherwin Goldman, "You know, we really ought to go back and do this again, before *Porgy*'s reputation is destroyed."

"Leonore and others of the copyright owners," Goldman said, later, "were getting more and more uneasy about letting opera companies do it, especially those in smaller cities."

A lawyer representative of the family eventually came to him and told him that the offers to do the opera were mounting, and was there any way he could get involved again? The small companies lacked the resources to do presentable versions of the work. Few localities could marshal up all the black singers required or enough funding. It was the lawyer's idea that in some way the various companies could get together and share resources.

The seed was planted. Gockley wrote to the heads of twenty-five opera companies about the idea of sharing costs, and, during the winter of 1986, Opera America, an association of opera companies, held a meeting in Washington, D.C., of the directors of the opera companies interested in putting on *Porgy and Bess,* Boston, Miami, San Francisco, Detroit, Cleveland, Columbus, and Omaha among them. The idea of opera companies working together to improve the quality of their presentations was relatively new. But in the Reagan years it was becoming harder and harder for them to stay afloat. "To our amazement," Goldman said, "they asked us to do it. But it took a complicated year of negotiation.

"We formed an American Opera Company production that used our sets from the Radio City Music Hall, and we produced it in cooperation with individual opera companies."

Thus, *Porgy and Bess* was staged in 1987 in opera houses in seventeen cities across the United States, an innovative joint venture by a group of independent opera companies. As before, Gockley and Goldman held national auditions for singers, who, when chosen, had long, welcome periods of employment. Each company was notified when the chorus was available, and part of the package was the accordionlike Music Hall set. John DeMain, of the Houston Opera, conducted most of the orchestras as the elements of the opera traveled from Miami to Houston, Austin, Los Angeles, San Diego, and on to other cities and its final stop in San Francisco.

The cost of the production was split several ways, and while not necessarily a profit-making venture, it also was not necessary to raise the great amount of cash usually required for so large an undertaking. Because of the popularity of Gershwin's music, and the highly professional nature of the production, newer companies were able to increase their sale of seasonal subscriptions.

So *Porgy and Bess* added another accomplishment to its luster. It provided the means, and pointed the way, to the healthy survival of opera in America.

A T T H E E N D of his novel, DuBose Heyward left his hero in a dispirited state. His Bess had gone, and he had no thought of following her. Heyward wrote:

> Maria saw that Porgy was an old man. The mellow mood that he had known for one summer had gone . . . she saw a face that sagged wearily, and the eyes of age lit only by a faint reminiscent glow from suns and moons that had looked into them, and had already dropped down to the west. . . . She closed the door, leaving Porgy and the goat in an irony of morning sunlight.

There would be a greater irony, but how could Heyward have known that a much happier fate lay in store for his Porgy? That his hero would be reborn and sing out in theatres and opera houses in many different lands, joined by a great host of glorious voices, and for generations to come.

SYNOPSIS OF *PORGY AND BESS*

DUSK HAS descended on Catfish Row, a dilapidated tenement in a fallen quarter of Charleston inhabited by poor black people—Gullah Negroes, as they are locally known. The walls of the tenement rise around a court where in this early evening hour the people of the community are relaxing. Couples stroll about, children play, there is impromptu dancing to a piano played by Jasbo Brown, and Clara, a sweet-faced young woman, sings a lullaby—"Summertime"—to her baby. Several of the men begin a crap game. Among them are Sportin' Life, Jake, Mingo, and Jim.

Jake, Clara's husband, is a captain of the fishing fleet, Jim is a fisherman, Mingo a young and lazy stevedore, and Sportin' Life is the bootlegger to Catfish Row and a sleazy seller of a drug he calls "happy dust." Robbins enters the game despite the pleas of his wife, Serena, a self-respecting woman who works for "white

folks" and is thus a kind of aristocrat of Catfish Row.

The life of Catfish Row goes on. Peter, the Honey Man, comes home, still crying his wares. Porgy, a crippled beggar, comes through the gate to the courtyard in his goat cart and enters the game, mocked by others who say he is sweet on Bess, the woman of Crown, the Row's bully. Soon enough, Crown, a hulking stevedore, arrives with Bess.

During the game, Crown, drunk, argues and fights with Robbins, the violent brawl ending in tragedy when Crown kills Robbins with his cotton hook. Crown flees, leaving Bess to look after herself. She would leave, too, but at the sound of a police whistle she knocks on doors to seek sanctuary. All doors are closed except Porgy's. She enters his room as the courtyard empties, leaving only Serena collapsed and moaning over her husband's body.

IN THE NEXT scene the body of Robbins is laid out in Serena's room, a saucer on his chest to hold contributions for his burial. Porgy and Bess, with other neighbors, come in to comfort the bereft woman. In their mourning they sing a spiritual, "Gone, Gone, Gone," and Porgy leads an impassioned prayer to the Lord to help them fill the saucer. The session is interrupted by a detective and two policemen looking for the killer. The detective fixes on an old man, Peter, accuses him of the crime, and takes him off as, if nothing else, "a material witness." The wake continues, with Serena singing "My Man's Gone Now." When the undertaker arrives, he agrees to bury Robbins for whatever is in the saucer. The curtain falls on the first act after the singing of "Leavin' for the Promise' Lan'," led by Bess, who, now that she is with Porgy, is accepted by the group.

IT IS A month later. Jake and other fishermen work on their nets in preparation for a fishing expedition. The dreaded hurricane season is due, and Jake's young wife, Clara, begs him not to take the boat out. Jake, though, is unmoved. He wants to earn enough money to ensure his baby son's college education. Porgy, rejuvenated by his love for Bess, sings of his own lack of need for money with "I Got Plenty o' Nuttin'."

The sinister Sportin' Life saunters over to where Maria, matriarch of the court, has laid out food on a table. Maria scolds him for peddling his happy dust around her food shop. When he urges her to be friendly, she grabs a carving knife, takes him by the throat, and informs him she would sooner lie down with a rattlesnake.

"Lawyer" Frazier visits the court and convinces Porgy that he needs to buy a divorce for Bess from Crown. When it turns out that Bess has never married Crown, Porgy still buys the divorce. Another visitor, this time a white man, Mr. Archdale, comes looking for Porgy to tell him that he'll put up old Peter's bond; Peter had once worked for his family. As Archdale is about to leave, a buzzard flies over the court, and the worried Porgy explains to Archdale that the bird is an ill omen, and in the "Buzzard Song" he expresses his fear of losing his newfound happiness.

IT IS THE day of the lodge picnic that takes place on Kitiwah Island. The people of Catfish Row are preparing for the picnic as Sportin' Life sneaks up to Bess and offers her a sample of his happy dust. Porgy sees this and sternly warns Sportin' Life to leave her alone, upon which the dope seller leaves in a hurry. Porgy and Bess sing of their love for each other in the duet "Bess, You Is My Woman Now."

Children enter, followed by the crowd of folk heading for the picnic and singing "Oh, I Can't Sit Down." Bess, fearful because of her intuition that Crown might be lurking on the island, doesn't want to attend the picnic, but Porgy generously urges her to go and have a good time.

ON KITIWAH Island, the picnickers have finished their meal and are enjoying themselves singing and dancing. Sportin' Life justifies his own credo with a song and dance — "It Ain't Necessarily So" — much to the pleasure of the crowd. Maria breaks up the festivities because it is time to get the boat that will take them back to the mainland. Bess has lagged behind, and just as she is about to leave too, she hears Crown's whistle. Her instinct that he has been hiding out on the island is true. She resists him at first, but finally gives way to his seduction. She misses the boat and stays with Crown on the island.

IT IS A week later on Catfish Row. Jake says his goodbye to his wife, Clara, and before going off with the other fishermen they sing "It Take a Long Pull to Get There." Bess has returned, ill and in delirium in Porgy's room. Several gather, including Serena and the forgiving Porgy, to pray for her recovery. Peter, the Honey Man, returns from his confinement in jail to be greeted happily by his neighbors. Other street vendors come along—among them the Strawberry Woman and the Crab Man—singing and crying their wares. Porgy hopes that Serena's invocation to "chase the devil" out of Bess will take effect. The bell of Saint Michael's chimes five times, and Bess's voice, stronger now, is heard from inside the room; then she comes out, to Porgy's joy. Bess sings "I Loves You, Porgy," and they go into his room.

In the court, Clara is concerned about her Jake; she has been on the wharf, where she was upset by about how sullen and black the water looks. Maria assures her there will be no hurricane, but suddenly the wind rises and the ominous sound of the hurricane bell is heard. Clara screams and faints, and now the hurricane hits Catfish Row with a terrible fury.

THE PEOPLE are huddled together singing and praying in Serena's room while, outside, the storm rages unabated. Their faces are filled with fear. One after another they take up the prayer "Oh, Doctor Jesus." In the midst of the storm the door to the room suddenly gives way and

Crown enters—they had thought him killed on the island by the storm. Clara, looking through a window, sees the wreck of Jake's boat and, thrusting her baby to Bess, rushes out into the storm to attempt to find her husband. Crown is the only one to go after her, but not before promising Bess that he will be back for her.

THE STORM is over and it is a calm evening in Catfish Row. But some of the fishermen have perished, Clara too, and the womenfolk can be heard mourning their dead in one of the rooms. Sportin' Life makes light of their grief to Maria and intimates to her slyly that Crown is still alive. Bess is heard singing "Summertime" to the dead Clara's baby. Crown appears at the courtyard gate and attempts to sneak into Porgy's room to find Bess, but before he can get inside, the cripple seizes him with his powerful hands. A struggle ensues, but it ends when Porgy strangles Crown to death and exults to Bess that she has a real man now.

THE FOLLOWING morning the police come to investigate the murder of Crown. The residents of Catfish Row refuse to talk. Exasperated, the coroner, aware that Porgy knew Crown, demands that he come with him to the inquest to identify the body. The superstitious Porgy is terrified at the thought of looking at his victim's body, and has to be dragged off by the police.

Sportin' Life sees his opportunity to move in and sidles up to the distraught Bess, suggesting that Porgy may be gone for a year and may even be hanged, and offers her a packet of happy dust. She spurns it at first, but he forces it into her hand, and she yields to the lure of the drug. Sportin' Life, sensing his victory, paints a picture for her of what life will be like for her if she goes with him to New York—"There's a Boat Dat's Leavin' Soon for New York." She is not impressed, but he offers her another packet. This she refuses, and, fleeing temptation, runs inside Porgy's room. Sportin' Life tosses the packet inside anyway. Suddenly, the door opens and Bess comes out, high on the drug. She takes Sportin' Life's arm, and they swagger through the gate.

ON A PLEASANT morning a week later, the clang of a patrol wagon is heard outside the court. Porgy, who has been locked up because of his refusal to look on the dead body of Crown, returns in high spirits with presents for Bess and his friends. He fails to notice that his friends stand around him sad and embarrassed, and calls to Bess. Only when she doesn't answer does he see that Serena is holding the baby that Clara had left with Bess. He crawls over to his room, opens the door, and calls again for Bess. In his despair he sings "Oh, Bess, Oh, Where's My Bess." Serena and Clara attempt to convince him that the woman isn't right for him, but finally, in answer to his pleading, they tell him the truth—that Bess has gone, that she's sold herself to the devil. But he also learns that Bess had thought him locked up forever before running off with Sportin' Life to New York. Where, he asks, is New York. A thousand miles away, they tell him. Despite their attempt to dissuade him he calls for his goat and cart; he's going to New York to find his Bess. He sings "Oh, Lawd, I'm on My Way," and the others join in as Porgy drives out through the gate of Catfish Row.

SELECTIVE BIBLIOGRAPHY

Angelou, Maya. *Singin' and Swingin' and Gettin' Merry Like Christmas*. New York: Random House, 1976.

Archer, Leonard C. *Black Images in the American Theatre*. Pageant-Poseidon, Ltd., 1973.

Armitage, Merle, ed. *George Gershwin*. New York: Longmans, Green, 1935.

———. *George Gershwin: Man and Legend*. New York: Duell, Sloan and Pearce, 1958.

Atkinson, Brooks. *Broadway*. New York: Macmillan, 1970.

Beahan, Charles. "Porgy and Me." Unpublished manuscript.

Behrman, S. N. *People in a Diary*. Boston: Little, Brown, 1972.

Bell, Era. "Why Negroes Don't Like Porgy and Bess." *Ebony*, October 1959.

Berg, A. Scott. *Goldwyn, A Biography*. New York: Alfred A. Knopf, 1989.

Calloway, Cab, and Rollins, Bryant. *Of Minnie the Moocher and Me*. New York: Thomas Y. Crowell Company, 1976.

Capote, Truman. *The Muses Are Heard*. New York: Random House, 1956.

Clarke, Gerald. *Capote, A Biography*. New York: Random House, 1988.

Crawford, Cheryl. *One Naked Individual: My Fifty Years in the Theatre*. Indianapolis, Ind.: Bobbs-Merrill, 1977.

Dandridge, Dorothy, and Conrad, Earl. *Everything and Nothing: The Dorothy Dandridge Story*. New York: Abelard-Schuman, 1970.

Duke, Vernon. *Passport to Paris*. Boston: Little, Brown, 1955.

Durham, Frank. *DuBose Heyward, The Man Who Wrote Porgy*. Columbia: University of South Carolina Press, 1954.

Ewen, David. *George Gershwin, His Journey to Greatness*. Englewood Cliffs, N.J.: Prentice-Hall, 1970.

Frischauer, Willi. *Behind the Scenes of Otto Preminger.* New York: William Morrow, 1974.

Gerber, Ella, and Heyward, Jenifer. "My Heart Pinched Me: A Saga of Travels Behind the Iron Curtain." Unpublished manuscript.

Gershwin, Ira. *Lyrics on Several Occasions.* New York: Alfred A. Knopf, 1959.

Goldberg, Isaac. *George Gershwin: A Study in American Music.* New York: Simon and Schuster, 1931. Reprinted with a supplement by Edith Garson. New York: Frederick Ungar, 1958.

Greene, Harlan. "Charleston Childhood: The First Years of DuBose Heyward." *South Carolina Historical Magazine* 83, 1982.

————. "The Little Shining Word: From Porgo to Porgy." *South Carolina Historical Magazine* 87, no. 1, January 1986.

Hamm, Charles. "The Theatre Guild Production of *Porgy and Bess.*" *Journal of the American Musicological Society,* 1987.

Heyward, Dorothy. "Porgy's Goat." *Harper's,* December 1957.

Heyward, Dorothy, and Heyward, DuBose. *Porgy, A Play in Four Acts.* New York: Doubleday, Doran, 1928.

Heyward, DuBose. *Porgy* (novel). New York: George H. Doran Company, 1925.

Isaacs, Edith J. R. "The Negro in the American Theatre, A Record of Achievement." *Theatre Arts Monthly,* November 1935.

Jablonski, Edward. *Gershwin, A Biography.* New York: Doubleday, 1987.

Jablonski, Edward, and Stewart, Lawrence D. *The Gershwin Years.* New York: Doubleday, 1973.

Kimball, Robert, and Simon, Alfred. *The Gershwins.* New York: Atheneum, 1973.

Knight, Arthur. "Catfish Row in Todd AO." *The Saturday Review,* July 4, 1959.

Kolodin, Irving. "Porgy and Bess: American Opera in the Theatre." *Theatre Arts Monthly,* August 1935.

Levant, Oscar. *A Smattering of Ignorance.* New York: Doubleday, Doran, 1940.

Lewis, David Levering. "Harlem's First Shining." *Modern Maturity Magazine,* February-March 1989.

Loften, Mitchell. *Black Drama.* New York: Hawthorn Books, 1967.

Poitier, Sidney. *This Life.* New York: Alfred A. Knopf, 1980.

Pratley, Gerald. *The Cinema of Otto Preminger.* New York: A. S. Barnes, 1971.

Preminger, Otto. *Preminger, An Autobiography.* New York: Doubleday, 1977.

Schwartz, Charles. *Gershwin, His Life and Music.* Indianapolis, Ind.: Bobbs-Merrill, 1973.

Seldes, Gilbert. *The Seven Lively Arts.* New York: Harper, 1924.

Shirley, Wayne D. "Porgy and Bess." *Quarterly Journal of the Library of Congress,* April 1974.

————. "Reconciliation on Catfish Row: Bess, Serena, and the Short Score of *Porgy and Bess.*" *Quarterly Journal of the Library of Congress,* Summer 1981.

Slavick, William H. *DuBose Heyward.* Boston: Twayne Publishers, 1981.

Taubman, Howard. *The Making of the American Theatre.* New York: Coward-McCann, 1965.

Wainwright, Loudon. "The One Man Gang Is in Action Again—at 76 Sam Goldwyn Conquers Crisis After Crisis to Produce *Porgy and Bess.*" *Life,* February 16, 1959.

Waters, Ethel, with Charles Samuels. *His Eye Is on the Sparrow*. New York: Doubleday, 1951.

Whipple, K. W. "Porgy, DuBose Heyward, and Charleston." Unpublished manuscript, 1943.

Woollcott, Alexander. "George the Ingenuous." *Hearst's International-Cosmopolitan,* November 1933.

ACKNOWLEDGMENTS

In searching out sources for this book it was immediately apparent that a nearly limitless amount of material existed concerning George and Ira Gershwin—biographies, articles, news clippings, criticism, letters, reminiscences, and more—but much less so for DuBose Heyward. Two rather thin biographical works were devoted to him; Heyward, perhaps purposely, left little in the way of documents about his life and career. Luckily for this author, Dorothy Heyward was a good deal less shy. She was proud of her husband's important contributions to *Porgy and Bess* and of her own, at one remove, as the coauthor of the play on which it was based.

It happened, long before I had any notion of writing this book, that I knew Dorothy Heyward. We were colonists together for two summers at the MacDowell Colony in New Hampshire, and I met her again on several visits there. I was aware at the time that she was busy on some mysterious and important negotiations regarding her husband's opera, but had no way of knowing these had to do with the attempt of Robert Breen and Blevins Davis to obtain the rights to produce it. She, too, was fascinated with the story behind the story, so to speak, and hoped to write it someday. She was unable to, but left behind some uncompleted reminiscences, and a store of letters and other documents, which were eventually given to the South Carolina Historical Society in Charleston.

Harlan Greene, the society's archivist, was of inestimable help in guiding me through this and a wealth of other material having to do both with *Porgy and Bess* and the intriguing figure of DuBose Heyward. Altogether knowledgeable himself on the subjects, a gifted fiction writer in his own right, he provided stimulation as well.

As for the Gershwins, there was the voluminous archive devoted to them in the Library of Congress, where Wayne Shirley led me to significant material. At the Theatre Collection of the Museum of the City of New York, where much Gershwin material resides, I received not only help but valuable research assistance from Lynn Doherty, who, not long after, became the curator of the collection. She could not have been more enthusiastic about the project, as was Patrick Hoffman from the same institution. Equally enthusiastic was my longtime literary agent, Mitch Douglas, who happens to be a mine of information on musical theatre and an avid collector of recordings and memorabilia. From him came rare recordings, audio and television tapes, liner notes, and tips on where to locate more information. He called me one day to advise me to get in touch with Nena Couch, the archivist for the Jerome Lawrence and Robert Lee Theatre Research Institute at Ohio State University. The newly formed institute had just made its first major acquisition—the Robert Breen Archives.

For many years, in a basement deep beneath the Hudson Theatre on West 44th Street, Robert Breen had stored literally tons of material, all having to do with his activities as actor and director, his tenure as executive secretary of ANTA, and, most important to me, his long years with *Porgy and Bess* and its remarkable international tours. Wilva Davis Breen was aware of the invaluable nature of the records kept so faithfully by her husband and eventually decided to donate this mass in two parts, the years through his WPA and ANTA involvement to George Mason University in Fairfax, Virginia, and that which mainly dealt with *Porgy and Bess* to Ohio State. Truckloads were dispatched just about the time I came on the scene.

One problem about making use of the material was that most of it was uncatalogued and some of it had to be fumigated. Michael Davis, an archeologist by profession and close friend of the Breens, had made a valiant cataloguing effort, but its sheer bulk required institutional support. At Ohio State, Nena Couch heroically (the only word) somehow managed to bring forth the relevant material needed for this book and make it accessible to the author, all neatly assembled. For several months she was constant with her help—far beyond the call of her normal duties. If more facts or photographs were asked for, she somehow found them. In addition, Michael Davis and Wilva Breen were always available to help make clear what might otherwise have been puzzling.

Sadly, Robert Breen is a neglected figure in our theatrical and cultural history. It lay beyond the scope of this book to tell his whole story, but let it be known that the needed material for it, along with enough theatrical research material for a good many master's theses, exists at George Mason University in the capable hands of Dr. Lorraine Brown, administrator of the Robert Breen Collection, and at Ohio State, where the Breen Archives are overseen by Dr. Alan Woods, director of the Lawrence and Lee Theatre Research Institute, and by curator Nena Couch. All three of the above became virtual colleagues during the writing of the book, and I owe them much. Dr. Woods had begun compiling an oral history dealing with the opera, and he generously made available to me his transcripts of audiotapes. Dr. Brown was similarly engaged in videotaping members of the Breen company. These tapes were also made available and I was able to participate in her lengthy taping session with William Warfield.

Then there was Wilva Breen, endlessly patient in providing information, in recalling her rich involvement with Robert Breen and the tour of the opera, and with leads to other participants. She generously granted permission for the use of letters, photographs, and memorabilia. She was always supportive and as much interested in an accurate account as I was. My gratitude to her and admiration for her gallant spirit hardly needs expressing.

There were others who I must specially thank, notably Ella Gerber, feisty acting coach, stage manager for Breen, and eventually director of several productions of the opera. I spent long enjoyable hours with her. Martha Flowers, too, Kay Swift, William Warfield, Miles Kreuger, Joan Burke, Lawrence D. Stewart, Robert Kimball. Sherwin M. Goldman was more than generous with his time in detailing for me his highly significant contributions to the opera's history and in providing photographs. For help in clarifying certain legal technicalities and in obtaining obscure research materials I am indebted to Anthony Hatab and equally so to my good friend Stanley Chase, who was associated with Robert Breen on the production of *Free and Easy*. Marc and Vicki Gershwin were notably gracious in providing details of family background and of more recent productions of the opera.

Certainly thanks are owed for courtesies at Yale University's Beinecke Library, with its Theatre Guild collection; to the custodians of the Theatre and Music collections at the Lincoln Center branch of the New York Public Library; to the press office of the Metropolitan Opera Association; and to Mary Corliss, curator of the Film Stills Archive at the Museum of Modern Art in New York.

Others whom I am grateful to for interviews or for advice and information are Sam Goldwyn, Jr., Professor David Rogers, George Stevens, Jr., Lillian Hayman, Dorothy McCurry, Mrs. Frances Godowsky, Mrs. Leonore Gershwin (for certain permissions), Ronald Blanc, Alfred Simon, Harold C. Schonberg, Steven Lemberg, John McGlinn, Seymour Weissman, Louis Aborn, Michael Sukin, Philip Cadgeano, Lou Valentino, Eva Jessye, Taina Elg, Friso Endt, Marnie Goodkind, Mark Jacobson, and Janet Olinkiewicz and the staff of the Shelter Island Public Library.

To my wife, Joan, I owe much for her patience, critical eye, and all-around support. Inspiration and expert guidance came when needed from my editor, Jonathan Segal. He wanted this book written as much as I wanted to write it.

INDEX

Note: Numbers in italics denote illustrations.

PERMISSIONS

Grateful acknowledgment is made to the following for permission to reprint previously published and unpublished material:

Robert and Wilva Breen: Excerpts from the papers of Robert Breen. Reprinted by permission of Robert and Wilva Breen.

The DuBose and Dorothy Heyward Memorial Fund: Excerpts from letters and recollections pertaining to the composition of the opera *Porgy and Bess.* Excerpts from *Porgy* by DuBose Heyward. Copyright 1925 by George H. Doran Company, New York. Reprinted by permission of The DuBose and Dorothy Heyward Memorial Fund.

Marc George Gershwin: Excerpts from the letters of George Gershwin. Reprinted by permission of Marc George Gershwin on behalf of The George Gershwin Estate.

Walter Kerr: Excerpt from March 10, 1953, article by Walter Kerr from *The New York Herald Tribune.* Reprinted by permission of Walter Kerr, *New York Times* drama critic, retired.

The New York Times Company: Excerpt from article by M.S. Handler, (November 2, 1955); and excerpt from a review of *Porgy and Bess* by Walter Kerr (October 10, 1976). Copyright © 1955, 1976 by The New York Times Company. Reprinted by permission.

Omni Publications International Ltd.: Excerpts from a review of *Porgy* by John Rosenfeld (*Saturday Review,* June 18, 1952); and excerpts from an article on *Porgy* by Horace Sutton (*Saturday Review,* December 8, 1956). Reprinted by permission.

Random House, Inc.: Excerpts from *Singin' and Swingin' and Gettin' Merry like Christmas* by Maya Angelou. Copyright © 1976 by Maya Angelou. Reprinted by permission of Random House, Inc.

A NOTE ABOUT THE AUTHOR

Former film critic for *The Saturday Review,* Hollis
Alpert is the author of several novels and theatrical
biographies. He has served on the fiction staff of *The
New Yorker,* was a senior editor at *The Saturday
Review,* managing editor of *World* magazine, and
founding editor and editor-in-chief of *American Film*
magazine. His short stories have appeared in *The
New Yorker* and many other magazines and his articles and profiles in *Esquire, Playboy, Partisan Review,* and *The New York Times Magazine.* He now
writes full-time and lives on Shelter Island, New
York.

A NOTE ON THE TYPE

The text of this book was set in Sabon, a typeface designed by Jan Tschichold (1902–1974), the well-known German typographer. Because it was designed in Frankfurt, Sabon was named for the famous Frankfurt type founder Jacques Sabon, who died in 1580 while manager of the Egenolff foundry.

Based loosely on the original designs of Claude Garamond (c. 1480–1561), Sabon is unique in that it was explicitly designed for hot-metal composition on both the Monotype and Linotype machines as well as for film composition.

Composed by The Sarabande Press
New York, New York

Printed and bound by Courier Companies, Inc.
Westford, Massachusetts

Designed by Valarie J. Astor